Legumi

Funghi

Dolci

Recipes from an ITALIAN SUMMER

Φ

Picnics

Salads

Barbecues

Light Lunches and Suppers

Summer Entertaining

Desserts

Ice Creams and Drinks

La dolce vita

In Italy, summer is the season of vacations and relaxation, of gathering together and eating with family and friends. Whether for a grand summer banquet held at long tables under the vines on a hot summer afternoon, or an informal picnic in a mountain meadow, Italian summer food is simple to prepare and makes the best possible use of a huge variety of seasonal produce.

Ferragosto

In Italy, almost everyone takes a vacation for the whole of August, and the most important date in the summer calendar is August 15th, or Ferragosto. It is a national holiday that traditionally involves a large meal with family and friends, such as a picnic in the countryside or at the beach.
The menus for special occasions such as the Ferragosto feast are carefully composed to present a tempting array of light, often cold, dishes, in which fresh, local and seasonal ingredients are artfully combined to create a meal that is both flavorful and colorful. It often takes the form of a cold buffet with a range of delicious dishes, which are organized from left to right, starting with the lighter dishes and antipasti and ending with the desserts. The most important principle of arranging a buffet is to present the food in the most appetizing way possible, showing the delicious seasonal ingredients to best advantage.

Vacation regions

Many of the recipes in this book
come from the regions most popular with
Italian vacationers: Sicily, Sardinia,
Campania, Tuscany, and the mountains
of northern Italy. The highly flavored
cuisine of Sicily often involves citrus
fruit and north African influences,
as well as their famous ice creams.
Sardinian food is simple and refined, and
makes great use of the wonderful seafood
caught on the island's shores, and cured
mullet roe, which is the island's best-
known food export.

The bold flavors of Campania are perfect
in summer, with fresh ingredients such as
olives, tomatoes, and goat cheese taking
center stage. Summer recipes from Tuscany
can turn the humblest of ingredients,
such as fresh borlotti beans, Swiss
chard, or salt cod, into stunning but
simple dishes. There are few finer
steaks for barbecuing than those from the
Tuscan Chianina cow, which, with simple
but careful cooking, are delicious
and tender. Finally, the food of the
mountains is fresh-tasting and
satisfying, and often includes fresh
herbs, late summer mushrooms, apples
and pears, and freshwater fish from the
mountain streams.

Summer cooking

The recipes in this book are organized
according to the different ways we like
to eat in summer, and to help inspire
tempting menus for all sorts of occasions.

The Picnics chapter contains cold dishes which can be easily transported and are good to eat outdoors, such as simple breads and salads, pies and frittatas, and desserts that can be prepared in advance. The Salads chapter provides recipes for leafy greens and vegetable salads, which work well as accompaniments to the main course and barbecue dishes in other parts of the book. Light Lunches and Suppers features simple meals that are quick to prepare, including substantial salads that can form a meal in their own right, as well as pizzas and light vegetable and fish dishes.

The Barbecues chapter contains vegetable, fish, and meat recipes that are excellent cooked on the barbecue, but many of them can also be cooked on a conventional broiler. The dishes found in Summer Entertaining require slightly more effort, but are perfect for cooking for larger gatherings, and range from canapés and antipasti to first courses and main dishes. The Desserts and Ice Creams and Drinks chapters feature a range of tempting recipes, some classic and some more unusual, using seasonal fruit.

Recipes from an Italian Summer is a celebration of the delicious ingredients that are available from May to September, and presents a comprehensive collection of authentic seasonal recipes from the team behind the best-selling Italian cookery bible, *The Silver Spoon*. With good ingredients, even the simplest of dishes can shine, and by cooking the recipes in this book, anyone can enjoy the taste of Italian summer, wherever they are.

Italian Food Festivals

Hundreds of food festivals take place in Italian towns and villages throughout the year. Often coinciding with religious feast days, they usually involve market stalls and food tastings as well as fireworks and music. This list is a selection of the best.

May

1st week: Sessame, Piedmont
Sagra del risotto (Risotto festival)

1st–3rd week: Mezzago, Lombardy
Sagra dell'asparagi
(Asparagus festival)

2nd week: Terricciola, Tuscany
Sagra della fragola
(Strawberry festival)

3rd week: Zoppola, Friuli Venezia Giulia
Sagra degli asparagi
(Asparagus festival)

4th week: Poggioreale, Sicily
Sagra del formaggio
(Cheese festival)

4th week: Vignola, Emilia Romagna
Sagra della ciliegia
(Cherry festival)

3rd–4th week May, 1st–2nd week June
Incisa in Valdarno, Tuscany
Sagra del fungo porcino
(Porcini mushroom festival)

June

4th week May–1st week June: Sesta al Reghena, Friuli Venezia Giulia
Sagra della trota (Trout festival)

1st week: Rovolon, Veneto
Festa del pane (Bread festival)

1st week: Genzano, Lazio
Sagra della fragola
(Strawberry festival)

1st–2nd week: Palaia, Tuscany
Sagra della ciliegia
(Cherry festival)

1st–2nd week: San Casciano Val di Pesa, Tuscany
Sagra del pinolo (Pine nut festival)

2nd–3rd week: Buti, Tuscany
Sagra del crostino
(Crostini festival)

2nd–4th week: Vicopisano, Tuscany
Sagra dell'anguilla (Eel festival)

3rd week: Rossiglione, Liguria
Sagra della fragola
(Strawberry festival)

4th week June–1st week July: Collesalvetti, Tuscany
Sagra del pane e pomodoro
(Bread and tomato festival)

July

2nd–4th week: Collebeato, Lombardy
Sagra delle pesche (Peach festival)

3rd week: Melpignano, Puglia
Sagra del cocomero
(Watermelon festival)

3rd week: Bagnara Calabra, Calabria
Sagra del pesce spada
(Swordfish festival)

3rd week: San Mango sul Calore,
Campania
Sagra dei fichi (Fig festival)

4th week: Piombino, Tuscany
Sagra del pesce (Fish festival)

4th week: Naples, Campania
Sagra della melanzana
(Eggplant festival)

4th week: Tropea, Calabria
Sagra di cipolla rossa
(Red onion festival)

4th week: Scarperia, Tuscany
Sagra del fungo porcino
(Porcini mushroom festival)

August

4th week July–1st week August:
Magliano Vetere, Campania
Sagra del cavatello
(Cavatelli pasta festival)

4th week July–1st week August:
Campello sul Clitunno, Umbria
Sagra del tartufo (Truffle festival)

3rd week: Castel di Lucio, Sicily
Sagra del caciocavallo
(Caciocavallo cheese festival)

3rd week: Prato Carnico, Friuli
Venezia Giulia
Fiesta della polenta
(Polenta festival)

3rd week: Gildone, Molise
Sagra dei pepperoni
(Pepper festival)

4th week: Alife, Campania
Festa della cipolla (Onion festival)

September

2nd week: Striano, Campania
Sagra del pomodoro (Tomato festival)

2nd week: Vezzano Ligure, Liguria
Sagra dell'uva e del vino
(Grape and wine festival)

2nd week: Greve in Chianti, Tuscany
Rassegna del Chianti Classico
(Chianti wine festival)

3rd week: Monterosso al Mare, Liguria
Sagra dell'acciuga salata
(Salted anchovy festival)

4th week September–1st week October:
Zagarolo, Lazio
Sagra dell'uva (Grape festival)

Seasonal
Food
Calendar

Fruit and vegetables are at their best during their natural growing season, and the typical seasons are listed here. They will vary from country to country and from year to year.

All summer

Apricots
Artichokes
Arugula
Bell peppers
Black currants
Broccoli
Cabbage (green)
Carrots
Corn salad
Cucumber
Fava beans
Fennel
Garlic
Gooseberries
Lettuce
Onion
Peaches
Peas
Potatoes
Radishes
Sorrel
Spinach
Strawberries
Swiss chard
Tomatoes
Watercress
Zucchini

Early summer

Asparagus
Cherries
Kiwifruits
Lemons
Melons
New potatoes
Oranges
Watermelon

Mid summer

Beets
Blueberries
Cherries
Corn
Eggplants
Figs
Gooseberries
Green beans
Melons
Nectarines
Raspberries
Red currants
Watermelon

Late summer

Apples
Blackberries
Blueberries
Borlotti beans
Celery
Corn
Damsons
Eggplants
Endive
Figs
Grapes
Green beans
Leeks
Mushrooms
Nectarines
Pears
Plums
Raspberries
Red currants

Picnics

Pic-nic

In Italy, the classic occasion for
a picnic is Ferragosto, a major feast
day on August 15th when friends and
family gather together for a vacation in
the countryside, often in the cooler
regions, such as in the mountains or by
the sea, and enjoy eating a range of
celebratory dishes in the open air. This
is often a grand occasion with many
courses and dishes, which are mostly
cold. However, picnics can also be very
simple affairs, from a sandwich on
a country walk, to a small family lunch
under an olive tree.

The huge range of antipasti, appetizers,
and salads in the Italian summer
repertoire provide a wonderful source of
inspiration for picnic food. Dishes such
as frittatas, cold risottos, pies, and
terrines are easy to transport, and
work very well at picnics alongside the
more traditional filled sandwiches, cold
meats, cheeses, and salads. Fresh,
ripe fruit provides the ideal dessert,
although a simple cake or fruit salad
can also be a pleasant way to end the
meal. All the recipes are simple to
prepare, delicious served cold, and easy
to take on a picnic.

Mayonnaise (Basic recipe)

Maionese (ricetta base)

Preparation time: 5 mins
Serves 4

2 egg yolks or 1 egg yolk
    plus 1 egg (see method)
scant 1 cup sunflower oil
2 tablespoons lemon juice
    or white-wine vinegar
salt and pepper

Mayonnaise is one of the best-loved and most
frequently eaten sauces in the world. Several
good store-bought brands are available,
but homemade tastes the best, and it is worth
savoring the delicacy of homemade mayonnaise
every now and again. It is useful to know how to
make it both by hand and in a food processor.
Both techniques are described here.

Always make sure that the oil and eggs are at
room temperature; if they are too cold, the
mayonnaise may not thicken correctly. Add the oil
a drop at a time and do the same with the lemon
juice or vinegar. If the mayonnaise separates,
whisk a fresh egg yolk in another bowl and
gradually whisk in the separated mixture a drop
at a time.

To make mayonnaise by hand, put the egg yolks in
a bowl and season with a pinch each of salt and
pepper. Add the oil, a drop at a time, beating
constantly with a small whisk or wooden spoon.
As soon as the mixture thickens, whisk in a drop
of lemon juice or vinegar. Continue adding the
oil and lemon juice or vinegar alternately,
beating constantly, until all the ingredients
are used.

To make mayonnaise in a food processor, place
an egg yolk and a whole egg in the food
processor, season with salt and pepper, and
add 2 tablespoons of the oil and a drop of the
lemon juice or vinegar. Process for a few
seconds at maximum speed. When the ingredients
are thoroughly mixed, slowly add the remaining
oil and lemon juice or vinegar and process for
1 minute.

For both methods, taste and adjust the seasoning
if necessary. Pour the mayonnaise into a
sauceboat and store in the refrigerator. Serve
with boiled or roasted meat, raw or cooked
vegetables, or as a garnish.

Herb mayonnaise

Maionese alle erbe

Preparation time: 10 mins

Cooking time: 5 mins

Serves 4

7 ounces spinach

1 sprig tarragon

½ bunch watercress

1 quantity Mayonnaise
    (see opposite)

salt

Cook the spinach in a pan of salted boiling water for 5 minutes, then drain well and let cool. When cool, place the spinach, tarragon, and watercress in a food processor and process to a puree. Stir the puree into the mayonnaise until the mixture is an even green color. Season with salt to taste. Serve with cold poached fish or hard-cooked eggs.

Tapenade

Tapenade

Preparation time: 15 mins

Serves 4

3½ ounces salted anchovy
    fillets, soaked in cold
    water for 10 mins and
    drained

1¾ cups pitted black olives

1 cup rinsed and drained
    capers

3½ ounces canned tuna in
    oil, drained

1 teaspoon Dijon mustard

olive oil, for drizzling

¼ cup brandy

2 tablespoons strained lemon
    juice

1 pinch fresh thyme

½ clove garlic, finely
    chopped

pepper

1 quantity Mayonnaise
    (see opposite), optional

Pat the anchovies dry, and chop with the olives, capers, and tuna. Place in a bowl and stir in the mustard.

Drizzle in olive oil to taste, stirring constantly. Add the brandy, lemon juice, thyme, and garlic. Season lightly with pepper. The fairly strong taste of this Provencal sauce may be made less intense by omitting the pepper.

Some people prefer to mix all the ingredients with mayonnaise. The result is equally pleasant. Store in the refrigerator. Serve with boiled meat, hard-cooked eggs, or fish.

Gorgonzola sauce

Salsa al gorgonzola

Preparation time: 5 mins

Serves 4
----

11 ounces mild Gorgonzola
   cheese, crumbled
2 tablespoons light cream
   or scant ½ cup milk
1 tablespoon grated
   horseradish
salt and pepper

Cream the Gorgonzola in a bowl with a fork, then gradually beat in the cream or milk. When the mixture has a creamy consistency, season with salt and pepper, and add the grated horseradish. Mix well and serve with canapés or raw vegetables.

Green sauce

Salsa verde

Preparation time: 15 mins

Cooking time: 15 mins

Serves 4
----

1 small potato
2 eggs, hard-cooked
2 salted anchovy fillets,
   soaked in cold water
   for 10 mins and drained
1 sprig flat-leaf parsley,
   leaves only
½ clove garlic
1 dill pickle, drained
scant 1 cup olive oil
2 tablespoons white-wine
   vinegar
salt and pepper

Cook the potato in a pan of lightly salted boiling water for 15 minutes or until tender. Drain and peel. While still hot, put in a bowl and mash well with a fork.

Shell and halve the eggs, then scoop the yolks into the bowl and mix with the mashed potato. Pat the anchovies dry, and chop finely with the parsley, garlic, and dill pickle. Add to the potato and mix well.

Gradually beat in the olive oil, a drop at a time. Season with salt and pepper and stir in the vinegar. Serve with boiled meat or cold, poached fish.

Focaccia

Focaccia

Preparation time: 3 hrs
(including rising)
Cooking time: 20-30 mins
Serves 6

4½ cups white bread flour,
    plus extra for dusting
½ teaspoon salt
2½ teaspoons active dry
    yeast
1½ tablespoons olive oil,
    plus extra for brushing
11 ounces stracchino or other
    soft cow's milk cheese,
    diced
12 basil leaves, chopped
coarse sea salt, for
    sprinkling

Sift together the flour and salt into a bowl and stir in the yeast. Make a well in the center and add the olive oil and ½–⅔ cup lukewarm water. Gradually incorporate the dry ingredients from the sides of the well, adding more lukewarm water to make a soft dough. Turn out onto a lightly floured counter and knead well until smooth and elastic. Shape the dough into a ball, put it into a bowl, cover with a clean dish towel, and let rise for 1½–2 hours, until doubled in volume.

Preheat the oven to 425°F and brush a roasting pan with oil. Flatten the dough and knead again, then roll out half on a lightly floured counter. Place the dough over the bottom and partly up the sides of the roasting pan. Sprinkle with the cheese, basil, and a little salt. Roll out the remaining dough, place it on top, and crimp the edges to seal.

Prick the surface with a fork, brush with a little water and oil, and sprinkle with sea salt. Bake for 20-30 minutes, then transfer to a wire rack to cool.

Photograph p.26

Frisedda

Frisedda

Preparation time: 10 mins
Cooking time: 10 mins
Serves 4

2 ring-shaped loaves of bread
1 large red tomato, halved
⅓ cup rinsed and drained
    small capers
1 fresh red chile, seeded and
    finely chopped
olive oil, for drizzling

Preheat the oven to 350°F. Cut the loaves in half horizontally and toast in the oven for 10 minutes, until lightly browned.

Remove from the oven and rub the cut surfaces vigorously with the tomato halves until they become red. Sprinkle with capers and chile and drizzle generously with oil.

Note: For a picnic, toast the bread in advance, prepare the rest of the ingredients, and take them separately. Rub with tomato and sprinkle with capers, chile, and oil just before serving.

Photograph p.27

Casatiello

Casatiello

Preparation time: 3¾ hrs
(including rising)
Cooking time: 1 hr
Serves 6–8

4½ cups white bread flour,
    plus extra for dusting
2½ teaspoons active dry
    yeast
generous ½ cup lard
scant ½ cup butter, softened
⅓ cup grated pecorino cheese
⅓ cup grated Parmesan cheese
⅓ cup diced salami
salt and pepper

Sift the flour with a pinch of salt into a bowl, adding the yeast, lard, and as much water as necessary to mix to a smooth dough. Shape it into a ball, transfer to a bowl, cover with a clean dish towel, and let rise for 1 hour.

Turn out onto a lightly floured counter and knead again, then knead in the lard, butter, cheeses, and a pinch of pepper. Knead for another 5 minutes, then knead in the salami. Shape into a ball, cover, and let rise for 2 hours.

Preheat the oven to 350°F. Shape the dough into a ring, put it onto a baking sheet, and bake for 1 hour, or until the loaf sounds hollow when tapped on the bottom. Transfer to a wire rack to cool.

/ Picnics /

Cheese and olive rolls

Panini di formaggio e olive

Preparation time: 10 mins
Serves 6

2⅔ cups cream cheese
24 green olives, pitted and
    finely chopped
¼–1 teaspoon olive oil
12 milk rolls
3½ ounces corn salad
salt and freshly ground
    white pepper

Combine the cream cheese and olives in a bowl. Season with salt and pepper and stir in a little olive oil to make a soft mixture. Cut the rolls in half and spread the cut sides with the cheese mixture. Put a few corn salad leaves on the bottom half of each roll and replace the tops.

Green bean tart

Torta di fagiolini

Preparation time: 30 mins
Cooking time: 1 hr
Serves 6

2¼ pounds green beans,
    trimmed
4 tablespoons butter, plus
    extra for greasing
1 clove garlic
1 pound 2 ounces store-bought
    puff pastry dough, thawed
    if frozen
all-purpose flour, for
    dusting
4 eggs
1¾ cups heavy cream
scant 1 cup milk
½ cup grated Parmesan cheese
salt and pepper

Cook the beans in a pan of salted boiling water for 5–8 minutes, until they are tender but still firm to the bite, then drain and chop. Melt the butter in a skillet. Add the garlic clove and cook, stirring frequently, for a few minutes, until golden, then remove and discard the garlic. Add the beans and cook, stirring occasionally, for 5 minutes. Remove the pan from the heat and let cool slightly.

Preheat the oven to 350°F and grease a tart pan or quiche pan with butter. Roll out the dough on a lightly floured counter to an ⅛-inch sheet and use it to line the prepared pan.

Beat the eggs with the cream and milk and season with salt and pepper. Spread out the beans in the pastry shell, pour in the egg mixture, and sprinkle with the grated Parmesan. Put the pan on a baking sheet and bake for about 45 minutes, or until the filling is set and the pastry is golden. Serve warm or cold.

Focaccia (p.21)

Piadina

Piadina

Preparation time: 45 mins
(including rising)
Cooking time: 15 mins
Serves 12

5¼ cups all-purpose flour,
    plus extra for dusting
2 teaspoons baking powder
    (optional)
¼ cup lard
olive oil, for brushing
12 slices prosciutto
salt

Sift together the flour, baking powder, and
2 pinches of salt into a large bowl. Add the lard
and as much warm water as necessary to mix to a
springy dough. Cover with a clean dish towel and
let rise for 30 minutes.

Divide the dough into 12 pieces and roll
them out into thin rounds on a lightly floured
counter. Brush a skillet with oil, add the
rounds in batches, and cook on both sides for
a few minutes, until lightly browned. Top each
piadina with a slice of prosciutto and fold in
half to serve.

Photograph p.30

Baguette with ratatouille

Baguette alla ratatouille

Preparation time: 50 mins
Cooking time: 1 hr 20 mins
Serves 16

14 ounces eggplants, diced
14 ounces red bell peppers
½ cup olive oil
2¼ pounds zucchini, diced
1 pound 5 ounces onions,
    diced
4 cloves garlic, lightly
    crushed
2¼ pounds tomatoes, peeled,
    seeded, and diced
2 bay leaves
3 sprigs thyme
1 teaspoon sugar
4 eggs, lightly beaten
salt and pepper
3 baguettes, approximately
    20 inches long and
    4 inches in diameter

First make the ratatouille. Put the eggplants
into a colander, sprinkle with salt, and let
drain. Hold the bell peppers over a naked flame
with a long-handled fork until blistered and
charred. Alternatively, halve and broil
them under a hot broiler, skin side up, until
blistered and charred. Peel off the skins,
remove and discard the seeds and stalks, and
dice the flesh.

Heat 1 tablespoon of the oil in a nonstick
skillet. Add the bell peppers and cook over low
heat, stirring occasionally, for 10 minutes.
Transfer to a separate colander and let drain.
Wipe out the pan with paper towels and heat
1 tablespoon of the remaining oil.

→

/ Picnics /

Add the zucchini and cook over low heat, stirring occasionally, for 10 minutes, then transfer to the colander. Wipe out the skillet, heat another tablespoon of oil, and cook the onions in the same way. Transfer to the colander. Wipe out the pan, heat another tablespoon of oil, and cook the eggplants in the same way. Transfer to the colander.

Heat the remaining oil in the pan. Add the garlic cloves and cook over low heat, stirring frequently, until browned, then remove with a slotted spoon and discard. Add the tomatoes, bay leaves, and thyme sprigs to the pan and bring to a boil. Season with salt and pepper and stir in the sugar and all the vegetables from the colander. Cover and cook over medium heat, stirring occasionally, for 30 minutes.

Add the eggs and stir rapidly for a few seconds to mix well. Remove the pan from the heat, adjust the seasoning, and transfer the mixture to a dish. Let cool, then cover and chill in the refrigerator.

To serve, cut each baguette into 5 pieces. Carefully remove the inside from each baguette slice and replace it with the ratatouille. Cut each piece of baguette in half before serving.

Photograph p.31

Piadina (p.28)

Baguette with ratatouille (p.28)

Rustic vegetable pie

Torta di verdure della lunigiana

Preparation time: 30 mins

Cooking time: 40 mins

Serves 6-8
----

1 pound 2 ounces spinach
1 pound 2 ounces Swiss chard
1 pound 2 ounces wild salad
    greens, such as borage,
    arugula, and dandelion
2 zucchini, sliced
2 leeks, trimmed and sliced
2 eggs
⅔ cup grated pecorino cheese
⅔ cup olive oil
2¾ cups all-purpose flour,
    plus extra for dusting
salt and pepper

Cook the spinach, Swiss chard, salad greens, zucchini, and leeks in a pan of salted boiling water for 5-10 minutes until tender. Drain, squeeze out as much liquid as possible, and chop coarsely. Beat the eggs with the pecorino, add the vegetables and generous ⅓ cup of the oil, and season with salt and pepper. Mix well and let stand.

Preheat the oven to 400°F and line a rectangular pie plate with parchment paper. Sift the flour with a pinch of salt into a mound on a counter. Make a well in the center, add the remaining oil, and generous 1 cup warm water, and gradually incorporate the flour using your fingers. Knead well to form a smooth pastry dough, then roll out on a lightly floured counter into 2 rectangles, one larger than the other.

Line the pie plate with the larger sheet and spoon in the vegetable mixture. Cover with the smaller sheet of dough, trim, and crimp the edges to seal. Make a hole in the center. Bake for 30 minutes. Serve warm or cold.

Spinach pie

Torta di spinaci

Preparation time: 35 mins
Cooking time: 50 mins
Serves 6

2¼ pounds spinach, coarse
    stalks removed
4 tablespoons butter, plus
    extra for greasing
1 clove garlic
generous 1 cup ricotta cheese
2 eggs
scant ½ cup heavy cream
1 pound 2 ounces puff pastry
    dough, thawed if frozen
all-purpose flour, for
    dusting
1 egg yolk, lightly beaten
salt and pepper

Wash the spinach and put it into a pan over low heat with just the water clinging to its leaves. Cook for 5 minutes, stirring occasionally. Drain the spinach well, pressing out as much liquid as possible. Melt the butter in a skillet. Add the garlic clove and cook, stirring frequently, for a few minutes, until golden brown, then remove and discard the garlic. Add the spinach to the skillet, and cook, stirring occasionally, for 5 minutes, then remove the skillet from the heat and let cool slightly.

Preheat the oven to 350°F and grease a pie plate with butter. Finely chop the spinach, put it into a bowl, and stir in the ricotta, eggs, and cream. Season with salt and pepper.

Roll out two-thirds of the pastry dough on a lightly floured counter and use it to line the prepared pie plate. Spoon the spinach mixture into the pastry shell. Roll out the remaining dough. Brush the rim of the pastry shell with egg yolk, place the dough on top, and press the edges together to seal. Brush the pie with egg yolk and prick the lid all over with a fork. Put the pie plate on a baking sheet and bake for about 40 minutes, until the pastry is risen and golden brown. Serve warm or cold.

Fennel pie

Torta di finocchi

Preparation time: 30 mins

Cooking time: 50 mins

Serves 6
----

scant ½ cup (1 stick) butter,
   plus extra for greasing
6 fennel bulbs, chopped
1 pound 2 ounces puff pastry
   dough, thawed if frozen
7 ounces Taleggio cheese,
   sliced
all-purpose flour, for
   dusting
3 eggs
¼ cup milk
1 egg yolk, lightly beaten
salt and pepper

Preheat the oven to 350°F and grease a large pie plate with butter. Melt the butter in a large pan, add the fennel, and cook over medium-low heat, stirring occasionally, for 8–10 minutes, until softened.

Roll out two-thirds of the dough on a lightly floured counter and line the pie plate with the dough. Trim the edges and brush the rim with water. Spoon the fennel into the pie plate and top with the slices of cheese.

Beat together the whole eggs and milk in a bowl, season with salt and pepper, and pour the mixture over the fennel and cheese. Roll out the remaining dough, place it over the pie, and press the edges to seal. Brush the surface with egg yolk and bake for about 40 minutes, until golden brown.

Photograph p.40

Wild greens and artichoke pie

Torta di erbette e carciofi

Preparation time: 50 mins
(including resting)
Cooking time: 55 mins
Serves 6

4½ cups all-purpose flour,
    plus extra for dusting
generous ⅓ cup olive oil
2 white bread slices, crusts
    removed
½ cup milk
1 pound 2 ounces leafy
    greens, such as Swiss
    chard, spinach, or turnip
    greens
juice of 1 lemon, strained
12 globe artichokes
butter, for greasing
1 onion, thinly sliced
generous 1 cup freshly grated
    pecorino cheese
⅔ cup freshly grated
    Parmesan cheese
1 tablespoon chopped marjoram
salt and pepper

Sift the flour with a pinch of salt into a mound on a counter, then add ¼ cup of the olive oil and just enough water to knead to a soft pastry dough. Set aside in the refrigerator to rest for 30 minutes.

Tear the bread into pieces, place in a bowl, and pour in the milk. Set aside to soak. Cook the greens in salted boiling water for 5–10 minutes until tender, then drain, squeezing out as much liquid as possible, and chop. Fill a bowl with water halfway and add the lemon juice. Remove and discard the outer leaves from the artichokes, cut off the top 2 inches of the remaining leaves, and remove and discard the chokes. Place in the water and set aside for about 10 minutes.

Preheat the oven to 400°F and grease a tart pan with butter. Drain the artichokes, chop, and put in a pan with the onion and the remaining oil. Cook over low heat for 10 minutes until softened. Squeeze out the bread and add to the pan with the greens and cheeses.

Mix well, season with salt and pepper, and sprinkle with the marjoram. Roll out the dough on a lightly floured counter into 2 rounds, one larger than the other. Place the larger one in the prepared pan, spoon in the vegetable mixture, cover with the second dough round, and crimp the edges to seal. Prick with a fork in a spiral pattern and bake for about 40 minutes. This pie may be served hot, warm, or cold.

Zucchini, goat cheese, and black olive frittata

Frittata di zucchini al caprino e olive nere

Preparation time:
40–50 mins
(including cooling)
Cooking time: 20 mins
Serves 6

3 tablespoons olive oil
1 pound 5 ounces zucchini,
    thinly sliced into
    rounds
1 sprig thyme
8 eggs
1 pinch curry powder
7 ounces goat cheese,
    crumbled
generous 1 cup grated
    Parmesan cheese
3 tablespoons chopped
    flat-leaf parsley
1 tablespoon snipped chives
1 tablespoon chopped chervil
¾ cup black olives,
    pitted and halved
milk, to loosen
salt and pepper

Heat the oil in a large skillet. Add the zucchini and thyme and cook over medium heat, stirring and turning occasionally, until the zucchini have softened and the moisture has evaporated. Season with salt and pepper, remove and discard the thyme, and set aside.

Beat the eggs with a small pinch of curry powder and salt and pepper in a bowl, then stir in the goat cheese, Parmesan, parsley, chives, chervil, and olives. If the mixture is too thick, loosen it with a little milk. Pour the egg mixture into the pan with the zucchini and cook over medium heat for about 5 minutes, until the eggs have set.

Remove the skillet from the heat, loosen the frittata with a spatula, and slide it onto a serving dish. Let cool to room temperature, then cut into slices and serve.

/ Picnics /

Frittata cake

Torta di frittate

Preparation time: 30 mins
Cooking time: 30 mins
Serves 6

7 ounces eggplants, sliced
7 ounces red or yellow bell
    peppers
6 eggs
1 sprig flat-leaf parsley,
    chopped
1 tablespoon freshly grated
    Parmesan cheese
1 tablespoon butter
3½ ounces fontina cheese,
    sliced
olive oil
salt and pepper

Preheat the broiler. Broil the eggplants until soft and golden brown. Broil the bell peppers until blackened and charred, then transfer to a plastic bag and seal the top. Preheat the oven to 475°F. When cool enough to handle, peel and seed the bell peppers and cut the flesh into strips.

Beat 2 eggs in one bowl and 2 eggs in another bowl, season both with salt and pepper, and divide the parsley between them. Beat the remaining eggs in a third bowl, season with salt and pepper, and stir in the Parmesan. Heat the butter and a tablespoon of oil in a skillet, pour in one bowl of the egg-and-parsley mixture, and cook until set on one side, but still quite soft on the other.

Slide the frittata out of the pan and cook 2 more in the same way, one with the remaining egg-and-parsley mixture and one with the egg-and-Parmesan mixture.

Line a cake pan with parchment paper and place one of the parsley frittatas, soft side up, in it. Cover with the eggplant and half the fontina. Place the Parmesan frittata on top of them, soft side up, and cover with the strips of bell pepper and the remaining fontina. Finally, place the second parsley frittata on top, soft side down. Bake for 10 minutes. Serve hot or cold.

Photograph p.41

Fennel pie (p.34)

Marinated mixed vegetables

Scapece misto

Preparation time: 12 hrs
(including overnight chilling)
Cooking time: 25 mins
Serves 6

2¼ pounds small yellow
   summer squash, peeled
   and sliced
3 eggplants, sliced
¾ cup olive oil
1¾ pounds zucchini, sliced
   into rounds
1 clove garlic, thinly sliced
2 sprigs mint, only leaves
mild white-wine vinegar,
   to taste
salt

Put the squash slices into a colander, sprinkle with salt, and let drain for 30 minutes. Put the eggplant slices into another colander, sprinkle with salt, and let drain for 30 minutes.

Rinse the squash and eggplant slices and pat them dry with paper towels. Heat generous ⅓ cup of the olive oil in a large skillet. Add the squash, eggplants, and zucchini and cook over medium-low heat, stirring frequently, for about 25 minutes, or until golden brown. Remove with a slotted spoon and drain on paper towels.

Put the vegetables into a bowl and sprinkle with the garlic and half the mint leaves. Heat the remaining olive oil in a small pan, add the vinegar, and whisk until combined, then pour the dressing over the vegetables. Cover the bowl with plastic wrap and chill in the refrigerator overnight. To serve, remove and discard the garlic and mint. Transfer the vegetables to a serving dish and garnish with the remaining mint leaves.

Spicy ditalini

Ditalini freddi aromatici

Preparation time: 2¼ hrs
(including marinating)
Cooking time: 8–10 mins
Serves 4

1 pound tomatoes, peeled,
    seeded, and diced
1 bunch mixed herbs, chopped
1 clove garlic, chopped
¼ cup olive oil
2¾ cups ditalini pasta or
    other small pasta shapes
1 tablespoon Worcestershire
    sauce
5 ounces canned tuna in oil,
    drained and flaked
salt and pepper

Combine the tomatoes, herbs, garlic, and olive oil in a bowl and season with salt and pepper. Cover with platic wrap and let stand in a cool place for 2 hours.

Cook the pasta in a large pan of salted boiling water for 8–10 minutes, or according to package directions, until it is tender but still al dente, or firm to the bite. Drain, rinse under cold running water, drain again, and transfer to a tureen.

Add the tomato marinade, the Worcestershire sauce, and the tuna, season with salt and pepper, and toss lightly. Chill in the refrigerator before serving.

Bean salad

Insalata di fagioli

Preparation time: 20 mins
Cooking time: 1 hr
Serves 4

scant 4¼ cups shelled fresh
    beans, such as borlotti
⅓ cup olive oil
3 sage leaves
1 clove garlic
salt and pepper

Put the beans, oil, sage, garlic, and 5 cups water into a pan and bring to a boil. Reduce the heat, cover halfway, and simmer for 1 hour, until the water has completely evaporated.

If the beans are still not tender, add a little hot water and cook until it has evaporated.

Remove the pan from the heat, discard the garlic and sage, and transfer the beans to a large bowl, seasoning them to taste with salt and pepper.

Fusilli salad

Fusilli in insalata

Preparation time: 20 mins
Cooking time: 8-10 mins
Serves 4

4 tomatoes, peeled, seeded,
    and diced
16 basil leaves
1 clove garlic
olive oil, for drizzling
12 ounces fusilli pasta
3 ounces canned tuna in oil,
    drained and flaked
12 black olives, pitted and
    cut into halves
4 ounces mozzarella cheese,
    diced
salt

Put the tomatoes into a salad bowl with the basil
and garlic, drizzle with olive oil, and season
with salt.

Cook the pasta in a pan of salted boiling water
for 8-10 minutes or according to package
directions. Once it is tender but still al dente,
or firm to the bite, drain it and put it into the
salad bowl with the tomatoes. Let cool, then
add the tuna, olives, and mozzarella. Toss well
and remove the garlic before serving.

Green rice salad

Insalata di riso al verde

Preparation time: 25 mins
Cooking time: 15-18 mins
Serves 6

1½ cups long-grain rice
generous ⅓ cup olive oil
2 tablespoons white-wine
    vinegar
1¾ cups basil
1¾ cups flat-leaf parsley
4 firm tomatoes, peeled,
    seeded, and diced
7 ounces fontina cheese,
    diced
salt and pepper

Cook the rice in a pan of salted boiling water
for 15-18 minutes, or according to package
directions, until it is tender. Drain, rinse
under cold water, and drain again, then spread
out the rice on a clean dish towel.

Whisk together the olive oil and vinegar in
a small bowl and season with salt and pepper.
Pour the mixture into a blender, add the basil
and parsley, and blend until combined. Put the
rice into a salad bowl, pour in the herb
sauce, add the tomatoes and cheese, and stir.

Farfalle giuliana

Farfalle alla giuliana

Preparation time: 12 hrs
(including overnight
chilling)
Cooking time: 25 mins
Serves 6

1 large eggplant, diced
2 red bell peppers
scant 1 cup olive oil
1 scallion, finely chopped
¾ cup pine nuts
juice of 2 lemons, strained
1 pound 5 ounces farfalle
    pasta
1 pinch dried oregano
1 sprig basil, chopped
salt and pepper

Put the eggplant into a colander, sprinkle with salt, and let drain. Meanwhile, hold the bell peppers over a naked flame with a long-handled fork until they are blistered and charred.

Alternatively, halve the bell peppers and place under a preheated broiler, skin side uppermost, until they are blistered and charred. Peel off the skins, then remove the seeds and stalks and cut into small squares. Rinse the eggplant and pat dry with paper towels. Heat half the oil in a large skillet. Add the eggplant and cook over medium heat, stirring frequently, for 10–15 minutes, until golden. Remove from the skillet with a slotted spoon and drain on paper towels. Put the bell peppers, scallion, eggplant, and pine nuts into a bowl and mix well. Whisk together the remaining oil and three-quarters of the lemon juice in a small bowl and season with salt and pepper. Pour the dressing over the vegetables and toss well.

Transfer a ladleful of the mixture to a food processor or blender and process. Cook the pasta in plenty of salted boiling water for 8–10 minutes, or according to package directions, until it is tender but still al dente, or firm to the bite. Drain, turn into a large salad bowl, drizzle over the pureed vegetable mixture, and toss. Sprinkle with the remaining vegetables and the herbs and stir. Add a little more oil and lemon juice, if necessary, season to taste with salt, then cover with plastic wrap and chill in the refrigerator overnight.

Note: This is a very tasty cold first course, which is also good for picnics. Its secret lies in the sauce, flavorings, and oil and lemon. Don't be afraid of overdoing it.

Maccheroncini salad

Maccheroncini in insalata

Preparation time: 45 mins
(including cooling)
Cooking time: 35 mins
Serves 4

11 ounces maccheroncini
    pasta, or other short
    pasta
2 yellow bell peppers
scant 1 cup shelled peas
7 ounces tomatoes, peeled,
    seeded, and chopped
1 bunch cicorino
    (see p.73), shredded
1 scallion, chopped
1 sprig basil, shredded
2 tablespoons mayonnaise
1 tablespoon anchovy paste
½ cup white wine
salt

Preheat the oven to 450°F. Cook the pasta in a large pan of salted boiling water for 8-10 minutes, or according to package directions, until tender but still al dente, or firm to the bite. Drain, rinse under cold running water, and drain again.

Put the bell peppers on a baking sheet and roast, turning occasionally, for 10-15 minutes, until blistered and charred. Remove from the oven, put them into a plastic bag, and seal the top. When they are cool enough to handle, peel off the skins, remove and discard the seeds, and cut the flesh into pieces.

Cook the peas in a pan of salted boiling water for 10 minutes, then drain and let cool. Put the bell peppers, peas, tomatoes, cicorino, scallion, and basil into a salad bowl and add the pasta. Combine the mayonnaise, anchovy paste, and wine in a bowl. Pour the sauce over the pasta salad, toss, and serve.

Baby octopus
and green bean salad

Insalata di moscardini e fagiolini

Preparation time: 15 mins
(including chilling)
Cooking time: 2½ hrs
Serves 6

2¼ pounds green beans,
    trimmed
juice of 1 lemon, strained
14 ounces baby octopuses,
    cleaned and skinned
    (see p.51)
¾ cup mild red-wine vinegar
2 tablespoons chopped basil
2 tablespoons chopped
    marjoram
1 tablespoon chopped flat-
    leaf parsley
1 clove garlic
1 fresh chile, halved and
    seeded
5 ounces canned tuna, drained
olive oil
salt and pepper

Cook the beans in a large pan of salted boiling
water for 5–10 minutes, until tender but still
firm to the bite, then drain and put into a salad
bowl. Bring a pan of water to the boil, add the
lemon juice and octopuses, and cook for 1 minute.
Drain and cut the largest ones in half, leaving
the rest whole.

Pour the vinegar into a small pan, add the basil,
marjoram, parsley, garlic, and chile, and bring
to a boil. Cook for a few minutes, until reduced.
Remove from the heat and strain into a bowl.

Flake the tuna and sprinkle it over the beans,
then top with the octopuses. Drizzle with olive
oil, spoon over the spiced vinegar, and season
with salt and pepper. Chill in the refrigerator
for 2 hours before serving.

Cold pennette with vegetables

Pennette fredde alle verdure

Preparation time: 2¾ hrs
(including cooling and
standing)
Cooking time: 25 mins
Serves 4

11 ounces pennette pasta or
    other tubular pasta
2 yellow bell peppers
1 large eggplant, sliced
3 zucchini, sliced
1 sprig basil, chopped
½ teaspoon grated fresh
    ginger
¼ cup olive oil, plus extra
    for drizzling
salt and pepper

Preheat the oven to 450°F. Cook the pasta in a large pan of salted boiling water for 8–10 minutes, or according to package directions, until tender but still al dente, or firm to the bite. Drain, rinse under cold running water, and spread out on a clean dish towel to dry.

Put the bell peppers on a baking sheet and roast, turning occasionally, for about 15 minutes, or until they are blistered and charred. Meanwhile, spread out the eggplant and zucchini slices on another baking sheet, drizzle with olive oil, and roast for 10 minutes. Remove the zucchini and eggplants from the oven and set aside.

Remove the bell peppers from the oven, put them into a plastic bag, and seal the top. When cool enough to handle, peel off the skins, remove and discard the seeds, and cut the flesh into small pieces. Put the pasta, bell peppers, eggplants, zucchini, basil, and ginger into a salad bowl, season with salt and pepper, and add the olive oil. Stir and let stand for 2 hours before serving to let the flavors mingle.

Cold octopus and eggplant salad

Insalata di polpo freddo e melanzane

Preparation time: 3 hrs
(including marinating and
cooling)
Cooking time: 40 mins
Serves 4

2 eggplants, thinly sliced
  lengthwise
2 tablespoons olive oil, plus
  extra for drizzling
1 clove garlic, crushed
1 fresh red chile, seeded and
  chopped
1 tablespoon chopped flat-
  leaf parsley
¾ cup white-wine vinegar
2¼ pounds octopus
2 tablespoons capers
  preserved in salt,
  rinsed, drained, and
  chopped
12 black olives, pitted and
  sliced
4 tomatoes, cut into wedges
4-5 basil leaves

Heat a nonstick skillet, sear the eggplant slices
for a few minutes, turning once, then remove from
the heat and put them into a salad bowl. In
a separate skillet, heat the olive oil with the
garlic and chile. Add the parsley and vinegar,
bring to a boil, and pour the mixture over the
eggplants, then let marinate for 2 hours.

Meanwhile, if it has not already been cleaned,
prepare the octopus. Turn the body inside out
and pull away the innards and the stiff strips
that stick to the sides. Cut off the stomach
sac. Rinse the octopus thoroughly under cold
running water and turn the body right side out.
Press out the beak and its soft surrounding
tissue from the center of the tentacles and cut
it out. Finally, beat it well with a meat mallet.
Put the octopus into a large pan of lightly
salted boiling water, cover, and simmer for
30 minutes, or until tender.

Remove the pan from the heat and let the octopus
cool in the cooking water. When the octopus is
cool, skin it and cut into very thin slices. Add
the slices to the eggplants, then add the capers
and olives, and season with salt and pepper.
Drizzle with olive oil, and garnish with the
tomatoes and basil leaves.

Panzanella

Panzanella

Preparation time: 10 mins

Serves 4
----

8 slices homemade or store-
    bought rustic white
    bread, crusts removed
8 basil leaves, torn
extra-virgin olive oil, for
    drizzling
4 firm red tomatoes, peeled
    and diced
salt and pepper

Tear the bread into pieces and soak in cold water for a few minutes, then squeeze out and put it into a salad bowl. Season with salt and pepper, sprinkle with the basil, and drizzle generously with oil. Toss the bread with 2 forks so that it crumbles, then add the tomatoes.

Photograph p.56

Rigatoni salad with tuna and green beans

Insalata di mezzi rigatoni
al tonno e fagiolini

Preparation time: 20 mins

Cooking time: 20 mins

Serves 4
----

5 ounces green beans
10 ounces mezzi rigatoni
    pasta or other medium
    pasta shapes
olive oil, for drizzling
5 ounces cherry tomatoes,
    halved and seeded
5 baby artichokes in oil,
    drained and cut into
    wedges
¾ cup pitted and sliced,
    mixed green and black
    olives
9 ounces canned tuna in oil,
    drained and flaked
salt and pepper

Cook the beans in a small pan of salted boiling water for 5–10 minutes, until tender. Drain, refresh under cold running water, and drain again, then cut the beans in half.

Cook the pasta in a large pan of salted boiling water for 8–10 minutes, or according to package directions, until it is tender but still al dente, or firm to the bite. Drain, rinse under cold running water, and drain again. Turn into a dish and drizzle with olive oil.

Put the tomatoes, artichokes, olives, beans, and tuna into a large salad bowl, add the pasta, and stir well. Season with pepper, drizzle with olive oil, and serve.

Piquant rice salad

Insalata di riso piccante

Preparation time: 15 mins

Cooking time: 15–18 mins

Serves 4

1¼ cups long-grain rice

½ cup shelled peas

1 red bell pepper, seeded and
    cut into strips

3 ounces canned anchovies,
    drained and chopped

scant 1 cup pitted olives

1 tablespoon rinsed and
    drained capers

generous ⅓ cup olive oil

2 tablespoons lemon juice,
    strained

salt and pepper

Cook the rice in a large pan of salted boiling
water for 15–18 minutes, or according to package
directions, until tender. Meanwhile, cook the
peas in a small pan of salted boiling water for
10 minutes, or until tender. Drain the rice,
rinse under cold running water, and drain again.
Drain the peas and refresh in cold water.

Put the rice and peas into a bowl and add the
strips of bell pepper, anchovies, olives, and
capers. Whisk together the oil and lemon juice,
season with salt and pepper, and pour over
the salad.

Photograph p.57

Conchiglie salad with robiola and pine nuts

Insalata di conchiglie alla robiola e pinoli

Preparation time: 10 mins

Cooking time: 25 mins

Serves 4

3½ ounces robiola cheese,
    diced

2 tablespoons heavy cream

2 tablespoons chopped basil

generous 1 cup pine nuts,
    coarsely chopped

10 ounces conchiglie pasta

salt and pepper

grated pecorino cheese,
    to serve (optional)

Put the cheese and cream into a small, shallow
pan and melt over very low heat, stirring
frequently, then remove the pan from the heat.
Stir in the basil and season with pepper, then
stir in the pine nuts. Transfer the mixture
to a salad bowl and keep cool, but do not chill
in the refrigerator.

Cook the pasta in a large pan of salted boiling
water for 8–10 minutes, or according to package
directions, until it is tender but still
al dente, or firm to the bite. Drain, rinse under
cold running water, drain again, and turn
into the salad bowl. Stir well, sprinkle with
the pecorino, if you like, and serve.

Note: Conchiglie pasta shells are ideal for
salads. Their shape makes them very suitable
for light sauces.

Panzanella (p.54)

Farfalle salad with smoked trout

Insalata di farfalle alla trota affumicata

Preparation time: 2 mins
Cooking time: 35 mins
Serves 4

5 ounces potatoes
5 ounces green beans,
    trimmed
9 ounces farfalle pasta
olive oil, for drizzling
11 ounces smoked trout,
    skinned and cut into
    thin strips
2 sprigs dill, chopped
salt and pepper

Cook the potatoes in salted boiling water for
20-25 minutes, until tender. Drain, cut into
dice, and let cool. Meanwhile, cook the beans
in another pan of salted boiling water for
5-10 minutes, until tender. Drain, refresh under
cold running water, drain again, and cut into
small pieces. Cook the pasta in a large pan of
salted boiling water for 8-10 minutes, until
it is tender but still al dente, or firm to the
bite. Drain, refresh under cold running water,
and drain again. Tip the pasta onto a large dish
and drizzle with olive oil.

Transfer the pasta to a salad bowl, add the
potatoes, beans, and trout and toss gently.
Sprinkle with the dill, drizzle with olive oil,
and season with salt and pepper. Cover with
clingfilm and keep in the refrigerator until
ready to serve.

Crabmeat with mustard

Polpa di granchio alla senape

Preparation time: 20 mins
Serves 4

2 hard-cooked eggs
2 tablespoons mild Dijon-
    style mustard
scant 1 cup sunflower oil
2 tablespoons lemon juice
4 ounces canned crabmeat,
    drained
1 large lettuce leaf
salt and pepper
thin slices of toast,
    to serve

Halve the eggs, remove the yolks, and crumble
them into a bowl. Add the mustard and mix until
thoroughly combined. Gradually stir in the oil
and lemon juice, a little at a time, as if making
mayonnaise. When the sauce is smooth and
thickened, season with salt and pepper to taste.

Pick over the crabmeat and remove any pieces of
shell and cartilage. Combine the crabmeat with
the sauce and heap the mixture in the middle of
the large lettuce leaf on a serving plate. Serve
with thin slices of toast.

Mortadella involtini

Involtini di mortadella

Preparation time: 15 mins

Serves 4

scant ½ cup cream cheese
8 shelled walnuts, chopped
20 shelled pistachio nuts,
    chopped
2 slices mortadella
salt and pepper
unsalted crackers or whole-
    wheat bread, to serve

Put the cheese into a bowl and beat until smooth and creamy. Stir in the walnuts and pistachios and season with salt and pepper.

Spread out the slices of mortadella and spread the cheese mixture over them, then roll each slice into a cylinder. Wrap them tightly in plastic wrap and twist the ends to seal. Chill them in the refrigerator until ready to serve.

Unwrap the cylinders and cut them into ⅛-inch thick slices. Arrange the slices, slightly overlapping, in a row on a serving dish and serve with unsalted crackers or whole-wheat bread.

Ham and kiwi mousse

Mousse di prosciutto e kiwi

Preparation time: 3¼ hrs
(including chilling)

Serves 6–8

2⅓ cups diced cooked ham
4 ounces robiola cheese
4 tablespoons butter,
    softened
3 kiwis, sliced
salt and pepper

Put the ham, cheese, and butter into a food processor, season with salt and pepper, and process until smooth. Line a mold with plastic wrap and transfer the mousse into the mold. Cover with plastic wrap and chill in the refrigerator for 3 hours.

Turn out onto a serving dish, garnish with sliced kiwis, and serve.

Chicken salami

Salame di pollo

Preparation time: 4–5 hrs
(including cooling and
chilling)
Cooking time: 1 hr
Serves 6

olive oil, for brushing
1 pound 2 ounces skinless,
    boneless chicken breasts,
    cut into pieces
4 scallions, chopped
1 clove garlic, chopped
3 tablespoons chopped
    tarragon
¼ cup pistachio nuts
1 cup fresh white bread
    crumbs
½ cup diced cooked ham
1 pinch freshly grated nutmeg
3 cups heavy cream
1 egg white
salt and pepper
salad greens, to garnish

Preheat the oven to 350°F and brush a large sheet of aluminum foil with oil. Put the chicken into a food processor and process until smooth. Transfer to a bowl, add the scallions, garlic, tarragon, pistachios, bread crumbs, ham, and nutmeg, season with salt and pepper, and mix well.

Whip the cream until stiff and fold it into the mixture. Whisk the egg white until stiff and fold it into the mixture. Shape the mixture into a sausage, place on the sheet of aluminum foil, fold the foil over, and seal well. Put the parcel on a baking sheet and bake for 1 hour.

Remove the parcel from the oven and let cool, then chill in the refrigerator. Unwrap the chicken salami, cut into slices, and serve garnished with salad leaves.

Baked figs

Fichi al forno

Preparation time: 10 mins
Cooking time: 10 mins
Serves 4

butter, for greasing
24 firm, ripe figs
scant 1 cup superfine sugar
⅓ cup rum
grated zest of 1 lemon
fig and walnut ice cream,
    to serve (optional)

Preheat the oven to 350°F and grease a large, deep ovenproof dish with butter. Wash the figs and, while they are still damp, dip them in the sugar so that it coats the skins. Put them into the prepared dish, in a single layer standing next to each other. Pour the rum into the bottom of the ovenproof dish and slowly add scant 1 cup water. Sprinkle with the grated lemon rind and bake for 10 minutes. Serve hot or cold. If serving cold, chill in the refrigerator for 1 hour before serving. They are delicious with fig and walnut ice cream.

Melons in port

Melone al porto

Preparation time: 35 mins
(including macerating)
Serves 4

2 small, firm, ripe melons
generous ⅓ cup port
4 mint leaves

Keep the melons in a cool place. Half an hour before serving, halve them, remove the seeds and membranes, and scoop out a little of the flesh around the cavities, then pour in the port. Serve each half garnished with a mint leaf. To take more easily on a picnic, prepare the melons in advance and pack them in a sealed container. Pour the port into the melon halves when you arrive.

Apple strudel

Strudel di mele

Preparation time: 1½ hrs
(including resting)
Cooking time: 45 mins
Serves 8

2¼ cups all-purpose flour,
    plus extra for dusting
1 egg, separated
sunflower oil, for brushing
5-6 firm apples
¼ cup rum
3 tablespoons pine nuts
1 pinch ground cinnamon
⅓ cup superfine sugar
scant ¼ cup raisins
2 tablespoons butter, plus
    extra for brushing
1¼ cups fresh white bread
    crumbs
salt

Sift the flour with a pinch of salt into a bowl, add the egg white and scant ½ cup water, and knead to a smooth dough. Shape it into a ball, brush with oil, wrap in plastic wrap, and let rest for 30 minutes. Preheat the oven to 350°F.

Meanwhile, peel, core, and thinly slice the apples. Put them into a bowl with the rum, pine nuts, cinnamon, sugar, and raisins and set aside to let the flavors mingle. Melt the butter in a small skillet. Add the bread crumbs and cook over low heat, stirring frequently, for a few minutes, until golden brown. Remove the skillet from the heat and set aside.

Unwrap the dough and roll it out on a lightly floured cloth, then place your hands underneath it, with palms facing downward, and gradually move them apart to stretch the dough in all directions until it is as thin as possible. If the cloth has a pattern, you should be able to see it through the dough.

Cut the dough into a neat rectangle and sprinkle evenly with the bread crumbs, followed by the apple mixture, leaving a 2-inch margin all the way around. Brush the margin with melted butter, then, using the cloth to help you, roll up the dough like a jelly roll, tucking in the sides. Lightly beat the egg yolk and brush it over the roll. Carefully transfer to a baking sheet and bake for 40 minutes.

Note: This dessert is particularly good for picnics, in which case it can be made the day before.

Salads

Insalate

Salads are healthy, natural, and tasty,
and they can be adapted to make use
of whatever leaves and vegetables are
at their best in the vegetable plot.
In this way, many delightful and unusual
combinations can be created, such as
arugula with melon, or watercress with
eggplant. When it comes to combining
ingredients for a salad, you can
use your imagination and your own good
taste, as well as following the
recipes here.

A salad can be a light accompaniment
to a main dish, or, when combined with
more substantial ingredients such
as meat or legumes and potatoes, it can
form a meal in itself. In Italy, this
kind of salad is usually referred to as
mista, or "mixed," and many of these can
be found in Light Lunches and Suppers.
The salads here are leaf and vegetable-
based, and are perfect alongside simple
broiled meat and fish dishes.

Salads are quick and easy to prepare,
with only a few rules to follow. First,
use extra-virgin olive oil and good-
quality vinegar. When preparing the
dressing, always add the salt to the
vinegar and whisk to dissolve it before
adding the oil. The salad should be
dressed just before serving to keep the
leaves as crisp as possible. Never add
too much dressing, because it can easily
mask the other flavors.

Pineapple, corn salad, and pine nut salad

Insalata di ananas, songino e pinoli

Preparation time: 10 mins
Serves 4

1 tablespoon balsamic vinegar
1 tablespoon soy sauce
3 tablespoons olive oil
1 bunch corn salad
1 small pineapple, peeled,
   cored, and cut into cubes
⅓ cup pine nuts
3 sprigs cilantro, coarsely
   chopped
salt and pepper

Whisk together the balsamic vinegar, soy sauce, and olive oil in a salad bowl and season with salt and pepper. Shred the corn salad and add it to the bowl with the pineapple and pine nuts, then toss. Sprinkle with cilantro and serve immediately.

Orange, walnut, and fennel salad

Insalata d'arance, noci e finocchi

Preparation time: 10 mins
Serves 4

4 fennel bulbs, thinly sliced
olive oil, for drizzling
2 oranges
6 walnuts, chopped
salt and pepper

Put the fennel into a salad bowl, drizzle with olive oil, and season with salt and pepper. Peel the oranges, removing all traces of bitter white pith, cut them into slices or segments, and add to the fennel. Sprinkle the salad with the walnuts, stir well, and keep cool until ready to serve.

Asparagus salad

Asparagi in insalata

Preparation time: 15 mins
Cooking time: 20–25 mins
Serves 4

2¼ pounds asparagus, trimmed
4 hard-cooked eggs
olive oil, for drizzling
juice of ½ lemon, strained
1 tablespoon chopped flat-
   leaf parsley
salt and pepper

Tie the asparagus together, stand them in a tall pan of salted boiling water without submerging the tips, cover, and cook for 5–10 minutes, until tender. Remove from the pan and arrange on a serving dish. Halve the eggs, scoop out the yolks, and crumble them over the asparagus. Drizzle with oil, sprinkle with lemon juice and parsley, and season with salt and pepper. Serve immediately.

Photograph p.68

Mixed beet salad

Insalata mista di barbabietole

Preparation time: 25 mins

Cooking time: 15-20 mins

Serves 4

11 ounces potatoes
5 ounces green beans
2 cooked beets, sliced
1 tomato, cut into wedges
3 hard-cooked eggs
3½ ounces Gruyère cheese,
    diced
2½ tablespoons rinsed and
    drained capers
3 dill pickles, drained and
    coarsely chopped
1 tablespoon chopped flat-
    leaf parsley
1 tablespoon white-wine
    vinegar
¾-1 cup olive oil
salt and pepper

Cook the potatoes in a pan of salted boiling water for 15-20 minutes, until they are tender. Cook the green beans in another pan of salted boiling water for 5-10 minutes, or until they are tender but still firm to the bite, then drain and refresh them under cold running water. Drain the potatoes and cut into slices.

Put the potatoes, beets, and tomato in the middle of a salad bowl. Shell the eggs. Cut 2 of the eggs into wedges and add to the bowl with the cheese. Surround these ingredients with the green beans.

Coarsely chop the remaining egg. Put the capers, dill pickles, chopped egg, parsley, vinegar, and ⅔ cup of the oil in a blender, season with salt and pepper, and blend to a thick sauce, adding more oil if necessary. Serve the salad, offering the sauce separately.

Avocado salad

Insalata di avocado

Preparation time: 25 mins

Serves 4

2 avocados
juice of 1 lemon, strained
2 mandarins or tangerines
1 romaine lettuce, separated
    into leaves
2 tomatoes, sliced
1 scallion, sliced
2 tablespoons chopped flat-
    leaf parsley
2 teaspoons Dijon mustard
generous ⅓ cup olive oil
salt and pepper

Peel, halve, and pit the avocados, then cut them into slices and sprinkle with the lemon juice to prevent discoloration. Peel the mandarins, remove all traces of white pith, and cut into round slices.

Arrange the lettuce leaves on individual dishes. Make a layer of tomato and scallion slices on the leaves, cover with avocado slices in a circle, and top with slices of mandarin. Sprinkle with the parsley.

Whisk together the mustard, oil, a pinch of salt, and a pinch of pepper in a bowl, pour over the salads, and serve.

Photograph p.69

Asparagus salad (p.66)

ocado salad (p.67)

Salad with capers

Insalatina ai capperi

Preparation time: 20 mins
Serves 6

3 carrots, cut into thin
  strips
1 bunch dandelion leaves,
  cut into thin strips
2 fennel bulbs, cut into
  thin strips
1 curly lettuce, cut into
  thin strips
generous ⅓ cup olive oil
2 tablespoons white-wine
  vinegar
3 tablespoons rinsed and
  drained capers preserved
  in salt
1 sprig basil, shredded
salt

Put the carrots, dandelion leaves, fennel, and lettuce into a salad bowl. Whisk together the oil and vinegar in a bowl and season with salt. Add the capers and basil, pour the dressing over the salad, toss, and serve.

Note: Dandelion leaves, with their pleasantly bitter taste, grow wild in Italy and are commonly used in salads.

Avocado and anchovy salad

Insalata di avocado e acciughe

Preparation time: 20 mins
Serves 4

2 avocados
6 olives, pitted and sliced
4 anchovy fillets in oil,
  drained and chopped
1 tablespoon rinsed and
  drained capers
generous ⅓ cup olive oil
juice of 1 lemon, strained
salt

Halve and pit the avocados, then scoop out the flesh and dice it. Put the avocados, olives, anchovies, and capers into a salad bowl.

Whisk together the olive oil and lemon juice in a small bowl and season with salt. Drizzle the dressing over the salad and keep it cool until ready to serve.

Carrot, celery and apple salad

Insalata di carote, sedano e mele

Preparation time: 15 mins
Serves 4

4 carrots, sliced
3 celery stalks, cut into
    small strips
2 apples, peeled, cored, and
    diced

For the sauce

⅓ cup whole-milk plain yogurt
2 tablespoons light cream
1 tablespoon chopped mixed
    herbs
1 tablespoon chopped flat-
    leaf parsley
salt and pepper

Make a layer of carrots, then a layer of celery, and, finally, a layer of apples in a salad bowl. To make the sauce, whisk together the yogurt and cream in a bowl, stir in the mixed herbs, and season with salt and pepper. Pour the sauce over the salad and sprinkle with the chopped parsley.

Note: The carrot is one of the most versatile vegetables and can be eaten in many ways, from raw in a *pinzimonio*, or dish of crudités, to braised, and also in savory tarts, soufflés, and smoothies. Tender and sweet new carrots can be eaten raw, grated, and dressed with oil, lemon, salt, and pepper.

Cucumbers in yogurt

Cetrioli allo yogurt

Preparation time: 20 mins
Serves 4

4 small cucumbers, thinly
    sliced
1 iceberg lettuce, shredded
2 hard-cooked eggs, cut into
    wedges
⅓ cup low-fat plain yogurt
1–2 tablespoons lemon juice,
    strained
salt and pepper

Put the cucumbers, lettuce, and wedges of hard-cooked egg into a salad bowl. Mix the yogurt with lemon juice to taste in a small bowl and pour over the salad. Season with salt and pepper, toss lightly, and serve.

Cucumber and horseradish salad

Cetrioli in insalata con cren

Preparation time: 20 mins
Serves 4

1 cucumber
4 ounces horseradish root
1 clove garlic
¾ cup plain yogurt
3 tablespoons white-wine
   vinegar
1 pinch ground ginger
1 pinch cayenne pepper
½ bunch watercress
salt and pepper

Peel the cucumber and horseradish and cut them into thin strips. Halve the garlic clove and rub the cut sides around the inside of a salad bowl. Pour the yogurt into the bowl, add the vinegar, ginger, and cayenne, and whisk well. Add the cucumber and horseradish strips, toss well, and garnish with the watercress.

Cucumbers with olives

Cetrioli alle olive

Preparation time: 45 mins
(including draining)
Serves 4

2 cucumbers, peeled
1 tablespoon chopped dill
1 tablespoon lemon juice
1 tablespoon olive oil
20 black olives, pitted and
   quartered
salt

Thinly slice the cucumber, place in a colander, sprinkle with salt, and let drain for 30 minutes. Rinse, drain, pat dry, and put them into a salad bowl. Sprinkle with the dill and drizzle with the lemon juice and olive oil. Add the olives, season with salt if necessary, and toss. Let stand for a few minutes, then serve.

Delicate lettuce

Lattuga delicata

Preparation time: 15 mins
Serves 4

5 ounces mild fontina cheese
olive oil, for drizzling
4 tomatoes, peeled and diced
1 lettuce
12–16 basil leaves
salt and white pepper

Dice the cheese and put it into a bowl, drizzle with olive oil, and season with a pinch of white pepper. Put the tomatoes into a bowl, season with salt and pepper, and drizzle with oil. Remove and discard the coarse outer lettuce leaves, then line 4 glass dishes with the tender leaves, sprinkle the cheese, tomatoes, and basil leaves on top, and serve.

Cicorino and Gorgonzola salad

Insalata di cicorino al gorgonzola

Preparation time: 15 mins
Serves 4

2 slices rustic bread, crusts
    removed
1 clove garlic, halved
3 bunches cicorino, cut into
    thin strips
3½ ounces Gruyère cheese,
    cut into thin strips
2 ounces strong Gorgonzola
    cheese
1 tablespoon Dijon mustard
generous ⅓ cup olive oil
2 tablespoons white-wine
    vinegar
1 teaspoon brandy
salt and pepper

Rub the slices of bread with the garlic, then discard the garlic. Cut the bread into cubes. Put the cicorino, Gruyère, and bread cubes into a salad bowl.

To make the dressing, crumble the Gorgonzola into a separate bowl and add the mustard, olive oil, vinegar, and brandy. Season with salt and pepper and whisk well until thoroughly combined and creamy. Spoon the dressing over the salad just before serving.

Note: Cicorino, along with endive, escarole, frisée, and radicchio, is a member of the chicory family and has the characteristic bitter flavor that adds a delicious piquancy to salads. It is not dissimilar to radicchio in appearance, and can be red or green.

Lettuce, Gruyère, and egg salad

Insalata di lattuga, groviera e uova

Preparation time: 15 mins
Serves 4

3 hard-cooked eggs
1 teaspoon curry powder
2 tablespoons white-wine
    vinegar
¼ cup olive oil
7 ounces lettuce, torn into
    large pieces
1¼ cups grated Gruyère
    cheese
salt and pepper

Halve the eggs and scoop out the yolks. Dice the whites and set them aside. Crumble the yolks into a bowl with the curry powder, vinegar, and oil, season with salt and pepper, and mix well. Put the lettuce leaves into a salad bowl and dress with the sauce. Sprinkle with the cheese and diced egg whites, toss gently, and serve.

Watercress
and eggplant salad

Insalata di crescione e melanzane

Preparation time: 15 mins
Cooking time: 8–10 mins
Serves 6

4 eggplants
generous ⅓ cup olive oil,
    plus extra for brushing
7 ounces watercress
1 red bell pepper, seeded and
    cut into strips
1 clove garlic
2 tablespoons white-wine
    vinegar
1 sprig flat-leaf parsley,
    chopped
3–4 mint leaves
salt

Preheat the broiler. Peel the eggplants, cut into slices, and brush with oil. Broil for 8–10 minutes, turning once, then set aside to cool.

Chop the eggplant slices and put them into a salad bowl with the watercress, red bell pepper, and whole garlic clove.

Whisk together the vinegar, oil, chopped parsley, and mint in a bowl, season with salt, and pour the dressing over the salad. Toss lightly and remove the garlic clove before serving.

Photograph p.78

Ligurian green bean salad

Insalata di fagiolini alla ligure

Preparation time: 15 mins
Cooking time: 5–10 mins
Serves 4

1 pound 2 ounces green beans
scant 1 cup pine nuts
2 tablespoons anchovy paste
2 tablespoons white-wine
    vinegar
generous ⅓ cup olive oil
4–5 mint leaves
salt

Bring a pan of salted water to a boil, add the beans, and cook for 5–10 minutes, or until just tender. Drain the pan, turn the beans into a salad bowl, and add the pine nuts.

Whisk together the anchovy paste and vinegar in a bowl, then whisk in the olive oil. Pour the dressing over the salad and toss lightly. Sprinkle with the mint leaves and serve.

/ Salads /

Green bean salad

Fagiolini in insalata

Preparation time: 45 mins
(including cooling)
Cooking time: 5-10 mins
Serves 4

1 pound 5 ounces green and
    yellow beans
1 onion, thinly sliced
1 clove garlic, thinly sliced
1 teaspoon mustard seeds
juice of ½ lemon, strained
1 sprig flat-leaf parsley,
    chopped
olive oil, for drizzling
salt and pepper

Trim the beans, then cook them in a pan of salted boiling water for 5-10 minutes, or until just tender. Drain, and turn into a salad bowl. Add the onion, garlic, mustard seeds, lemon juice, and parsley, drizzle with olive oil, and season with salt and pepper. Toss and set aside in a cool place for 30 minutes to let the flavors mingle before serving.

Fig salad

Fichi in insalata

Preparation time: 15 mins
Serves 4

4 black figs
4 green figs
3½ ounces pecorino cheese
¾ cup shredded arugula
1 lettuce, shredded
scant ⅓ cup olive oil
salt and pepper

Peel the figs and cut them into segments. Dice the cheese. Put the arugula, lettuce, figs, and cheese into a salad bowl, season with salt, and stir gently. Whisk together the olive oil and a pinch each of salt and pepper in a bowl. Pour the dressing over the salad, toss, and serve.

Fennel, celery, and apple salad

Insalata di finocchio, sedano e mele

Preparation time: 15 mins
Serves 4

2 fennel bulbs
2 green apples
2 celery hearts
⅔ cup plain yogurt
2 tablespoons snipped chives
salt and pepper

Thinly slice the fennel and core and thinly slice the apples. Slice the celery hearts into rounds. Combine the fennel, apples, and celery hearts in a salad bowl. Combine the yogurt and chives in a bowl, season with salt and pepper, and add to the salad. Toss lightly and serve.

Photograph p.79

Watercress and eggplant salad (p.76)

Mushroom carpaccio on a bed of cabbage

Carpaccio di funghi su letto
di insalata cappuccio

Preparation time: 15 mins
Serves 4

1 pound 2 ounces very fresh
    young porcini mushrooms
3 tablespoons olive oil
½ tablespoon balsamic vinegar
1 tablespoon sherry vinegar
1 white cabbage, shredded
2 celery stalks, cut into
    short lengths
1 tablespoon snipped chives
2 ounces Parmesan cheese,
    shaved
salt and pepper

Remove and discard the stems of the mushrooms and cut the caps into very thin slices. Whisk together the olive oil and balsamic and sherry vinegars in a bowl and season with salt and pepper.

Put the cabbage and celery into a bowl, pour in half the dressing, and toss, then divide among 4 plates. Top with the mushroom slices, sprinkle with the chives, and pour the remaining dressing over the top. Sprinkle with the Parmesan and serve.

Strawberry salad

Insalata di fragole

Preparation time: 20 mins
Serves 4

1 cup hulled and sliced
    strawberries
1 curly lettuce, shredded
5 ounces mixed salad greens,
    such as arugula and corn
    salad, shredded
scant ⅓ cup olive oil
2 tablespoons balsamic
    vinegar
salt and pepper

Put the strawberries, lettuce, and mixed greens into a salad bowl and mix gently. Whisk together the olive oil and balsamic vinegar in a small bowl and season with salt and pepper. Pour the dressing over the salad, toss gently, and serve.

Photograph p.82

Peach salad

Insalata di pesche

Preparation time: 20 mins
Serves 4

1 lollo rosso lettuce, cut
    into strips
1 frisée lettuce, cut
    into strips
3 yellow peaches, peeled,
    pitted, and cut
    into eighths
⅔ cup low-fat plain yogurt
scant 1 cup chopped walnuts
salt and pepper

Put the lettuce and frisée into a salad bowl
and add the peaches. Season the yogurt with salt
and pepper, drizzle it over the salad, and
stir gently. Sprinkle with the walnuts and serve.

Carnation salad

Insalata con garofani

Preparation time: 25 mins
(including soaking)
Serves 4

1 ounce unsprayed pink
    carnation petals
3½ ounces radicchio
3½ ounces small-leafed
    lettuce, such as Boston
5–6 radishes, trimmed
1 small smoked scamorza
    cheese
1 green apple
generous ⅓ cup olive oil
2 tablespoons white-wine
    vinegar
salt and pepper

Put the carnation petals in a bowl of cold water
and let soak for about 10 minutes. Meanwhile, cut
the radicchio and lettuce into strips, thinly
slice the radishes, dice the scamorza, and core
and slice the apple, then put them all into a
salad bowl.

Whisk together the oil and vinegar in a bowl and
season with salt and pepper. Pour the dressing
over the salad and toss. Drain the carnation
petals, sprinkle them over the salad, and serve.

Photograph p.83

Strawberry salad (p.80)

Radish salad with olives

Insalata di ravanelli con olive

Preparation time: 20 mins
(including standing)
Serves 4

6 red radishes, trimmed
juice of 1 lemon, strained
3½ ounces corn salad
10 pitted black olives
olive oil, for drizzling
salt

Cut the radishes into very thin horizontal slices, put them into a salad bowl, and sprinkle with the lemon juice. Add the corn salad and olives, drizzle with olive oil, and season with salt to taste. Mix gently and let stand for 10 minutes before serving.

Lettuce hearts with herbs

Cuori di lattuga alle erbe

Preparation time: 20 mins
(including standing)
Serves 4

4 lettuce hearts
1 tablespoon Dijon mustard
2 tablespoons balsamic
    vinegar
about ⅓ cup olive oil
1 sprig tarragon, chopped
4 chives, snipped
1 sprig chervil, chopped
salt and pepper

Cut each lettuce heart into 4 and place in a salad bowl. Mix together the mustard and vinegar in a bowl and season with salt and pepper. Gradually whisk in the olive oil. Sprinkle the lettuce with the herbs and pour the dressing over the salad. Toss and let stand for 10 minutes before serving.

Lettuce with orange and olives

Insalata di lattuga all'arancia e olive

Preparation time: 10 mins
Serves 4

1 romaine lettuce, cut into
    large strips
½ cup olive oil
juice of 1 lemon, strained
1 orange, peeled and thinly
    sliced
12 black olives, pitted
salt and pepper

Put the lettuce into a salad bowl. Whisk together the olive oil and lemon juice in a bowl and season with salt and pepper. Pour the dressing over the lettuce and toss. Add the orange slices and olives and serve immediately.

/ Salads /

Lettuce, green bean, and beet salad

Insalata di lattuga,
fagiolini e barbietole

Preparation time: 20 mins
Cooking time: 10 mins
Serves 6

¼ cup olive oil
juice of ½ lemon, strained
1 tablespoon Dijon mustard
1 clove garlic, very thinly
    sliced
1 sprig flat-leaf parsley,
    chopped
4 ounces green beans
2 large cooked beets,
    peeled and cut into
    2-inch sticks
1 cucumber, peeled, halved
    lengthwise, and thinly
    sliced
1 lettuce, shredded
3 shallots, chopped
½ green bell pepper, seeded
    and cut into strips
7 ounces Emmenthal cheese,
    diced
salt and pepper

Whisk together the olive oil, lemon juice, mustard, and garlic in a bowl and season with salt and pepper. Stir in the parsley. Bring a pan of salted water to a boil, add the beans, and cook for 10 minutes, then drain and refresh the beans under cold running water. Drain the beans again, pat them dry with paper towels, and cut them in half.

Put the beans, beet, cucumber, lettuce, shallots, green bell pepper, and cheese into a salad bowl, add a few tablespoons of the dressing, and toss. Serve immediately, offering the remaining dressing separately.

Sunflower petal salad

Insalata di petali di girasole

Preparation time: 15 mins
Serves 4

1 unsprayed sunflower
7 ounces small-leafed
    lettuce, such as Boston,
    separated into leaves
2¾ cups thinly sliced white
    mushrooms
olive oil, to taste
white-wine vinegar, to taste
salt

Pull off the petals from the sunflower, then rinse and pat dry with paper towels. Put the petals, lettuce, and mushrooms into a salad bowl. Whisk together the oil and vinegar in a bowl, season with salt, and pour the dressing over the salad. Toss lightly and serve.

Photograph p.88

Mushroom salad
with speck and cicorino

Insalata di funghi allo speck e cicorino

Preparation time: 10 mins

Cooking time: 15 mins

Serves 4

5 tablespoons olive oil
1 clove garlic
5⅔ cups sliced white
    mushrooms
2 ounces speck or bacon, cut
    into strips
1 teaspoon balsamic vinegar
3½ ounces cicorino
    (see Note, p.73)
salt and pepper

Heat 2 tablespoons of the oil with the garlic in a shallow pan. Cook until the garlic has browned, then add the mushrooms and speck or bacon, and cook over medium-high heat, stirring occasionally, for 10 minutes. Remove and discard the garlic and season with salt and pepper. Remove the pan from the heat and let cool.

Whisk together the remaining olive oil and the balsamic vinegar in a bowl and season with salt and pepper. Put the cicorino into a salad bowl, add the mushroom mixture, pour the dressing over the salad, and serve.

Sunshine salad

Insalata solare

Preparation time: 45 mins
(including salting)

Serves 4

1 eggplant
generous ⅓ cup olive oil,
    plus extra for drizzling
1 green bell pepper, seeded
    and sliced
1 red bell pepper, seeded
    and sliced
1 tomato, thinly sliced
scant 1 cup green olives,
    pitted
3 tablespoons rinsed and
    drained capers
1 fresh red chile,
    seeded and chopped
salt and pepper

Peel and dice the eggplant. Put it into a colander, sprinkle with salt, and let drain for 30 minutes. Rinse it, pat dry with paper towels, put it into a salad bowl, and drizzle with olive oil. Put the green and red bell pepper slices on top. Pat the tomato slices dry with paper towels and put them on top of the bell peppers.

Sprinkle the olives, capers, and chile over the salad. Put the olive oil in a bowl, season with salt and pepper, and pour over the salad. Toss just before serving. The salad may be dressed 30 minutes beforehand.

Photograph p.89

Corn and
mozzarella salad

Insalata di mais e mozzarella

Preparation time: 10 mins

Serves 6

1¼ cups drained and rinsed
    canned corn kernels, or
    cooked corn kernels
3 tomatoes, peeled and diced
1 medium-size mozzarella,
    diced
2 celery hearts, chopped
1 green bell pepper in olive
    oil, drained and cut
    into strips
¼ cup olive oil
white-wine vinegar,
    for drizzling
salt and pepper

Put the corn, tomatoes, mozzarella, celery
hearts, and green bell pepper into a salad bowl.
Add the olive oil, season with salt and pepper,
and drizzle with the vinegar. Stir well
and serve.

Note: Cow's milk mozzarella should be eaten
fresh, while still soft and springy. It can be
kept for 2–3 days in the refrigerator in its
milky liquid.

Lettuce with
roasted vegetables

Insalata di lattuga con verdure arrosto

Preparation time: 1¼ hrs

(including cooling)

Cooking time: 1 hr

Serves 4
----

7 small potatoes
1 large mealy potato, sliced
1 carrot, sliced
1 turnip, sliced
1 red bell pepper, seeded
    and diced
8 pearl onions
2 sprigs fresh rosemary
1 clove garlic
olive oil, for drizzling
3 zucchini, sliced
4 mint leaves, shredded
1 tablespoon balsamic vinegar
1 lettuce, shredded
salt and pepper

Preheat the oven to 400°F. Put the potatoes,
carrot, turnip, red bell pepper, onions,
rosemary, and garlic into an ovenproof dish,
drizzle with oil, and season with salt and
pepper. Roast for 30 minutes, then remove from
the oven and loosen the vegetables with a
spatula. Add the zucchini, return the dish to the
oven, and roast for another 30 minutes.

Remove the dish from the oven, sprinkle the mint
over the vegetables, drizzle with the vinegar,
and let cool. Make a bed of lettuce on a serving
dish, top with the cooled vegetables, and serve.

Sunflower petal salad (p.85)

Minted eggplant salad

Insalata di melanzane alla menta

Preparation time: 45 mins
(including salting)
Cooking time: 10 mins
Serves 4

2 eggplants, thickly sliced
    lengthwise
scant ½ cup olive oil, plus
    extra for brushing
3 tomatoes, cut into wedges
2 scallions, sliced
1 tablespoon anchovy paste
1 tablespoon white-wine
    vinegar
1 sprig flat-leaf parsley,
    chopped
4–5 basil leaves
1 sprig oregano, chopped
1 sprig mint, chopped
salt and pepper
10 black olives, to garnish
mint leaves, to garnish

Put the eggplant slices into a colander, sprinkle with salt, cover, and let drain for 30 minutes, then rinse and pat dry with paper towels. Meanwhile, preheat the broiler. Spread out the eggplant slices on a baking sheet, brush with olive oil, and broil for 5 minutes, then turn, brush with more oil, and broil for another 5 minutes. Remove from the heat and let cool, then cut into strips.

Put the eggplants, tomatoes, and scallions into a salad bowl. Whisk together the anchovy paste and vinegar in a bowl, then whisk in the olive oil, parsley, basil, oregano, and mint, and season with salt and pepper. Pour the dressing over the salad and toss lightly. Garnish with the olives and mint leaves and serve.

Tomato tartare with basil

Tartare di pomodori al basilico

Preparation time: 45 mins
(including salting)
Serves 4

16 cherry tomatoes, seeded
    and diced
11 ounces primo sale
    (see Note), diced
16 black olives, pitted
1 bunch of basil, shredded
olive oil, for drizzling
salt

Put the tomatoes into a colander, sprinkle with salt, and let drain for 30 minutes. Drain well, transfer to a large salad bowl, add the cheese, olives, and basil leaves, drizzle generously with olive oil, and season with salt. Mix carefully and keep cool until ready to serve.

Note: To make this tartare a success, the tomatoes and cheese must be diced quite finely and should be fairly firm. *Primo sale* is a soft fresh cheese and can be replaced with buffalo mozzarella.

Photograph p.94

/ Salads /

Raw leek salad

Insalata di porri

Preparation time: 45 mins
(including standing)
Serves 4

4 tender leeks, white
    parts only
Parmesan cheese (see method)
olive oil, for drizzling
salt and pepper

Cut the white parts of the leeks into very thin slices and weigh them. Cut a piece of Parmesan the same weight as the leeks, and make shavings of cheese with a vegetable peeler. Mix the leeks and Parmesan shavings in a bowl, drizzle with olive oil, and season with salt and pepper. Let stand for 30 minutes before serving to let the flavors mingle.

Melon balls with arugula

Palline di melone con rucola

Preparation time: 10 mins
Serves 4

1 small melon
¾ cup shredded arugula
¼ cup olive oil
2 tablespoons white-wine
    vinegar
salt and freshly ground white
    pepper

Halve the melon and remove and discard the seeds. Using a melon baller, scoop out small balls from the melon flesh. Put them into a large bowl and add the arugula.

Whisk together the olive oil and vinegar in a small bowl and season with salt and pepper. Pour the dressing over the salad, stir gently, and serve.

Melon salad

Insalata di melone

Preparation time: 15 mins
Serves 4

1 melon
4 tomatoes, sliced
1 lettuce, cut into strips
generous 1 cup drained and
    rinsed canned corn
    kernels, or cooked corn
    kernels
⅓ cup plain yogurt
juice of ½ lemon, strained
2 tablespoons olive oil
salt

Cut the melon in half and scoop out the seeds. Using a melon baller, scoop out balls from the melon flesh and put them into a salad bowl. Add the tomatoes, lettuce, and corn. Combine the yogurt, lemon juice, olive oil, and a pinch of salt in a bowl. Add to the salad, toss gently, and serve.

Red currant
and blueberry salad

Insalata di ribes e mirtilli

Preparation time: 15 mins
Serves 4

2 hard-cooked eggs, sliced
9 ounces salad greens,
    shredded
4 carrots, cut into strips
4 goat cheeses, diced
1¼ cups red currants
1¼ cups blueberries
scant ⅓ cup olive oil
3 tablespoons balsamic
    vinegar
salt and pepper

Put the hard-cooked eggs, salad greens, carrots, cheese, red currants, and blueberries into a salad bowl. Whisk together the olive oil and balsamic vinegar in a small bowl and season with salt and pepper. Pour the dressing over the salad, toss, and serve.

Sicilian citrus
fruit salad

Insalata siciliana d'agrumi

Preparation time: 40 mins
(including standing)
Serves 6

4 oranges
2 fennel bulbs, thinly sliced
4 slightly green lemons,
    thinly sliced
1 cup pitted and chopped
    black olives
olive oil, for drizzling
salt and freshly ground
    white pepper

Peel the oranges, removing all traces of bitter white pith, and cut them into segments, slicing between the membranes, then put them into a salad bowl. Add the fennel, lemons, and olives, drizzle with the olive oil, and season with salt and white pepper. Stir gently, cover, and let stand in the refrigerator for 20 minutes to let the flavors mingle, then serve.

/ Salads /

Baby zucchini salad

Insalata di zucchine novelle

Preparation time: 45 mins
(including standing)
Serves 4

6 baby zucchini, thinly
    sliced lengthwise
2 ounces Parmesan cheese,
    shaved
1 pinch dried oregano
3 tablespoons olive oil
2 tomatoes, peeled and sliced
salt and pepper

Put the zucchini in a salad bowl, add the
Parmesan, oregano, and olive oil, and season with
salt and pepper. Mix well and set aside in
a cool place for at least 30 minutes to let
the flavors mingle. Add the tomatoes just before
serving.

Photograph p.95

Zucchini salad
with basil

Zucchine in insalata con basilico

Preparation time: 10 mins
Serves 4

1 pound 5 ounces young
    zucchini, thinly sliced
6 sprigs basil, chopped
juice of 1 lemon, strained
generous ⅓ cup olive oil
salt and pepper

Put the zucchini slices into a salad bowl and
sprinkle with the basil. Whisk together the
lemon juice and olive oil in a bowl and season
with salt and pepper. Pour the dressing over
the zucchini and basil and mix well.

Mixed zucchini salad

Insalata mista di zucchine

Preparation time: 15 mins
Serves 4

1 fennel bulb
4 small zucchini, thinly
    sliced into rounds
2 celery stalks, chopped
1 scallion, sliced
1 bunch arugula, finely
    chopped
juice of ½ lemon strained
generous ⅓ cup olive oil
salt and pepper

Cut the fennel into quarters and thinly slice
them. Put the fennel into a salad bowl with the
zucchini, celery, scallion, and arugula. Whisk
together the lemon juice and oil in a bowl,
season with salt and pepper, and pour the
dressing over the salad. Toss lightly and serve.

Tomato tartare with basil (p.90)

by zucchini salad (p.93)

Panzanella with vegetables

Panzanella di verdure

Preparation time: 1½ hrs
(including chilling)
Cooking time: 5 mins
Serves 4

2 young zucchini
5 ounces rustic bread, crusts
    removed, and cut into
    cubes
olive oil, for drizzling
2 plum tomatoes, peeled,
    seeded, and diced
1 scallion, thinly sliced
8 black olives, pitted and
    chopped
balsamic vinegar, for
    drizzling
4–5 basil leaves, torn,
    plus extra to garnish
salt and pepper

Preheat the oven to 350°F. Blanch the zucchini
in a pan of boiling water for 3 minutes until
just tender, then drain and let cool. Spread out
the cubes of bread on a baking sheet, drizzle
with oil, season with salt and pepper, and bake
for 5 minutes.

Cut the zucchini into rounds and put them into
a bowl with the tomatoes, toasted bread,
scallion, and olives. Drizzle with olive oil and
balsamic vinegar, season with salt and pepper,
and gently stir in the basil leaves.

Fill small molds with this mixture, pressing it
down gently. Chill in the refrigerator for
1 hour. To serve, turn out onto individual plates
and garnish with basil leaves.

Couscous and onion salad

Insalata di cus-cus alle cipolle

Preparation time: 2¾ hrs
(including soaking and
chilling)
Serves 4

generous 1 cup couscous
scant ⅓ cup olive oil
juice of 2 lemons, strained
1¼ cups chopped onions
1 pound 2 ounces tomatoes,
    diced
1 sprig flat-leaf parsley,
    chopped
1 sprig cilantro, chopped
1 sprig mint, chopped
1 sprig basil, chopped
salt and pepper

Put the couscous into a bowl, pour in boiling
water to cover, stir with a fork, cover, and let
soak for 30 minutes, or according to package
directions, until the liquid has been absorbed.
Separate the grains with a fork. Whisk together
the olive oil and lemon juice in a bowl and
season with salt and pepper. Pour the dressing
over the couscous and add the onions, tomatoes,
and herbs. Stir, then cover, and chill in the
refrigerator for 2 hours before serving.

/ Salads /

Artichoke, mushroom, and fennel salad

Insalata di carciofi, funghi e finocchi

Preparation time: 25 mins

Serves 4

juice of 1 lemon, strained
3 very tender young
    artichokes
2 cups white mushrooms
6 tablespoons olive oil
1 fennel bulb
1 large sprig flat-leaf
    parsley, finely chopped
salt and pepper

Fill a bowl with water halfway and add 1 tablespoon of the lemon juice. Trim the artichokes and remove the coarse outer leaves, then put them into the acidulated water. Slice the mushrooms and put them into another bowl. Combine the remaining lemon juice and 4 tablespoons of the olive oil in a pitcher, season with salt and pepper, and pour the mixture over the mushrooms.

Trim the fennel, cut it into strips, and put it into a salad bowl. Drain the artichokes and arrange the leaves around the fennel. Spoon the mushrooms into the middle. Combine the parsley and remaining oil in a bowl, season with salt and pepper, pour the dressing over the salad, and toss just before serving.

Mixed vegetable salad

Insalata mista

Preparation time: 30 mins

Cooking time: 20-30 mins

Serves 4

3 potatoes
2 carrots
scant 1 cup shelled peas
juice of 1 lemon, strained
3 very tender young
    artichokes
3½ ounces Edam cheese, diced
generous ⅓ cup olive oil
16 green and black olives,
    pitted
2 hard-cooked eggs, cut
    into wedges
salt and pepper

Cook the potatoes in a pan of salted boiling water for 20-30 minutes, until they are tender. Meanwhile, cook the carrots in another pan of salted boiling water for 20-25 minutes, until they are tender, and cook the peas in a third pan of salted boiling water for 15-25 minutes, until they are tender.

Meanwhile, fill a bowl with water halfway and stir in 1 tablespoon of the lemon juice. Trim the artichokes, cut them into wedges, and put them into the acidulated water. Drain all the cooked vegetables and dice the carrots and potatoes.

Put the potatoes, carrots, peas, artichokes, and cheese into a salad bowl. Whisk together the olive oil and remaining lemon juice in a bowl, season with salt and pepper, pour the dressing over the salad, and toss gently. Garnish with the olives and hard-cooked eggs.

Gourmet salad

Insalata del gourmet

Preparation time: 25 mins
Cooking time: 25-30 mins
Serves 4

2 red bell peppers
4 pearl onions, quartered
1 sprig flat-leaf parsley,
    chopped
1 sprig basil, chopped
4 new potatoes, boiled,
    drained, and diced
2 carrots, boiled, drained,
    and sliced
3½ ounces lean ham, cut into
    strips
⅝ cup heavy cream
1 tablespoon Worcestershire
    sauce
generous ⅓ cup olive oil
juice of 2 lemons, strained
salt

Preheat the oven to 350°F. Put the bell peppers on a baking sheet and roast, turning occasionally, for 25-30 minutes, until they are blistered and charred. Remove from the oven, put into a plastic bag, and tie the top. When they are cool enough to handle, peel off the skins, remove and discard the seeds, and cut the flesh into strips.

Put the bell pepper strips, onions, parsley, basil, potatoes, carrots, and ham into a salad bowl. Whisk the cream in a small bowl. Whisk together the Worcestershire sauce, olive oil, and lemon juice in another bowl, season with salt, and fold in the cream. Dress the salad with this sauce, stirring carefully, and serve.

Tomato and quails' egg salad

Insalata di pomodori e uova di quaglia

Preparation time: 15 mins
Cooking time: 8 mins
Serves 4

12 quails' eggs
4-6 lettuce leaves
7 ounces ham, cut into
    strips
4 green tomatoes, seeded and
    sliced
olive oil and white-wine
    vinegar, for drizzling
salt

Cook the quails' eggs in a pan of boiling water for 2-3 minutes, then drain and refresh under cold running water. Shell the eggs and cut them in half. Line a salad bowl with lettuce leaves and arrange the strips of ham, tomato slices, and egg halves on top. Season with a pinch of salt and drizzle with olive oil and a little vinegar. Mix gently at the table.

Raw spinach salad

Insalata di spinaci

Preparation time: 10 mins

Serves 4
----

12 ounces young spinach
    leaves, coarse stalks
    removed
white-wine vinegar, for
    drizzling
olive oil, for drizzling
salt
Parmesan cheese shavings, to
    garnish

Cut the spinach leaves into strips and put them
into a salad bowl. Season with salt and drizzle
with vinegar and oil to taste. Sprinkle with
Parmesan shavings and serve.

Celery and Roquefort salad

Insalata di sedano al roquefort

Preparation time: 15 mins

Serves 4
----

1 apple
9 ounces white mushrooms
juice of ½ lemon, strained
5 celery stalks, cut into
    1¼-inch pieces
scant 1 cup diced ham
3½ ounces Roquefort cheese,
    diced
10 walnuts, halved
1 tablespoon chopped
    flat-leaf parsley

For the sauce

¼ cup mayonnaise
¼ cup mustard
⅔ cup whole-milk plain yogurt
salt and pepper

Peel, core, and dice the apple. Slice the
mushrooms and drizzle with the lemon juice. Put
the apple, mushrooms, celery, ham, and cheese
into a salad bowl.

To make the sauce, combine the mayonnaise,
mustard, and yogurt in a bowl and season with
salt and pepper. Pour the sauce over the salad,
garnish with the walnuts, sprinkle with
the parsley, and let stand for a few minutes
before serving.

Barbecues

Grigliata

Cooking outdoors is the perfect way to
entertain during the summer months,
and the scents and sounds of cooking on
the barbecue create a wonderful appetite
for a feast. Another advantage is that
cooking on a barbecue means that nobody
has to spend their time in the kitchen.
A good barbecue should be very simple,
and only requires good-quality
ingredients to be grilled over hot
embers, seasoned with salt and pepper,
and perhaps drizzled with a little
extra-virgin olive oil.

In Italy, the ancient Chianina breed
of cattle produces steaks so highly
prized that strict rules accompany the
technique for grilling them, such as
never pricking the meat with a fork
so that the tasty juices cannot escape
(see Florentine T-bone steak, p.124).
There are also many fish and vegetables
that can be grilled very successfully,
such as radicchio, eggplants, shrimp,
and sardines. These are often cooked
with fresh herbs and dressed simply
with lemon and extra-virgin olive oil.

The recipes here can also be cooked
indoors in a broiler, if a barbecue is
not available. All they need to accompany
them is a salad and some good bread.

Aromatic marinade

Marinata aromatica

Preparation time: 5 mins,
plus marinating time

1 onion, sliced
3 tablespoons chopped flat-
    leaf parsley
1 tablespoon chopped thyme
2 bay leaves, torn into
    pieces
2 cloves garlic, thinly
    sliced
scant ¼ cup olive oil
2 teaspoons lemon juice,
    strained
salt and pepper

This marinade is good for sliced beef or lamb or chicken breast portions. Season the meat with salt and pepper and cover with the onion, parsley, thyme, bay leaves, and garlic. Combine the olive oil and lemon juice and pour over the meat. Marinate in the refrigerator for about 2 hours.

Quick lemon marinade

Marinata veloce al limone

Preparation time: 5 mins,
plus marinating time

1¾ cups olive oil
juice of 1 lemon, strained
2 sprigs flat-leaf parsley,
    leaves only
1 small shallot, chopped
1 sprig thyme, leaves only
1 bay leaf
salt and pepper

This marinade is good for fish or steaks. Combine the olive oil, lemon juice, parsley, shallot, thyme, and bay leaf in a bowl and season with salt and pepper. Marinate for 30 minutes.

Yogurt marinade

Marinata allo yogurt

Preparation time: 10 mins,
plus marinating time

1 onion, coarsely chopped
2¼ cups low-fat plain yogurt
salt and pepper

This marinade is good with lamb or kid. Put the onion in a food processor and process to a puree, then push it through a strainer into a bowl. Add the yogurt and season with salt and pepper. Marinate in the refrigerator for 3-4 hours.

Vinegar marinade

Marinata all'aceto

Preparation time: 5 mins,
plus marinating time

scant 1 cup white-wine
    vinegar
scant 1 cup olive oil
juice of 1 lemon, strained
2 teaspoons finely chopped
    rosemary
1 tablespoon finely chopped
    flat-leaf parsley
1 pinch dried oregano
salt and pepper

This marinade is good with fish. Combine the vinegar, olive oil, and lemon juice in a large bowl. Add the rosemary, parsley, and oregano and season with salt and pepper. Marinate for 30 minutes.

White wine marinade

Marinata al vino bianco

Preparation time: 5 mins,
plus marinating time

1 onion, sliced
4 cups dry white wine
1 cup olive oil
juice of 1 lemon, strained
salt and pepper

This marinade is good with fish. Put the onion in a bowl, add the wine, olive oil, and lemon juice, and season with salt and pepper. Marinate for 30 minutes.

Anchovy butter

Burro all'acciuga

Preparation time: 5 mins

7 tablespoons butter,
    softened
2 ounces anchovy fillets,
    well rinsed and drained
1 teaspoon anchovy paste

Cream the butter in a bowl. Beat in the anchovies, then beat in the anchovy paste. Good with grilled red meat.

Basil butter

Burro al basilico

Preparation time: 5 mins
Cooking time: 5 mins

7 tablespoons butter, diced
1 large bunch of basil,
    leaves torn into pieces
2-3 tablespoons lemon juice,
    strained
salt and pepper

Put the butter in the top of a double boiler or in a heatproof bowl and melt over barely simmering water. Remove the pan from the heat, whisk in the basil and lemon juice, and season with salt and pepper. Good with fish or shellfish.

Fennel butter

Burro al finocchio

Preparation time: 10 mins

1 clove garlic
7 tablespoons butter,
    softened
2 teaspoons fennel seeds
juice of ½ lemon, strained
white pepper

Blanch the garlic in a small pan of boiling water for about 1 minute, then drain, peel, and mash well with a fork. Cream the butter in a bowl and beat in the garlic. Grind the fennel seeds in a mortar with a pestle or in a spice grinder and beat into the butter. Beat in the lemon juice and a pinch of white pepper. Good with red meat or grilled fish.

Gorgonzola butter

Burro al gorgonzola

Preparation time: 5 mins

7 tablespoons butter,
    softened
2¾ ounces Gorgonzola cheese,
    crumbled
1 sprig flat-leaf parsley,
    chopped

Beat together the butter and Gorgonzola in a bowl until smooth and even. Beat in the parsley. Good with grilled red meat.

/ Barbecues /

Sage butter
Burro alla salvia

Preparation time: 1 min
Cooking time: 5 mins

7 tablespoons butter
15 sage leaves
salt

Melt the butter in a small pan over low heat. As soon as it starts to color, add the sage leaves and season with salt. When the leaves are crisp, remove the pan from the heat and serve the butter immediately. Good with boiled rice, grilled meat, or ravioli.

Grilled Treviso radicchio
Radicchio de Treviso alla griglia

Preparation time: 10 mins
Cooking time: 5 mins
Serves 4

1 pound 5 ounces Treviso
    radicchio
¼ cup olive oil
juice of 1 lemon, strained
salt and pepper

Light the barbecue. Remove the coarse outer leaves from the radicchio, trim the stalks to 1¼ inches, and rinse. Toss with the olive oil, place on the barbecue, and grill, turning occasionally, for about 5 minutes.

Transfer to a serving dish, season with salt and pepper, and sprinkle with the lemon juice. Serve immediately.

Grilled eggplants
Melanzane arrosto

Preparation time: 1¾ hrs
(including draining
and cooling)
Cooking time: 10–15 mins
Serves 6

3 eggplants, thickly sliced
3 cloves garlic, thinly
    sliced
18 basil leaves
olive oil, for drizzling
salt and pepper

Put the eggplant slices in a colander, sprinkle with salt, and let drain for about 30 minutes. Light the barbecue. Rinse the eggplant slices and pat dry with paper towels, then place them on the barbecue and grill on both sides for a few minutes. Remove from the heat and let cool.

Arrange the eggplant slices in layers on a serving dish, sprinkling each layer with garlic, basil leaves, salt, and pepper and drizzling with plenty of olive oil. Set aside in a cool place for at least 1 hour to let the flavors mingle before serving.

Photograph p.114

Potatoes in aluminum foil

Patate d'argento

Preparation time: 10 mins
Cooking time: 40 mins
Serves 6

18 even-size white-fleshed
    potatoes, such as
    russet

Wash and dry the potatoes and season with salt.
Wrap each potato in aluminum foil and puncture
each potato several times with a toothpick. Roast
the potatoes in the ashes of the barbecue for
about 40 minutes. Meanwhile, prepare your chosen
filling (see below) by mixing together the
ingredients listed to make a paste. Remove the
potatoes carefully with tongs, unwrap them, and
transfer to individual plates. Spoon the filling
on the side and serve immediately.

To serve, prepare one or more of the following
fillings, adding the flavorings to taste:

Brie creamed with chopped aromatic herbs, such
as marjoram, thyme, and chervil.

Smoked salmon and butter with chopped wild
fennel, olive oil, and pureed black olives.

Cooked shrimp, butter, and paprika.

Black olives, capers, canned tuna, anchovies,
lemon juice, and olive oil.

Mascarpone cheese, 2 finely chopped shallots,
curry powder, and fresh tomato juice.

Mascarpone cheese, Gorgonzola cheese, chopped
pistachios, and brandy.

Mascarpone cheese, plain yogurt, chopped basil,
salt, and pepper.

Photograph p.115

Grilled stuffed squid

Calamari ripieni alla griglia

Preparation time: 20 mins
Cooking time: 10–15 mins
Serves 4

4 squid, cleaned, tentacles
and body sacs reserved
(see p.265)
1 sprig flat-leaf parsley,
plus extra to garnish
½ clove garlic
1 cup fresh bread crumbs
olive oil, for drizzling and
brushing
salt and pepper
lemon wedges, to garnish

Light the barbecue. Chop the squid tentacles
with the parsley and garlic. Put the mixture in
a bowl, add the bread crumbs, drizzle with olive
oil, and season with salt and pepper. Spoon
the mixture into the body sacs of the squid and
secure with toothpicks.

Brush the outside of the squid with olive oil
season with salt and pepper, place on the
barbecue, and grill, turning frequently, until
golden brown and tender. Serve hot with lemon
wedges and sprigs of parsley.

Grilled porgy

Orata ai ferri

Preparation time: 3 hrs
(including marinating)
Cooking time: 15 mins
Serves 4

¼ cup olive oil
juice of 1 lemon, strained
1 sprig flat-leaf parsley,
chopped
4 porgy, 9–11 ounces each,
scaled and cleaned
3–4 cups fine fresh bread
crumbs
salt and pepper

Combine the olive oil, lemon juice, and parsley
in a dish, season with salt and pepper, add
the fish, turning to coat, then let stand in the
refrigerator to marinate for 3 hours.

Light the barbecue. Drain the fish, reserving
the marinade, and sprinkle with the bread crumbs,
pressing them on with your fingers. Place the
fish on the barbecue and grill, turning and
brushing with the reserved marinade 2 or 3 times,
for about 15 minutes, until the flesh
flakes easily.

Grilled eggplants (p.109)

Grilled langoustines

Scampi grigliati

Preparation time: 50 mins
(including marinating)
Cooking time: 12 mins
Serves 4

20 langoustines (Norwegian
    lobsters) or crayfish,
    peeled
1 sprig flat-leaf parsley,
    finely chopped
1 sprig chervil, finely
    chopped
1 sprig marjoram, finely
    chopped
juice of 1 lemon, strained
¼ cup olive oil, plus extra
    for brushing
salt and pepper

Put the langoustines in a large bowl, sprinkle
with the herbs, add the lemon juice and olive
oil, and season with salt and pepper. Let marinate
for about 45 minutes.

Light the barbecue. Drain the langoustines,
reserving the marinade, place them on the
barbecue and grill, turning twice and
occasionally drizzling with a little reserved
marinade, for about 12 minutes.

Photograph p.117

Langoustines with sage

Scampi alla salvia

Preparation time: 1¼ hrs
(including marinating)
Cooking time: 10–12 mins
Serves 4

20 langoustines (Norwegian
    lobsters) or crayfish,
    peeled
juice of 2 lemons, strained
20 smoked pancetta slices
20 small sage leaves
olive oil, for brushing
salt and pepper

Put the langoustines in a bowl, season with salt
and pepper, pour in the lemon juice, and
let marinate for about 1 hour. Light the barbecue.
Drain the langoustines, reserving the marinade,
wrap each in a slice of pancetta together with a
sage leaf, and secure with a toothpick. Brush
lightly with olive oil, arrange on the barbecue,
and cook, turning twice and occasionally
drizzling with the reserved marinade, for 10–12
minutes.

Grilled langoustines

Grilled sardines

Sardine alla griglia

Preparation time: 50 mins
(including standing)

Cooking time: 4 mins

Serves 4

thinly pared zest of
    ½ orange, chopped
1 clove garlic, chopped
2 teaspoons finely chopped
    rosemary
2¼ pounds sardines, scaled
    and cleaned
olive oil, for drizzling
salt and pepper

Combine the orange zest, garlic, and a little rosemary in a bowl and use to stuff the cavities of the sardines.

Put the sardines on a plate, sprinkle with the remaining stuffing mixture, season with salt and pepper, and drizzle with a little olive oil. Let stand to absorb the flavor for 30 minutes.

Light the barbecue. Arrange the sardines on the barbecue and grill for about 2 minutes on each side. Serve immediately.

Photograph p.119

Stuffed sardines

Sardine farcite

Preparation time: 25 mins

Cooking time: 6–8 mins

Serves 6

½ cup cooked fine couscous,
    cooked
scant ⅓ cup harissa
1 tablespoon ground cumin
1 tablespoon paprika
1 tablespoon ground turmeric
3 cloves garlic, chopped
1 bunch cilantro, chopped
⅔ cup olive oil
24 small sardines, scaled
    and cleaned salt

Light the barbecue. Combine the couscous, harissa, cumin, paprika, turmeric, garlic, and cilantro in a bowl. Stir in 1 tablespoon of the oil to blend the mixture thoroughly. Stuff the cavities of the sardines with this mixture, then brush them with olive oil.

Place the sardines on the barbecue and cook for 3–4 minutes on each side, turning them over carefully. When they are golden brown, drain them on paper towels. Season lightly with salt and serve immediately.

Note: Harissa is a north African spice paste made from chiles, garlic and ground spices, often including caraway, cumin, and coriander.

Mixed fish kebabs

Spiedini misti di pesce

Preparation time: 1 hr
(including marinating)
Cooking time: 10 mins
Serves 4

2¼ pounds mixed fish fillets
    and other seafood, such
    as tuna, monkfish, and
    Norwegian lobsters
scant ⅓ cup olive oil
1 clove garlic, finely
    chopped
2 tablespoons finely chopped
    flat-leaf parsley
8 black olives, pitted
8 small mushrooms
8 cherry tomatoes
salt and pepper

Cut the fish fillets into large cubes and peel
the langoustines, if using. Combine the olive
oil, garlic, and parsley, and coat the seafood in
the mixture. Let marinate for 30 minutes. Light
the barbecue and soak wooden skewers, if using,
in water for 30 minutes.

Drain the seafood, reserving the marinade,
and thread onto long skewers, alternating with
the olives, mushrooms, and tomatoes. Brush
with the marinade and grill on the medium-hot
barbecue, turning frequently, for 10 minutes.
Serve immediately.

Photograph p.122

Lamb chops with mint

Costolette alla menta

Preparation time: 1–2¼ hrs
(including marinating)
Cooking time: 4–8 mins
Serves 4

juice of 1 lemon, strained
plenty of olive oil, for
    brushing
1 sprig mint, chopped
8 lamb rib chops
salt and pepper
peas or zucchini cooked
    in butter, to serve
    (optional)

Combine the lemon juice, 3 tablespoons of the
oil, and the mint in a dish, add the lamb chops,
and let marinate, turning occasionally, for
1–2 hours.

Light the barbecue. Drain the lamb chops, place
on the barbecue grill, and cook for 2–4 minutes
on each side, basting with more oil as necessary.
Season with salt and pepper and serve with peas
or zucchini, if desired.

Photograph p.123

/ Barbecues /

Marinated mutton kebabs

Spiedini marinati

Preparation time: 1¼ hrs
(including marinating)
Cooking time: 3–5 mins
Serves 4

scant ⅓ cup olive oil
1 clove garlic
1 sprig thyme
6 black peppercorns
1 pound 2 ounces boneless leg
   of mutton, cut into cubes
salt

Combine the oil, garlic, thyme, and peppercorns in a dish, season with salt, and add the meat. Stir well and let marinate for 1 hour.

Light the barbecue. Drain the mutton and divide it among four metal skewers. Place them on a very hot barbecue and cook, turning frequently, for 3 minutes, or until they are almost crisp on the outside and tender in the middle.

Lamb chops
with anchovy butter

Costolette al burro d'acciuga

Preparation time: 5 mins
Cooking time: 8 mins
Serves 4

8 lamb rib chops
olive oil
1 quantity Anchovy butter
   (see p.105)
salt

Light the barbecue. Brush the chops on both sides with olive oil, place on the barbecue, and grill for 2–4 minutes on each side, depending on how well done you like your lamb. Season with salt, transfer to a warm serving dish, and dot with the anchovy butter.

Mixed fish kebabs (p.120)

Meatballs in lemon leaves

Polpette in foglie di limone

Preparation time: 30 mins
Cooking time: 15 mins
Serves 6

5 slices white bread
    (about 5 ounces),
    crusts removed
generous ⅓ cup milk
11 ounces ground beef
11 ounces ground veal
generous 1 cup grated
    Parmesan cheese
2 eggs
2 tablespoons finely chopped
    flat-leaf parsley
olive oil, for brushing
36 lemon leaves
salt and pepper

Tear the bread into pieces and put them into
a bowl. Pour in the milk and let soak for
10 minutes, then remove the bread and set aside,
squeezing out excess liquid. Put the bread,
beef, veal, cheese, eggs, and parsley into a
bowl, season with salt and pepper, and mix well,
adding a little milk if the mixture is too thick.

Light the barbecue. Shape the mixture into balls
about the size of a walnut, brush with oil,
and wrap each meatball in 2 lemon leaves,
securing them with wooden toothpicks. Grill on
each side for about 15 minutes.

Florentine T-bone steak

Costata alla fiorentina

Preparation time: 15 mins
Cooking time: 10 mins
Serves 4

2 T-bone steaks, 1 pound
    5 ounces each
olive oil, for drizzling
salt and pepper

Light the barbecue, preferably using oak charcoal.
Do not season the steaks. When the coals are hot,
position the grill about 8 inches above the
embers. Put the steaks on the grill and cook for
about 5 minutes on each side, turning only once.
Remove from the grill and season with salt and
pepper. To serve, lightly drizzle a warm serving
dish with olive oil and arrange the seasoned
steaks on it.

Note: The Association of the Florentine T-bone
Steak Academy, founded in 1991 by the Florentine
Butchers' Association, has set out rules about
the preparation of steaks. For over 200 years,
a Florentine steak has been defined as a T-bone
steak cut from a Chianina breed calf and hung
for 5–6 days. The steak must be cut from the loin
through the fillet and sirloin with the T-bone
in the middle. The meat must be ¾–1¼ inches thick
and weigh 1 pound 5 ounces–1¾ pounds.

Photograph p.126

Steak with herbs

Bistecche alle erbe

Preparation time: 5 mins
Cooking time: 8-10 mins
Serves 4

4 sirloin or Delmonico
    steaks, 7 ounces each
4 sage leaves
1 tablespoon rosemary leaves
¼ cup olive oil
1 teaspoon crushed black
    peppercorns
salt
4 seeded rolls, to serve

Light the barbecue. Rub the steaks all over with the sage leaves and rosemary. Pour the oil into a shallow dish, stir in the peppercorns, and dip the steaks into the mixture, turning to coat. Drain, place on the barbecue, and grill for about 4 minutes on each side, or until the steak is cooked to your liking. Season with salt and serve immediately in seeded rolls.

Photograph p.127

Mixed grill

Grigliata mista

Preparation time: 10 mins
Cooking time: 8-10 mins
Serve 6

2 sirloin steaks
2 boneless pork leg or
    shoulder steaks
2 tablespoons olive oil
2 teaspoons dried sage
2 teaspoons dried rosemary
6 lamb chops
3 Italian sausages
6 slices calf's liver
salt and pepper
bread rolls, to serve

Trim off any fat from the sirloin and pork steaks. Put them between 2 sheets of plastic wrap and pound them with a meat mallet until they are thin and even. Rub them all over with the oil, sage, and rosemary, season with pepper, and put them into a bowl. Put the lamb chops, sausages, and liver in another bowl.

Light the barbecue. Just before cooking, prick the sausages with a skewer and brush the liver with olive oil. Place the sirloin and pork steaks on the barbecue and grill for 1 minute on each side, then add the lamb chops and grill for another 2 minutes. Finally, add the sausages and liver and grill, turning all the meat once, for another 4-6 minutes, or until tender. Season with salt and pepper and serve in bread rolls.

Florentine T-bone steak (p.124)

Colorful kebabs

Spiedini colorati

Preparation time: 20 mins

Cooking time: 8-10 mins

Serves 4

14 ounces beef tenderloin
7 ounces lean bacon
    in one piece
4 small tomatoes, halved
2 onions, sliced into
    thick rings
8 green olives, pitted
olive oil, for brushing
salt and pepper

Cut the beef and bacon into 8 cubes each. Sprinkle the cut sides of the tomatoes with salt and leave upside down to drain. Light the barbecue To assemble the kebabs, thread a tomato half, a cube of bacon, a slice of onion, a cube of beef, and an olive onto each of 4 skewers, followed by another cube of bacon, another slice of onion, another cube of beef, another olive, and another tomato half. Brush with oil, place on the barbecue, and grill, turning once, for 8-10 minutes, until the meat is cooked through and tender. Season with salt and pepper and serve immediately.

Chicken on the spit

Pollo allo spiedo

Preparation time: 15 mins

Cooking time: 35-50 mins

Serves 4

1 chicken
3 tablespoons olive oil
salt and pepper
salad greens or roast new
    potatoes with rosemary,
    to serve

Light the barbecue. Folding the wings against the back of the chicken, season the bird with salt and pepper inside and out, and brush well with the oil.

Thread the chicken onto a spit, place over the barbecue, and turn slowly, basting occasionally with the cooking juices, for 35-50 minutes, or until it is tender and cooked through.

To test if it is cooked, insert a skewer into the thickest part of the leg. If the juices run clear, the chicken is cooked. Remove the chicken from the spit and season with salt and pepper. Serve hot with salad greens or roast new potatoes with rosemary.

Note: The chicken can also be cooked in a conventional oven, turning regularly.

Turkey kebabs

Spiedini di tacchino

Preparation time: 50 mins
(including standing)
Cooking time: 20-25 mins
Serves 4

11 ounces turkey breast,
    cut into thin strips
3 eggplants, sliced
5 zucchini, sliced
12 pearl onions
2 tablespoons olive oil,
    plus extra for brushing
1 pinch dried oregano
2 red bell peppers, seeded
    and sliced
1 sprig basil, chopped
salt and pepper

Light the barbecue and soak wooden skewers, if
using, in water for 30 minutes. Wrap the strips
of turkey in the eggplant slices, then in
the zucchini slices, making sure that some of
the eggplant and zucchini is reserved.

Thread the rolls onto 4 skewers, alternating them
with the onions. Brush with oil, sprinkle with
oregano, put them into a dish, and let stand for
30 minutes to let the flavors mingle.

Place the remaining eggplant slices and zucchini
slices on the barbecue, together with the
bell peppers, and cook, turning once, for about
10 minutes. Transfer the grilled vegetables
to a salad bowl, season with salt and pepper,
and sprinkle with the chopped basil and oil.

Place the kebabs on the barbecue and grill,
turning occasionally, for 10-15 minutes,
until they are cooked through. Season with salt
and pepper and serve immediately with the
grilled vegetables.

Light Lunches and Suppers

Pranzi e cene leggeri

Summers in Italy can be extremely hot, and many people prefer to eat simple cold food, and often a one-dish meal, in order not to have to spend too much time in the kitchen. However, they still want to eat something tasty, appetizing, and refreshing. Italian summer dishes are ideal for this purpose as they are extremely varied and versatile: many dishes can be served as appetizers, *primi piatti* (first courses), side dishes, or salads, as well as a meal in their own right.

The recipes in this chapter are simple, casual, quick to prepare, and work perfectly as a light lunch or supper. All they need to accompany them is some good country bread. They range from salads and carpaccios with fish, meat, and cheese, to pizzas and pasta dishes with seasonal vegetables, and light vegetable and fish dishes.

Smoked duck salad with fava beans and arugula

Insalata di anatra affumicata
alle fave e rucola

Preparation time: 15 mins

Cooking time: 8 mins

Serves 4
----

2 smoked duck breasts,
    thinly sliced
¼ cup basil-flavored oil
4¼ cups shelled fava beans
9 ounces arugula, separated
    into leaves
1 tablespoon chopped chervil
salt and pepper

Put the duck in a dish, sprinkle with 1 tablespoon of the oil, and turn to coat. Cook the fava beans in a pan of salted boiling water for 8 minutes, then drain them and refresh in ice water. Drain the beans again and skin them by squeezing gently between a thumb and index finger. Put the beans into a salad bowl, add the remaining oil, and toss lightly. Add the duck and arugula and toss lightly again. Season with salt and pepper, sprinkle with the chervil, and serve.

Note: Fresh fava beans are also excellent raw, with bread, salami, or pecorino cheese.

Allegria salad

Insalata allegria

Preparation time: 25 mins

Serves 4
----

1 bunch of mixed herbs,
    finely chopped
3 tablespoons rinsed and
    drained capers preserved
    in salt
1 clove garlic, crushed
scant ½ cup heavy cream
3 tablespoons mayonnaise
3 tablespoons chopped walnuts
thinly pared zest of
    1 orange, chopped
4 slices rustic bread
3½ ounces mixed salad
    greens, shredded
3½ ounces fontina cheese,
    diced
7 ounces cherry tomatoes,
    halved
2 hard-cooked eggs
olive oil, for drizzling
salt and pepper

Put the herbs, capers, and garlic into a large bowl. Whisk the cream in another bowl until just thickened, then stir it into the herb mixture with the mayonnaise, walnuts, and half the orange zest, and season with salt and pepper.

Spread the mixture on each slice of bread, put the slices of bread on a serving dish, and divide the salad greens, cheese, and tomatoes among them. Halve the eggs, remove the yolks, and crumble them into a bowl. Sprinkle the yolks and the remaining orange zest over the cheese and tomatoes, drizzle with olive oil, and serve.

Note: Herbs are added to salads as a finishing touch or to enhance the flavor of the other ingredients. They usually include chives, mint, cilantro, flat-leaf parsley, tarragon, and basil and may be chopped with varying fineness before being added to the salad.

Avocado and shrimp salad

Insalata di avocado e gamberetti

Preparation time: 15 mins

Serves 4

½ cup shelled and chopped
    pistachio nuts
2 avocados
juice of 1 lemon, strained
7 oz cooked, peeled shrimp
olive oil, for drizzling
salt and freshly ground
    white pepper

Mix the pistachios with a pinch of pepper in
a small bowl. Peel, halve, and pit the avocados.
Slice thinly and drizzle with the lemon juice.
Put the slices into a salad bowl, add the shrimp,
and stir gently, then sprinkle with the pistachio
mixture. Season lightly with salt, drizzle with
olive oil, and serve immediately.

Farmhouse salad

Insalata del contadino

Preparation time: 10 mins

Serves 4

1 pound 2 ounces cooked
    potatoes, diced
7 ounces cooked green beans
scant 1½ cups cooked or
    drained, canned borlotti
    beans
1 small onion, thinly sliced
    into rings
2 tablespoons white-wine
    vinegar
generous ⅓ cup olive oil
4-6 basil leaves, torn
salt

Combine the potatoes, green beans, and borlotti
beans in a serving dish and sprinkle with the
onion rings. Pour the vinegar into a bowl and
whisk in a generous pinch of salt. Add the olive
oil and whisk well again. Pour the dressing over
the salad, sprinkle with the basil, and serve.

Photograph p.136

Octopus salad

Insalata di polpo

Preparation time: 1 hr
(including cooling)
Cooking time: 1 hr
Serves 4

1¼ pounds octopus
1 bay leaf
2 sprigs flat-leaf parsley
1 clove garlic, coarsely
    chopped
1 hot fresh red chile,
    seeded and coarsely
    chopped
scant ⅓ cup olive oil
juice of 1 lemon, strained
salt

If the octopus has not already been cleaned and tenderized, turn the body inside out and pull away the innards and the stiff strips that stick to the sides. Cut off the stomach sac. Rinse the octopus thoroughly under cold running water and turn the body right side out. Press out the beak and its soft surrounding tissue from the center of the tentacles and cut it out. Finally, beat well with a meat mallet. Bring a large pan of salted water to a boil. Add the octopus and bay leaf and cook for about 1 hour, testing with a fork to check whether it is tender. Remove the pan from the heat, discard the bay leaf, and let the octopus cool in the water.

When cold, remove it from the pan, peel away and discard the skin, then chop the octopus into pieces and put them into a serving dish. Put the parsley, garlic, chile, olive oil, lemon juice, and a pinch of salt into a blender and blend until thoroughly combined. Pour the dressing over the octopus and serve.

Note: Octopus works very well in salads. It can also be dressed simply with a drizzle of olive oil, or with vinegar, lemon, spices, salt, and pepper.

Photograph p.137

/ Light lunches and suppers /

Onion, trout, and sorrel salad

Insalata di cipolla, trota e acetosella

Preparation time: 30 mins
(including cooling and
standing)
Cooking time: 1½ mins
Serves 4

12 quails' eggs
4 onions, thinly sliced
7 ounces smoked trout,
    skinned and flaked
7 ounces sorrel

For the sauce

1 orange
¼ cup light cream
2 teaspoons Dijon mustard
salt and pepper

Put the quails' eggs into a pan, add water to cover, and bring to a boil. Boil for 1½ minutes, then drain the pan. Put the eggs into a bowl of cold water and let them cool completely.

To make the sauce, peel the orange, removing all traces of the bitter white pith, then halve it. Squeeze the juice from 1 half of the orange into a bowl, stir in the cream and mustard, and season with salt and pepper.

Cut the second orange half into segments, slicing between the membranes, and set the segments aside. Shell the quails' eggs and put them into a salad bowl with the reserved orange segments and the onions, trout, and sorrel. Pour the dressing over the salad and let stand in a cool place for 5 minutes before serving.

Farro and shrimp salad

Insalata di farro e gamberetti

Preparation time: 30 mins
Serves 4

1 cucumber, peeled and sliced
1 tablespoon apple vinegar
3 tablespoons olive oil
juice of 1 lemon, strained
1 sprig flat-leaf parsley,
    chopped
1 sprig tarragon, chopped
scant 1½ cups cooked farro
    or spelt, drained
11 ounces cooked, peeled
    shrimp
1 carrot, finely grated
generous 1 cup shredded
    arugula
salt and pepper

Put the cucumber slices into a bowl and drizzle with the vinegar. Whisk together the olive oil, lemon juice, parsley, and tarragon in a bowl and season with salt and pepper. Put the farro, shrimp, carrot, cucumber, and arugula into a salad bowl, pour the dressing over the salad, stir, and serve.

Farmhouse salad (p.133)

topus salad (p.134)

Pork loin salad with melon and strawberries

Insalata di lonza di maiale
al melone e fragole

Preparation time: 1 hr
(including cooling)
Cooking time: 20 mins
Serves 4

5 tablespoons olive oil
1 pound 2 ounces loin of
    pork, diced
3 tablespoons sherry
1 tablespoon white-wine
    vinegar
½ honeydew melon, seeded,
    peeled, and diced
12 strawberries, hulled
    and quartered
12 ounces insalatine, or
    mixed small salad greens
    (see Note)
salt and pepper

Heat 2 tablespoons of the oil in a skillet. Add
the pork and cook over medium-high heat, stirring
frequently, for 5–10 minutes, until all the
pieces are seared. Reduce the heat, season with
salt and pepper, and cook, stirring occasionally,
for 10 minutes. Remove the skillet from the heat
and set the pork aside to cool.

Put the sherry, vinegar, remaining oil, and a pinch
of salt into a blender and blend at high speed
until combined. Pour the dressing into a bowl and
season with pepper. Put the pork, melon,
strawberries, and salad greens into a salad bowl,
pour the dressing over the salad, toss lightly,
and serve.

Note: The Italian word *insalatine* refers to
small salad greens, either with a sweet flavor,
such as corn salad and oakleaf lettuce, or
bitter, such as radicchio and arugula. They add
a delightful flavor to cold meat or fish dishes.

Mozzarella and cicorino

Ciliegine di mozzarella al cicorino

Preparation time: 10 mins

Serves 4

2 bunches cicorino, shredded
(see p.73)
1 curly lettuce, such as
Quattro Stagioni, shredded
11 ounces cherry tomatoes,
halved
1 yellow bell pepper, seeded
and cut into thin strips
7 ounces canned tuna in brine
or spring water, drained
and flaked
7 ounces small mozzarella
balls
4–5 basil leaves, torn
generous ⅓ cup olive oil
2 tablespoons white-wine
vinegar
1 tablespoon Dijon mustard
salt and pepper

Put the cicorino and lettuce into a salad bowl,
add the tomatoes, bell pepper, tuna, and
mozzarella balls, and sprinkle with the
basil leaves.

Whisk together the oil, vinegar, mustard, and
a pinch each of salt and pepper in a bowl. Pour
the dressing over the salad, toss, and serve.

Lettuce with
skate and walnuts

Insalata di lattuga con razza e noci

Preparation time: 15 mins

Cooking time: 15 mins

Serves 6

6¼ cups fish stock
2¼ pounds skate wings
1 tablespoon sherry vinegar
2 tablespoons whole-grain
mustard
2 tablespoons olive oil
1 lettuce, shredded
12 walnuts, halved
salt and pepper

Pour the stock into a wide pan, add the skate
wings, and bring just to a boil. Reduce the
heat so that the surface is barely trembling and
poach the fish for 15 minutes. Meanwhile, whisk
together the vinegar, mustard, and olive oil
in a bowl and season with salt and pepper.
Lift the skate out of the pan with a slotted
spatula, remove the skin, and cut the fish into
thin slivers.

Toss the lettuce with the dressing and spread
it out on a serving dish. Put the fish on top and
sprinkle with the walnuts. Serve immediately,
while the fish is still warm.

Lettuce omelet

Omelette alla lattuga

Preparation time: 10 mins
Cooking time: 15 mins
Serves 4

3 tablespoons butter
1 lettuce, cut into strips
5 eggs
salt and freshly ground
    white pepper

Melt 2 tablespoons of the butter in a pan.
Add the lettuce strips and cook over low heat,
stirring occasionally, for 10 minutes. Remove
the pan from the heat and season with salt and
white pepper. Beat the eggs with a pinch of
salt in a bowl, then stir in the lettuce. Melt
the remaining butter in a skillet. Pour in
the egg mixture and cook over low heat until the
underside of the omelet has set but the
top is still soft. Slide it out of the pan and
serve immediately.

Radicchio, turkey, and snow pea salad

Insalata di radicchio, tacchino e taccole

Preparation time: 20 mins
Cooking time: 3–4 mins
Serves 4

2⅔ cups trimmed snow peas
scant 1½ cups diced, cooked
    turkey breast
2⅓ cups shredded radicchio
olive oil, for drizzling
2 hard-cooked eggs, sliced
salt and white pepper

For the tuna sauce

4 ounces canned tuna, drained
    and flaked
scant 1 cup mayonnaise
1 tablespoon white-wine
    vinegar
2 tablespoons rinsed,
    drained, and chopped
    capers

Blanch the snow peas in a pan of salted boiling
water for 3–4 minutes until just tender, then
drain and set aside. To make the sauce, combine
the tuna and mayonnaise in a bowl until creamy,
then stir in the vinegar and capers.

Put the turkey, radicchio, and snow peas into
a salad bowl and mix, then drizzle with olive
oil and season lightly with white pepper.
Garnish with the slices of hard-cooked eggs, pour
the tuna sauce over the salad, and serve.

/ Light lunches and suppers /

Chicken salad with plums

Insalata di pollo con le prugne

Preparation time: 20 mins
Cooking time: 3 hrs
Serves 4

14 ounces tomatoes, peeled,
    seeded, and cut into
    wedges
6 tablespoons olive oil
2 skinless, boneless chicken
    breasts
13 ounces plums, pitted, and
    cut into quarters
11 ounces mixed lettuce
    leaves, shredded
1 tablespoon white-wine
    vinegar
salt and pepper

Preheat the oven to 300°F. Spread out the tomatoes on a baking sheet and season lightly with salt. Bake for 2–3 hours, until dried. Heat 2 tablespoons of the olive oil in a skillet. Add the chicken and cook over medium-high heat, turning once, for 7–8 minutes, until evenly browned. Season with salt and pepper and remove from the skillet. Add the plums to the skillet and cook, stirring occasionally, for 5–8 minutes, then remove from the skillet.

Cut the chicken into small pieces. Make a bed of shredded lettuce on a serving dish, top with the chicken, and add the plums and tomatoes. Whisk together the remaining olive oil, the vinegar, and a pinch of salt in a small bowl. Pour the dressing over the chicken salad, season with pepper, and serve.

Royal salad

Insalata reale

Preparation time: 1 hr
(including cooling)
Cooking time: 40 mins
Serves 4

2¾ cups shelled fresh
    haricot beans
7 ounces potatoes
1 apple
juice of 1 lemon, strained
3 tablespoons white-wine
    vinegar
generous ⅓ cup olive oil
4 heads Belgian endive, cored
    and cut into pieces
7 ounces corn salad
salt and pepper

Cook the beans in a pan of salted boiling water for about 40 minutes, until they are tender, then drain and let cool.

Meanwhile, boil the potatoes in a separate pan of salted boiling water for about 30 minutes, until they are tender. Drain the pan, leave the potatoes until cool enough to handle, then peel and cut them into rounds. Peel, core, and dice the apple, put it into a bowl, and sprinkle it with the lemon juice to prevent discoloration.

Pour the vinegar into a small bowl and stir in a pinch of salt, then whisk in the oil and season with pepper. Drain the apple and put it into a salad bowl with the beans, potatoes, Belgian endive, and corn salad. Pour the dressing over the salad, toss gently, and serve.

Rice, shrimp, and green apple salad

Insalata di riso, gamberetti e mele verdi

Preparation time: 50 mins
(including cooling)
Cooking time: 50 mins
Serves 4

1¼ cups long-grain rice
olive oil, for drizzling
1 carrot, cut into chunks
1 leek, cut into short
   lengths
1 onion, quartered
1 sprig sage
1 sprig flat-leaf parsley
1 sprig rosemary
11 ounces uncooked shrimp
2 green apples, peeled, cored
   and diced
1½ tablespoons butter
1 teaspoon all-purpose flour
scant 1 cup dry white wine
1 tablespoon finely chopped
   flat-leaf parsley
salt and pepper

Cook the rice in a large pan of salted boiling water for about 15 minutes, until it is tender, then drain and rinse it under cold running water, and drain well again. Turn it into a salad bowl, drizzle with olive oil, and set aside in a cool place. Pour 4 cups water into a pan, add the carrot, leek, onion and herbs, and bring to a boil. Simmer for a few minutes, then add the shrimp and cook for another 10 minutes. Drain, discard the vegetables and herb sprigs, and let the shrimp cool, then peel them.

Melt the butter in a skillet. Stir in the flour, then gradually stir in the white wine. Add the apples and cook, stirring occasionally, until they are softened but not disintegrating. Remove the skillet from the heat, sprinkle with the chopped parsley, and let cool. Stir the shrimp-and-apple mixture into the rice, drizzle with olive oil, and season with salt and pepper. Mix well and serve.

Rice salad niçoise

Insalata di riso alla nizzarda

Preparation time: 10 mins
Cooking time: 15 mins
Serves 4

1 cup long-grain rice
1 red bell pepper, seeded and
   cut into strips
1¼ cups pitted olives, cut
   into strips
3½ ounces canned tuna in
   oil, drained and flaked
generous ⅓ cup olive oil
juice of 1 lemon, strained
2 hard-cooked eggs, cut into
   wedges
salt and pepper

Cook the rice in a pan of salted boiling water for 15 minutes, or according to package directions, until it is tender, then drain and rinse it under cold running water. Drain well. Turn it into a bowl and add the red bell pepper strips, olives, and tuna. Whisk together the olive oil and lemon juice in a bowl and season with salt and pepper. Pour the dressing over the salad and toss gently. Garnish with the hard-cooked eggs and serve.

Note: Niçoise is also the name given to a classic salad made with green beans, potatoes, tuna, olives, anchovies, tomatoes, and eggs with herbs.

Arugula and veal salad

Insalata di rucola e vitello

Preparation time: 15 mins
(including standing)

Serves 4

¾ cup coarsely shredded
    arugula
11 ounces cold roast veal,
    thinly sliced
3½ ounces fresh cheese, such
    as robiola, sliced
3 tablespoons olive oil
juice of 1 lemon, strained
salt and pepper

Cover the bottom of a serving dish with the arugula. Put the slices of veal on top and cover with the slices of cheese. Whisk together the olive oil and lemon juice in a bowl and season with salt and pepper. Pour the dressing over the salad and let stand for 5 minutes before serving to let the flavors mingle.

Tasty salad

Insalata gustosa

Preparation time: 20 mins
Cooking time: 12–15 mins

Serves 4

2 potatoes, diced
2 zucchini, diced
1 cup shelled fava beans
1½ cups diced mortadella
⅔ cup mayonnaise
juice of ½ lemon, strained
1 tablespoon store-bought
    cocktail sauce
salt

Cook the potatoes, zucchini, and beans in a pan of salted boiling water for 12–15 minutes, until tender, then drain and turn into a salad bowl. Add the mortadella. Combine the mayonnaise, lemon juice, and cocktail sauce in a bowl. Pour the dressing over the salad, toss to mix, and serve.

Beef and radicchio salad

Manzo in insalata con radicchio

Preparation time: 10 mins

Serves 4

7 ounces Treviso radicchio
11 ounces cold cooked beef,
    thinly sliced
3½ ounces latteria or other
    mild cheese, sliced
strained lemon juice, for
    drizzling
olive oil, for drizzling
salt and pepper

Cut the radicchio into pieces and use them to cover the bottom of a rectangular serving dish. Put the slices of beef between 2 sheets of plastic wrap and pound with a meat mallet or a rolling pin until they are very thin and even. Lay the slices of beef over the radicchio and top with the slices of cheese. Season with salt and pepper, drizzle with lemon juice and oil, and serve.

Salmon and onion salad

Preparation time: 15 mins

Cooking time: 10 mins

Serves 4

1 cup milk

1 tablespoon black
     peppercorns

14-ounce salmon fillet

2 tablespoons light cream

juice of 1 orange, strained

2 tablespoons olive oil

1 lettuce, cut into strips

1 red onion, thinly sliced
     into rings

¼ cup chopped pistachio nuts

1 sprig flat-leaf parsley,
     leaves only

salt and pepper

Pour the milk and 1 cup water into a large shallow pan, add the peppercorns, and bring to a boil. Reduce the heat so that the surface is barely simmering, add the salmon, and poach for 10 minutes. Whisk together the cream, orange juice, and olive oil in a bowl and season with salt and pepper. Remove the salmon from the pan with a slotted spatula, draining it well.

Remove and discard the skin on the fish and flake the flesh into a small bowl. Arrange the lettuce, onion rings, and salmon on a serving dish and sprinkle with the pistachios and the parsley leaves. Drizzle with the sauce and serve.

Langoustine, fig, and melon salad

Preparation time: 25 mins

Cooking time: 4–5 mins

Serves 4

1 pound 5 ounces langoustines
     (Norwegian lobsters)
     or crayfish

4 plum tomatoes, peeled,
     seeded, and coarsely
     chopped

juice of ½ lemon, strained

juice of ½ grapefruit,
     strained

dash of Tabasco sauce

olive oil, for drizzling

1 melon, halved and seeded

4 white figs

1 bunch of arugula, separated
     into leaves

salt and pepper

Boil the langoustines in a pan of salted water for 4–5 minutes, then drain the pan, peel them, and set them aside. Put the tomatoes, lemon juice, grapefruit juice, and Tabasco into a food processor or blender, season with salt and pepper, and process until thoroughly combined. Pour the sauce into a bowl, drizzle with olive oil, stir, and set aside.

Using a melon baller, make about 40 balls from the melon flesh. Peel the figs and cut each into 4 segments with a dampened and very sharp knife. Put the arugula into the center of 4 individual dishes, arrange the figs, langoustines, and melon balls around the arugula in a sunburst pattern. Pour the tomato sauce over the salad before serving.

Escarole and speck salad

Insalata di scarola e speck

Preparation time: 15 mins

Cooking time: 8–10 mins

Serves 4

3 tablespoons olive oil

4 thick slices speck or
    bacon, about 7 ounces in
    total, cut into thin
    strips

1 head escarole, shredded

3 scallions, sliced

2 tablespoons white-wine
    vinegar

2 hard-cooked eggs

salt and pepper

Heat the oil in a small skillet. Add the speck
or bacon and cook over very low heat for 3–4
minutes. Remove from the skillet, reserving the
oil, and drain on paper towels. Put the escarole,
scallions, and bacon into a salad bowl. Stir
the vinegar into the oil in the skillet and cook
for a few minutes, until thickened.

Remove from the heat and pour the dressing over
the salad. Halve the eggs, scoop out the yolks,
and crumble them over the salad. Dice the whites
and sprinkle them over the salad. Season with
salt and pepper and serve immediately.

Escarole and shrimp salad

Insalata di scarola e gamberi

Preparation time: 15 mins

Cooking time: 3 mins

Serves 4

11 ounces shelled, uncooked
    shrimp

1 head escarole, cut
    into strips

3 tomatoes, peeled, seeded,
    and cut into wedges

½ tablespoon capers
    preserved in salt,
    rinsed and drained

scant ½ cup olive oil

juice of 1 lemon, strained

1 tablespoon chopped
    flat-leaf parsley

salt and pepper

Cook the shrimp in a pan of boiling salted
water for 3 minutes, drain, and let cool. Put
the escarole, tomatoes, shrimp, and capers
into a salad bowl. Whisk together the olive oil
and lemon juice in a bowl and season with salt
and pepper. Pour the dressing over the salad,
toss lightly, sprinkle with the chopped parsley,
and serve.

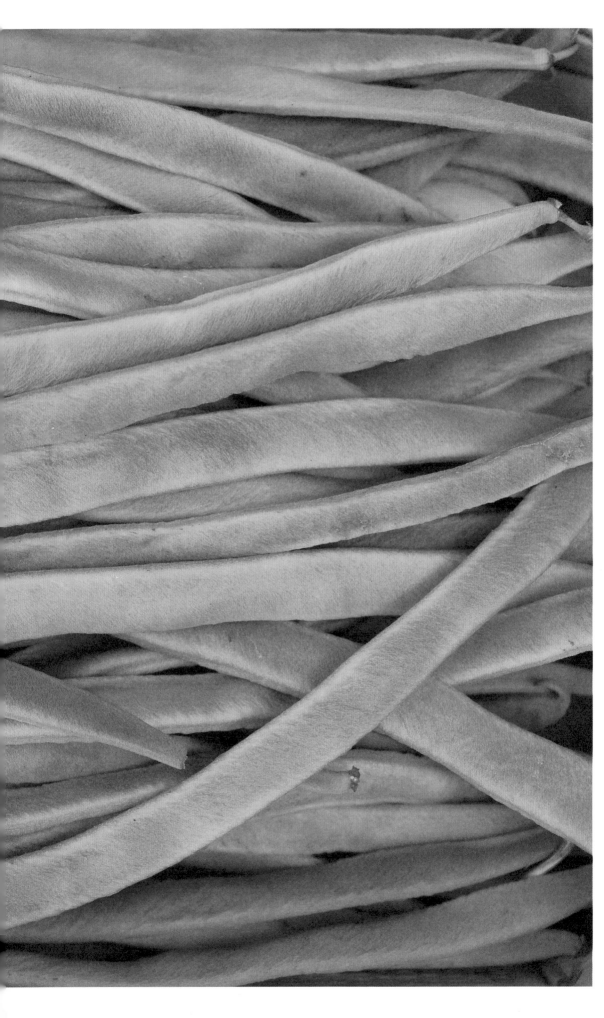

Salmon trout
and cucumber salad

Insalata di trota salmonata e cetrioli

Preparation time: 1¼ hrs
(including chilling)
Cooking time: 8-10 mins
Serves 4

4 salmon trout fillets
4 ripe tomatoes, sliced
1 cucumber, peeled and sliced
    into rounds
1 tablespoon chopped basil
1 tablespoon snipped chives
salt

For the dressing

generous ⅓ cup olive oil
2 tablespoons white-wine
    vinegar
1 tablespoon chopped shallot
1 clove garlic, chopped
salt and white pepper

Cut each fish fillet in half, put into a shallow pan, pour in water to cover, and add a pinch of salt. Bring to a boil, then reduce the heat so that the surface of the water is barely simmering, and poach for 3 minutes. Remove the fish from the pan and set aside.

To make the dressing, whisk together the oil, vinegar, shallot, and garlic in a bowl and season with salt and pepper. Pour half the dressing onto a serving dish and chill in the refrigerator for 1 hour. To serve, arrange the tomato and cucumber slices on the serving dish, put the fish fillets on top, and sprinkle with the basil and chives, then pour over the remaining dressing.

Photograph p.154

Potato pizza

Pizza di patate

Preparation time: 25 mins
Cooking time: 40-50 mins
Serves 4

2 tablespoons olive oil, plus
    extra for brushing
1 pound 2 ounces potatoes,
    unpeeled
generous ¾ cup all-purpose
    flour
2 tablespoons butter
1 egg
5 ounces mozzarella cheese,
    sliced
5 canned anchovy fillets,
    drained and chopped
3 tomatoes, peeled and diced
pinch of dried oregano
salt and pepper

Preheat the oven to 425°F and brush a roasting pan with oil. Put the potatoes in a large pan with salted water to cover. Bring to a boil and cook, covered, for 20-30 minutes, until tender, then drain, let cool slightly, and peel. Press the warm potatoes through a potato ricer into a bowl, add the flour, butter, and egg, and mix well until thoroughly combined. Spoon the potato mixture into the roasting pan and smooth the surface. Cover with the mozzarella slices and sprinkle with the anchovies and tomatoes. Season with salt and pepper, drizzle with oil, and sprinkle with the oregano. Bake for about 20 minutes, until golden and the cheese is bubbling. Serve immediately.

Photograph p.155

/ Light lunches and suppers /

Cheese pizza

Pizza al formaggio

Preparation time: 15 mins
Cooking time: 20 mins
Serves 4

olive oil, for brushing
    and drizzling
1 quantity Pizza dough
    (see p.156)
all-purpose flour,
    for dusting
5 ounces mozzarella
    cheese, sliced
5 ounces Gorgonzola
    cheese, crumbled
pinch of dried oregano
salt and pepper
lettuce, to serve

Preheat the oven to 425°F and brush a baking sheet with oil. Roll out the dough to a ⅛-inch thick sheet on a lightly floured counter and lift it onto the prepared baking sheet. Cover the surface evenly with the mozzarella and Gorgonzola, sprinkle with the oregano, season with salt and pepper, and drizzle with oil. Bake for about 20 minutes, until the cheese is golden and bubbling. Serve with a side dish of lettuce.

Eggplant pizza

Pizza alle melanzane

Preparation time: 50 mins
(including salting)
Cooking time: 30 mins
Serves 4

2 eggplants, thinly sliced
olive oil, for brushing
    and drizzling
1 quantity Pizza dough
    (see p.156)
all-purpose flour,
    for dusting
7 ounces canned tomatoes,
    drained and chopped
5 ounces mozzarella cheese,
    cut into strips
4-5 basil leaves, chopped
salt and pepper

Put the eggplant slices into a colander, sprinkling each layer with salt, and let drain for 30 minutes, then rinse and pat dry with paper towels. Preheat the oven to 425°F and brush a baking sheet with oil.

Roll out the dough on a lightly floured counter to a ¾-inch thick sheet and transfer to the prepared baking sheet. Cover with the eggplant slices, sprinkle with the tomatoes, and top with the strips of mozzarella. Season with salt and pepper, drizzle with oil, and sprinkle with the basil. Bake for 30 minutes and serve immediately. It may also be eaten cold.

Salmon trout and cucumber salad (p.152)   1

tato pizza (p.152)

Shrimp and arugula pizza

Pizza con gamberi e rucola

Preparation time: 3½ hrs
(including rising)
Cooking time: 20 mins
Serves 4

For the dough

4 cups flour, preferably
    Italian type 00, plus
    extra for dusting
1 cake fresh yeast, scant
    1 tablespoon (1 envelope)
    active dry yeast, or 2¼
    teaspoons instant yeast
1 cup lukewarm water
salt

For the topping

olive oil, for brushing and
    drizzling
9 ounces canned tomatoes,
    drained and chopped
9 ounces cooked, peeled
    shrimp
1 bunch arugula, chopped
salt and pepper

To make the dough, sift the flour with a pinch
of salt into a mound on a counter and make
a well in the center. Mash the fresh yeast, if
using, into 1 cup lukewarm water with a fork
until smooth and pour it into the well. If using
active dry yeast, add to the water and set aside
for 10 minutes, until bubbles form on the
surface. Pour the yeast mixture into the well.

Gradually incorporate the flour with your fingers,
then knead well until smooth and elastic. If
using instant yeast, sift together the flour and
yeast into a mound on a counter and make a well
in the center. Pour the water into the well.
Gradually incorporate the dry ingredients with
your fingers, then knead well until smooth and
elastic. Shape the dough into a ball, put it into
a bowl, cover with a dish towel, and let rise in
a warm place for about 3 hours, until almost
doubled in size.

Preheat the oven to 425°F and brush a baking
sheet with oil. Flatten the dough with your hand
and roll out on a lightly floured counter to form
a ½-inch thick round. Put the dough on the baking
sheet and make a rim around the edge. Sprinkle
with the tomatoes, then the shrimp, and finally
the arugula. Season with salt and pepper and
drizzle with olive oil, then bake for 20 minutes.
Serve immediately.

/ Light lunches and suppers /

Fisherman's pizza
Pizza alla pescatora

Preparation time: 30 mins
Cooking time: 45 mins
Serves 4

11 ounces baby octopuses,
    cleaned and skinned
    (see p.134)
2 tablespoons olive oil,
    plus extra for brushing
    and drizzling
11 ounces uncooked shrimp
11 ounces clams, scrubbed
11 ounces mussels, scrubbed
    and beards removed
1 onion, thinly sliced
4 cloves garlic, thinly
    sliced
1 fresh chile, seeded
    and chopped
1 tablespoon chopped flat-
    leaf parsley
1 quantity Pizza dough
    (see p.156)
all-purpose flour,
    for dusting
11 ounces cherry tomatoes,
    peeled and quartered
salt

Cook the octopuses in a pan of salted boiling water for 2 minutes, or until tender, then drain well. Preheat the oven to 425°F. Brush a baking sheet with oil and line it with parchment paper. Cook the shrimp in a pan of boiling water for 2–3 minutes, then drain, peel, and devein them. Discard any clams or mussels with broken shells or that do not shut immediately when sharply tapped. Place the remaining clams and mussels in a dry skillet and set over high heat for 5 minutes, until the shells have opened. Remove the clams and mussels from their shells, discarding any that remain closed.

Heat the oil in a skillet, add the onion, garlic, and chile and cook over low heat, stirring occasionally, for 5 minutes, then add the octopuses, mussels, clams, and shrimp. Season with salt and cook, stirring frequently, for 5 minutes. Remove from the heat and add the parsley.

Roll out the dough on a lightly floured counter, then press it out on the baking sheet. Sprinkle the tomatoes on top, drizzle with oil, and bake for about 15 minutes. Arrange the seafood on top and return the pizza to the oven for another 7–8 minutes (no longer, or the seafood will become tough).

/ Light lunches and suppers /

Mini pizzas with Parmesan

Pizzelle con parmigiano

Preparation time: 2½ hrs
(including rising)
Cooking time: 30 mins
Makes 25 mini pizzas

For the dough

4 cups white flour,
    preferably Italian type
    00, plus extra for
    dusting
⅗ cake fresh yeast,
    2 teaspoons active dry
    yeast, or 1½ teaspoons
    instant yeast

For the topping

3 tablespoons olive oil,
    plus extra for frying
1 clove garlic
2¼ pounds tomatoes, peeled,
    seeded, and chopped
pinch of sugar
pinch of dried oregano
3-4 basil leaves
generous 1 cup grated
    Parmesan cheese
salt

To make the topping, heat the oil in a large pan and add the garlic clove. When the garlic is browned, remove it with a slotted spoon and discard. Add the tomatoes and sugar and season lightly with salt. Cover and simmer gently for about 25 minutes, until the sauce thickens. Remove the pan from the heat and stir in the oregano and basil leaves.

To make the dough, sift the flour into a mound on a counter and make a well in the center. Using a fork, mash the fresh yeast, if using, with 1 cup lukewarm water in a small bowl to create a smooth paste, or for active dry yeast, add to the water and set aside for 10 minutes, until bubbles form on the surface. Add the yeast to the well in the flour. Gradually incorporate the flour, then knead the dough until it is soft and elastic. If using instant yeast, sift together the flour and yeast into a mound on a counter and make a well in the center. Pour the water into the well. Gradually incorporate the dry ingredients with your fingers, then knead well until smooth and elastic. Shape it into a ball, put it in a bowl, cover with a dish towel, and let it rise in a warm place for 2 hours.

Turn out the dough onto a lightly floured counter and break off a piece the size of a large walnut. Stretch it out, pulling with your hands, then shape into a round 2½-2¾ inches in diameter. Repeat with the remaining dough to make 25 mini pizza bases. Gently reheat the sauce. Pour oil into a skillet to a depth of about 2 inches and heat. When it is very hot, add the pizza bases, in batches, and fry for only 15 seconds. Remove from the skillet and drain on paper towels.

When all the pizza bases have been cooked, spread 1 teaspoon of the sauce on top of each and sprinkle with 1 teaspoon of the Parmesan. Transfer to a serving dish and serve immediately.

Pasta with cuttlefish ink

Pasta col nero di seppie

Preparation time: 40 mins

Cooking time: 1¼ hrs

Serves 6

2½ pounds cuttlefish
scant ½ cup olive oil
1 onion, finely chopped
1 clove garlic, finely
    chopped
scant ½ cup dry white wine
2 teaspoons tomato paste
12 ounces tomatoes, chopped
1 fresh red chile, seeded and
    finely chopped
1 pound linguine
2 tablespoons finely chopped
    flat-leaf parsley
salt

To clean the cuttlefish, cut off the tentacles just in front of the eyes, then remove and discard the beak from the middle. Separate the tentacles and pull off the skin from each. Pull off the skin from the body sac then cut down the center of the sac, and remove the cuttlebone. Open out the body sac, carefully remove the ink sac from the innards, and place in a bowl of water. (The ink sac is pearly white.) Remove and discard the innards and the head. Wash the body sac and tentacles under cold running water and cut into pieces.

Heat the oil in a shallow pan. Add the onion and garlic and cook over low heat, stirring occasionally, for 5 minutes, or until softened. Add the cuttlefish, increase the heat to medium, and cook, stirring frequently, for 10 minutes. Pour in the wine and cook for a few minutes to let the alcohol evaporate, then stir in the tomato paste, tomatoes, chile, and the ink from the cuttlefish sac, then season with salt and pepper. Reduce the heat and simmer for about 1 hour, stirring occasionally and adding a little water, if necessary.

Cook the linguine in a large pan of salted boiling water for 8–10 minutes, or according to package directions, until it is tender but still al dente, or firm to the bite. Drain the pasta and turn it into a serving dish. Pour the cuttlefish sauce over the pasta, sprinkle with the parsley, and serve immediately.

Spaghetti with lobster

Spaghetti all'aragosta

Preparation time: 15 mins
Cooking time: 30 mins
Serves 6

scant ½ cup olive oil
1 onion, finely chopped
11 ounces ripe tomatoes,
    peeled, seeded, and diced
14 ounces lobster meat, diced
1 pound spaghetti
salt
1 sprig flat-leaf parsley,
    to garnish

Heat the oil in a shallow pan. Add the onion and cook over low heat, stirring occasionally, for 5 minutes, or until softened. Stir in the tomatoes and cook for another 5 minutes, then add the lobster meat and cook gently for about 10 minutes, or until tender. Meanwhile, cook the spaghetti in a large pan of salted boiling water for 8–10 minutes, or according to package directions, until it is tender but still al dente, or firm to the bite. Drain the pasta and toss with the lobster sauce. Transfer to a warm serving dish, garnish with a parsley sprig, and serve immediately.

Note: Sardinian lobster, with its delicate flesh and intense flavor, is considered by many Italians to be the best lobster available.

Colorful ruote with bell peppers

Ruote colorate ai peperoni

Preparation time: 30 mins
(including cooling)
Cooking time: 50 mins
Serves 4

12 ounces mixed red and green
    ruote pasta
¼ cup olive oil, plus extra
    for drizzling
1 red bell pepper
1 yellow bell pepper
1 green bell pepper
1 bunch mixed herbs, such
    as basil, marjoram, and
    tarragon, shredded
1 clove garlic, chopped
salt

Preheat the oven to 350°F. Cook the pasta in a large pan of salted boiling water for 8–10 minutes, or according to package directions, until tender but still al dente, or firm to the bite. Drain the pan, rinse the pasta under cold running water, and drain again. Turn into a salad bowl and drizzle with olive oil. Put the bell peppers on a baking sheet and roast them, turning occasionally, for 35–40 minutes, until they are blistered and charred. Remove from the oven, put them into a plastic bag, and seal the top. When they are cool enough to handle, peel off the skins, remove and discard the seeds, and cut the flesh into ½-inch wide strips. Put the bell peppers into a bowl, season with salt, and add the olive oil, herbs, and garlic. Add the dressed bell peppers to the cold pasta, stir thoroughly, and serve.

Seafood linguine

Linguine ai frutti di mare

Preparation time: 30 mins
Cooking time: 20 mins
Serves 4

14 ounces clams
11 ounces mussels
2 tablespoons olive oil
3 cloves garlic
1 pinch dried oregano
12 ounces linguine
14 ounces canned chopped
    tomatoes
1 tablespoon chopped basil
salt and pepper

Scrub the shellfish under cold running water and pull off the "beards" from the mussels. Discard any with damaged shells, and any that do not shut when sharply tapped.

Heat 1 tablespoon of the oil in a skillet and add 1 garlic clove and the oregano. Add the clams and cook over medium-high heat for 3–5 minutes, until the shells have opened. Remove the pan from the heat and discard any clams that remain shut.

Put the mussels into a medium pan, pour in ⅔ cup water, cover, and bring to a boil over high heat. Cook, shaking the pan occasionally, for 3–5 minutes, until the shells have opened. Remove the pan from the heat and discard any mussels that remain shut.

Lift out the clams and mussels from the pans, reserving 1 tablespoon of the clam cooking juices. Remove most of the clams and mussels from the shells and set aside.

Preheat the oven to 425°F. Cook the linguine in a large pan of salted boiling water for 8–10 minutes, or according to package directions, or until al dente, or firm to the bite, and then drain it.

Heat the remaining oil in a medium pan. Add the remaining garlic and cook, stirring frequently, for a few minutes, until golden brown, then remove and discard. Add the tomatoes, linguine, shellfish, chopped basil, and reserved cooking juices, and season with salt and pepper. Mix well, then spoon the mixture into the middle of a large sheet of aluminum foil. Fold the foil over and seal the edges. Put the package on a baking sheet and bake for 5 minutes. Serve immediately.

Photograph p.166

Spaghetti with raw tomato

Spaghetti al pomodoro crudo

Preparation time: 45 mins
(including standing)
Cooking time: 8-10 mins
Serves 4

1 pound 2 ounces ripe vine
    tomatoes, peeled, seeded,
    and chopped
¼ cup olive oil
10 leaves fresh basil,
    chopped
2 cloves garlic
12 ounces spaghetti
salt and pepper

Put the tomatoes into a salad bowl, add the oil,
basil, and garlic, and season with salt and
pepper. Mix well, cover, and set aside in a cool
place for 30 minutes to let the flavors mingle,
then remove and discard the garlic.

Cook the spaghetti in a large pan of salted
boiling water for 8-10 minutes, or according to
package directions, until it is tender but
al dente, or firm to the bite, then drain and toss
with the raw tomato sauce and serve immediately.

Photograph p.167

Fusilli with eggplant caponata

Fusilli con caponata di melanzane

Preparation time: 30 mins
Cooking time: 35 mins
Serves 4

5 tablespoons olive oil,
    plus extra for drizzling
2 eggplants, peeled
    and diced
2 onions, sliced
3 plum tomatoes, peeled,
    seeded, and diced
1 tablespoon rinsed and
    drained capers
6 black olives, pitted
    and halved
6 basil leaves, torn
11 ounces fusilli pasta
salt and pepper

Heat 3 tablespoons of the oil in a large skillet.
Add the eggplants and cook over medium-low heat,
stirring occasionally, for 10 minutes, until they
are softened and golden brown. Remove the skillet
from the heat and set aside.

Heat the remaining oil in a shallow pan.
Add the onions and cook over low heat, stirring
occasionally, for 5 minutes, or until softened.
Add the tomatoes and cook, stirring occasionally,
for another 5 minutes. Add the capers, olives,
and eggplants and cook for a few minutes,
then remove the pan from the heat and add the
basil leaves.

Cook the pasta in a large pan of salted boiling
water for 8-10 minutes, or according to package
directions, until tender but still al dente,
or firm to the bite. Drain and turn into a salad
bowl. Drizzle with olive oil, season with pepper,
and stir. Add the warm eggplant caponata, stir
again, and serve immediately.

Cold spaghetti
with tuna and chives

Spaghetti freddi al tonno ed erba cipollina

Preparation time: 40 mins
(including standing)
Cooking time: 10 mins
Serves 4

12 ounces spaghetti
1 red bell pepper, seeded and
    cut into small strips
2 teaspoons snipped chives
olive oil, for drizzling
4 ounces canned tuna in oil,
    drained and flaked
salt and pepper

Cook the pasta in a large pan of salted boiling water for 8–10 minutes, or according to package directions, until it is tender but still al dente, or firm to the bite. Drain, rinse under cold running water, and drain again.

Meanwhile, put the bell pepper strips and chives into a large bowl. Add the spaghetti, drizzle generously with olive oil, and season with pepper. Stir and let stand for 30 minutes to let the flavors mingle. Transfer to a serving dish, sprinkle with the tuna, and serve.

Gnocchetti with turkey

Gnocchetti profumati al tacchino

Preparation time:
2¼–3¼ hrs
(including standing)
Cooking time: 15 mins
Serves 4

7 ounces firm tomatoes, diced
7 ounces thickly sliced roast
    turkey, diced
20 black olives, pitted
    and chopped
1 bunch mixed herbs, chopped
dash of Tabasco sauce
olive oil, for drizzling
12 ounces Sardinian
    gnocchetti or malloreddus
salt and pepper

Put the tomatoes, turkey, olives, herbs, and a few drops of Tabasco into a bowl and stir well. Season with pepper, drizzle with olive oil, stir again, and let stand for 2–3 hours to let the flavors mingle.

Cook the pasta in a large pan of salted boiling water for 8–10 minutes, or according to package directions, until tender but still firm to the bite. Drain and let cool. Turn the pasta into a serving dish, pour the sauce over it, season with salt, and serve.

Note: Sardinian gnocchetti, or malloreddus, is one of the island's traditional types of pasta, a tasty mixture of pure durum wheat flour, water, and salt. Other small shell-like pasta shapes can be substituted.

Seafood linguine (p.163)

ghetti with raw tomato (p.164)

Country salad

Insalata rustica

Preparation time: 40 mins

Cooking time: 1 hr

Serves 6

2¾ cups shelled fresh
    cannellini beans
5 ounces pearl onions
5 ounces baby carrots
generous 1 cup diced,
    cooked ham

For the green sauce

1 small potato
2 hard-cooked eggs
4 canned anchovy fillets,
    soaked in cold water
    for 10 mins and drained
1 sprig flat-leaf parsley
1 sprig basil
¼ clove garlic
1 dill pickle, drained
scant 1 cup olive oil
2 tablespoons white-wine
    vinegar
salt and pepper

First, make the green sauce. Cook the potato in lightly salted boiling water for 15 minutes, or until it is tender, then drain, peel, and mash in a bowl with a fork. Shell and halve the eggs, then scoop the yolks into the bowl and mix with the potato.

Pat the anchovies dry with paper towels, and chop finely with the parsley, basil, garlic, and dill pickle. Stir into the potato mixture, then gradually beat in the olive oil, a little at a time. Season to taste with salt and pepper and stir in the vinegar.

Put the beans into a pan, add water to cover and bring to a boil, then reduce the heat, and simmer for about 40 minutes, until tender. Set a few onions and 2-3 carrots aside. Cook the remaining onions in boiling water for 10 minutes, or until they are tender. Cook the remaining carrots in another pan of salted boiling water for 5-10 minutes, until they are tender. Drain all the vegetables when they are cooked. Peel the onions, including those set aside, leaving them whole.

Chop the carrots, including those set aside. Mix together the beans, onions, carrots, and ham in a salad bowl, stir in the green sauce, and serve.

/ Light lunches and suppers /

Sweet-and-sour caponata

Caponata in agrodolce

Preparation time: 55 mins
(including salting)
Cooking time: 30 mins
Serves 4

2¼ pounds eggplants, diced
2 tablespoons raisins
1 cup olive oil
1 celery stalk, chopped
1 onion, sliced
11 ounces ripe tomatoes,
    peeled and diced
1½ teaspoons sugar
scant ½ cup red-wine vinegar
1 tablespoon pine nuts
scant 1 cup pitted and halved
    green olives
3 tablespoons rinsed and
    drained capers
4–5 basil leaves
12 slices provolone or other
    medium-flavored cheese
salt and pepper

Put the eggplants into a colander, sprinkle with salt, and let drain for 30 minutes, then rinse and pat dry with paper towels. Meanwhile, put the raisins into a bowl, pour in warm water to cover, and let soak for 15 minutes, then drain.

Heat scant ⅓ cup of the olive oil in a large skillet. Add the eggplants and cook over medium heat, stirring frequently, for 8–10 minutes, until golden brown.

Meanwhile, heat the remaining oil in another shallow pan. Add the celery, onion, and tomatoes and cook over low heat, stirring occasionally, for 10 minutes, until thickened, then season with salt and pepper. Stir the sugar, vinegar, pine nuts, olives, raisins, and capers into the sauce and cook for a few minutes more. Add the eggplants and simmer for 10 minutes. Serve the caponata warm, sprinkled with basil and with the provolone cheese on the side.

Green beans with tomato

Fagiolini al pomodoro

Preparation time: 15 mins
Cooking time: 25 mins
Serves 4

1 pound 5 ounces green
    beans, trimmed
2 tablespoons olive oil
1 onion, chopped
1 clove garlic
5 tomatoes, peeled, seeded,
    and chopped
6 green olives, pitted and
    quartered
6 basil leaves, chopped
salt and pepper

Cook the beans in a pan of salted boiling water for 5–10 minutes, or until just tender. Meanwhile, heat the oil in another pan, add the onion and garlic, and cook over low heat, stirring occasionally, for 5 minutes. Drain the beans, add to the pan, and mix well. Stir in the tomatoes, season with salt and pepper, then remove and discard the garlic. Simmer over low heat for about 10 minutes, then stir in the olives and basil and cook for another 5 minutes. Serve warm.

Fava beans with ham

Fave al prosciutto

Preparation time: 30 mins
Cooking time: 20 mins
Serves 4

4½ pounds fresh fava beans,
    shelled
3 tablespoons butter
generous ½ cup diced, cooked
    ham
1 onion, chopped
1 carrot, chopped
scant 1 cup meat stock
1 sprig flat-leaf parsley,
    chopped
salt and pepper

Put the beans in a pan, add cold water to cover, bring to a boil, and cook for 10 minutes.

Meanwhile, melt half the butter in another pan, add the ham, onion, and carrot, and cook, stirring occasionally, for 5 minutes. Drain the beans and add to the ham mixture, then pour in the stock and season with salt and pepper. Simmer until the sauce is very thick, then stir in the remaining butter, transfer to a warm serving dish, and sprinkle with the parsley.

Eggplant fricassee

Fricassea di melanzane

Preparation time: 1 hr
(including salting)
Cooking time: 25 mins
Serves 4

5 eggplants, thickly sliced
2 tablespoons butter
3 tablespoons olive oil
1 onion, chopped
1 pound 2 ounces ripe plum
    tomatoes, peeled,
    seeded, and chopped
1 sprig flat-leaf parsley,
    chopped
1 clove garlic, chopped
2 eggs
juice of 1 lemon, strained
salt and pepper

Put the eggplant slices in a colander, sprinkle with salt, and let drain for 30 minutes. Meanwhile, melt the butter with the oil in a pan, add the onion, and cook over low heat, stirring occasionally, for 5 minutes.

Rinse the eggplants, pat them dry, and add them to the pan, then add the tomatoes, parsley, and garlic, and season with salt and pepper. Mix well and cook over medium heat for about 15 minutes, or until the eggplants are tender. Remove the pan from the heat.

Beat the eggs with the lemon juice and pour them over the eggplant mixture. Stir rapidly, so that the eggs do not scramble but coat the mixture like a cream. Transfer the fricassee to a warm serving dish and serve immediately.

Marinated eggplants

Melanzane marinate

Preparation time: 6¾ hrs
(including marinating)

Cooking time: 20 mins

Serves 4

1 pound 5 ounces eggplants,
   cut into ¼-inch thick
   slices
1 fresh chile, seeded
   and chopped
3 cloves garlic, finely
   chopped
1 tablespoon rinsed, drained,
   and chopped capers
   preserved in salt
10 mint leaves, chopped
¾ cup olive oil
salt and pepper

Put the eggplant slices in a colander, sprinkle with salt, and let drain for about 30 minutes. Meanwhile, combine the chile, garlic, capers, and mint in a bowl and season with salt and pepper. Heat a heavy, nonstick skillet. Rinse the eggplants, pat them dry, and brush with some of the oil. Add the eggplant slices to the skillet, in batches if necessary, and cook over high heat until they are golden brown on both sides.

Make a layer of eggplant slices in a salad bowl, sprinkle with a tablespoon of the chile dressing, and continue making layers until all the ingredients are used. Pour in the remaining olive oil and let marinate in a cool place for at least 6 hours.

Stuffed eggplants

Melanzane ripiene

Preparation time: 30 mins

Cooking time: 30 mins

Serves 4

4 eggplants
6 tablespoons butter, plus
   extra for greasing and
   dotting
olive oil, for frying
7 ounces ground beef
¼ cup all-purpose flour
2¼ cups milk
1 pinch freshly grated nutmeg
1 egg
¾ cup grated Parmesan cheese
1 cup fresh bread crumbs
salt and pepper

Halve the eggplants lengthwise and scoop out and reserve most of the flesh from each half. Sprinkle the eggplant skins with salt and turn them upside down to let the excess water drain. Preheat the oven to 350°F and grease an ovenproof dish with butter. Heat a little oil in a skillet, add the ground beef, and cook over medium-high heat for a few minutes until browned. Set aside.

To make the béchamel sauce, melt 4 tablespoons of the butter in a medium pan over low heat. Stir in the flour and cook, stirring constantly, for 1 minute. Gradually stir in the milk and bring to a boil. Cook and continue to stir until the sauce is thickened. Remove the pan from the heat, stir in the nutmeg, season with salt and pepper, and let cool slightly. Rinse the eggplant shells and pat dry with paper towels.

→

→ Chop the reserved eggplant and stir it into the sauce with the egg, meat, and cheese, then season with salt and pepper. Fill the eggplant shells with this mixture, put them into the prepared dish, dot with the remaining butter, and sprinkle with the bread crumbs. Bake for 30 minutes, until the topping is crisp and golden. Serve immediately.

Photograph p.174

Bell pepper frittata
Frittata ai peperoni

Preparation time: 15 mins

Cooking time: 35 mins

Serves 4
----

3 tablespoons butter
¼ cup olive oil
2 yellow bell peppers,
    halved, seeded, and diced
3 tomatoes, peeled, seeded,
    and diced
6 eggs, lightly beaten
salt and pepper

Heat half the butter and the oil in a skillet, add the bell peppers, and cook, stirring, for 2 minutes. Add the tomatoes, season with salt and pepper, cover, and cook over low heat for 15–20 minutes. Add the eggs to the skillet. Melt the remaining butter in another skillet and pour the entire mixture into it. Cook the frittata for 5–8 minutes on each side until golden, and serve.

Photograph p.175

Eggs with tomatoes
Uova al piatto con pomodori

Preparation time: 25 mins

(including draining)

Cooking time: 25 mins

Serves 4
----

2 teaspoons olive oil, plus
    extra for brushing
4 large tomatoes
1 pinch dried oregano
4 eggs
1 sprig flat-leaf parsley,
    chopped
salt and pepper

Preheat the oven to 350°F. Brush an ovenproof dish with olive oil. Cut the tops off the tomatoes and scoop out the seeds and some of the flesh. Sprinkle the insides with a little salt and turn upside down on paper towels for 10 minutes to drain. Season the insides of the tomatoes with oregano and pepper and divide the olive oil among them. Place the tomatoes in the prepared dish and bake for 20 minutes.

Remove the dish from the oven, break an egg into each tomato, return the dish to the oven, and bake for another 5 minutes, until the eggs are just set. Garnish with parsley and serve.

Pea mold

Flan di piselli

Preparation time: 20 mins
Cooking time: 1 hr
Serves 6

5 tablespoons butter, plus
    extra for greasing
½ onion, chopped
⅓ cup diced, cooked ham
5¼ cups shelled fresh peas
2 tablespoons all-purpose
    flour, plus extra for
    dusting
1 cup milk
1 pinch freshly grated nutmeg
3 eggs, separated
salt

Melt 1½ tablespoons of the butter in a medium pan. Add the onion and cook over low heat, stirring occasionally, for 5 minutes, until softened. Add the ham, peas, and ¾ cup hot water and simmer for 10–15 minutes, until the peas are tender. Preheat the oven to 350°F, then grease a mold with butter, and dust it with flour.

To make the béchamel sauce, melt 2 tablespoons of the remaining butter in a medium pan over low heat. Stir in the flour and cook, stirring constantly, for 1 minute. Gradually stir in the milk and bring to a boil, stirring constantly. Cook, stirring, until thickened, then remove from the heat, stir in the nutmeg, season with salt and pepper, and let cool slightly.

Transfer two-thirds of the ham-and-pea mixture to a food processor. Process to a puree, then add the remaining butter and process again to combine. Put the puree into a bowl, stir in the béchamel sauce and the remaining peas and ham, and let cool. Stir the egg yolks, one at a time, into the mixture. Whisk the egg whites to stiff peaks in a grease-free bowl, then fold them into the mixture. Pour the mixture into the prepared mold and smooth the surface.

Stand the mold in a roasting pan, pour in boiling water to come about halfway up the sides, carefully transfer to the oven, and bake for 40 minutes. Turn out and serve immediately.

Stuffed eggplants (p.171)

spring onion & pepper frittata (p.172)

Tomatoes
with zucchini

Pomodori alle zucchine

Preparation time: 20 mins
Cooking time: 40 mins
Serves 4

olive oil, for brushing and
    drizzling
8 tomatoes
2 zucchini, trimmed
1 sprig flat-leaf parsley,
    chopped
1 clove garlic, chopped
7 ounces mozzarella cheese,
    sliced
½ teaspoon dried oregano
salt and pepper

Preheat the oven to 350°F. Brush an ovenproof
dish with oil. Thinly slice the tomatoes without
cutting all the way through, leaving them joined
at the bottom. Halve the zucchini lengthwise,
then slice them into thin strips. Slip the strips
of zucchini between the slices of tomato.

Place the tomatoes in the prepared dish, sprinkle
with the parsley and garlic, season with salt and
pepper, and drizzle them with olive oil. Bake
for 30 minutes. Remove the dish from the oven but
do not switch the oven off.

Carefully slip slices of mozzarella between
the slices of tomato and zucchini, sprinkle with
the oregano, and return to the oven for
10 minutes until the mozzarella starts to melt
and form strings. Transfer to a warm serving
dish and serve immediately.

Tomatoes with
saffron pilaf stuffing

Pomodorini ripieni di riso pilaf
allo zafferano

Preparation time: 1½ hrs
(including cooling)
Cooking time: 40 mins
Serves 4

2 tablespoons butter
½ onion, chopped
1 pinch saffron threads
1 cup hot vegetable stock
generous ¾ cup long-grain
    rice
12 large vine tomatoes
1 tablespoon olive oil, plus
    extra for drizzling
1 zucchini, diced
2 tablespoons chopped flat-
    leaf parsley
salt and pepper

Preheat the oven to 350°F. Melt the butter
in a shallow, ovenproof heavy pan. Add the onion
and cook over low heat, stirring occasionally,
for 5 minutes, or until softened. Meanwhile,
lightly crush the saffron threads and mix with
2 tablespoons of the hot stock in a small bowl.

Add the rice to the pan, season lightly with
salt, and cook, stirring constantly, for a few
minutes until all the grains are coated with
butter. Pour in the remaining hot stock and bring
back to a boil. Stir in the saffron mixture,
cover the pan, and transfer it to the oven. Cook
for 18-20 minutes without removing the lid
or stirring. Remove the dish from the oven and
let cool.

Meanwhile, cut off the tops of the tomatoes and
scoop out the flesh and seeds with a teaspoon.
Sprinkle the insides of the tomatoes with salt
and leave them upside down to drain. Heat the
olive oil in a skillet. Add the zucchini and cook
over medium-low heat for 10 minutes, or until it
is softened, then season with salt. Combine the
cooled rice, zucchini, and parsley in a bowl,
drizzle with olive oil, and season with salt and
pepper. Stir well and spoon the mixture into the
tomato shells. Serve warm or cold.

Grocer's bag

Sacchetti dell'ortolano

Preparation time: 30 mins

Cooking time: 20 mins

Serves 4
----

4 yellow bell peppers
2 tablespoons olive oil,
    plus extra for brushing
4 eggplants, diced
1 clove garlic
1 tablespoon tomato paste
1 tablespoon rinsed and
    drained capers
6 basil leaves, chopped
8 black olives
5 ounces mozzarella cheese,
    diced
salt and pepper
4 basil leaves, to garnish

Preheat the broiler. Put the bell peppers on a baking sheet and place under the broiler, turning frequently, until they are charred and blackened. Transfer them to a plastic bag, tie the top, and let cool. Peel off the bell pepper skins, cut off the tops, and remove the seeds and membranes, without piercing the sides.

Preheat the oven to 350°F. Brush an ovenproof dish with oil. Heat the olive oil in a skillet. Add the eggplants and garlic and cook over low heat for 5 minutes, or until they are golden brown. Mix the tomato paste with 1 teaspoon hot water and add it to the pan with the capers, basil leaves, and olives. Cook for a few more minutes. Remove and discard the garlic and season with salt and pepper.

Remove the pan from the heat and add the mozzarella. Fill the bell peppers with the mixture and place them in the prepared dish. Bake for 10 minutes. Garnish each bell pepper with a basil leaf and serve warm.

Tomatoes with eggplants

Pomodori alle melanzane

Preparation time: 1¼ hrs

(including salting)

Cooking time: 20 mins

Serves 4
----

4 tomatoes
2 tablespoons olive oil
1 eggplant, peeled and diced
1 clove garlic, chopped
1 scallion, finely chopped
1 tablespoon rinsed, drained,
    and chopped capers
    preserved in salt
1 sprig basil, chopped
3 tablespoons white-wine
    vinegar
salt and pepper

Cut off the tops of the tomatoes and reserve. Scoop out the tomato seeds and some of the flesh, sprinkle the "shells" with salt, and turn them upside down on paper towels to drain for 1 hour. Heat the oil in a pan, add the eggplant and garlic, and cook over high heat, stirring frequently, until the eggplant is lightly browned all over. Add the scallion, capers, and basil and season with salt and pepper. Pour in the vinegar and cook until it has evaporated. Remove from the heat and let cool. Fill the tomatoes with the eggplant mixture, replace the tops, and serve.

Photograph p.182

/ Light lunches and suppers /

Stuffed zucchini flowers

Fiori di zucchine ripieni

Preparation time: 15 mins
Serves 4

7 ounces robiola or other
    soft cheese, cut into
    pieces
7 ounces Gorgonzola cheese,
    crumbled
3 dill pickles, drained
    and chopped
1 egg yolk
12 zucchini flowers, trimmed
salt

Put the cheeses in a bowl and beat with a wooden spoon until smooth. Stir in the dill pickles and egg yolk and season with salt. Mix carefully. Fill the zucchini flowers with the cheese mixture, arrange them on a serving dish in the shape of a star, and serve.

Photograph p.183

Zucchini capricciose

Zucchine capricciose

Preparation time: 40 mins
Cooking time: 30 mins
Serves 4

3 tablespoons olive oil,
    plus extra for brushing
6 zucchini, halved lengthwise
4 salted anchovies, soaked
    in water and drained
1 clove garlic, chopped
1 sprig flat-leaf parsley,
    chopped
1 sprig basil, chopped
scant 1 cup pitted green
    olives
2 tomatoes, peeled, seeded,
    and chopped
5 ounces mozzarella cheese,
    diced
salt and pepper

Preheat the oven to 400°F. Brush an ovenproof dish with olive oil. Scoop out the flesh from the zucchini with a small sharp knife, being careful not to pierce the sides. Chop the flesh and set aside. Place the zucchini shells, skin side up, in the prepared dish and bake for 10 minutes. Remove from the oven and set aside. Reduce the oven temperature to 350°F.

Place the anchovies skin side up, press along the backbones with your thumb, then turn them over and remove the bones. Chop the flesh and put it into a bowl, add 2 tablespoons of the oil, and beat the mixture with a wooden spoon until smooth.

Combine the garlic, parsley, basil, zucchini flesh, and olives in another bowl, then stir in the tomatoes. Pour in the remaining oil, add the anchovy mixture, and season with salt and pepper. Mix well and spoon the mixture into the zucchini shells. Top with the mozzarella and bake for 20 minutes, until golden.

Tomatoes with eggplants (p.180)

stuffed zucchini flowers (p.181)

Zucchini
and beet carpaccio

Carpaccio di zucchine e barbabietole

Preparation time: 45 mins
(including chilling)
Cooking time: 5 mins
Serves 4

1¼ cups pine nuts
scant ½ cup olive oil
1 teaspoon Dijon mustard
juice of 1 lemon, strained
4 baby zucchini, thinly
    sliced lengthwises
4 cooked beets, sliced into
    rounds
7 ounces smoked scamorza
    cheese, cut into thin
    strips
salt and pepper

Put the pine nuts into a nonstick pan and cook over low heat for a few minutes, shaking the pan occasionally, until the nuts are a light golden brown, then remove from the pan and set aside. Whisk together the olive oil, mustard, and lemon juice in bowl and season with salt and pepper. Arrange the zucchini slices in an overlapping pattern on a serving dish or on individual plates, sprinkle with the pine nuts, drizzle with half the dressing, and chill in the refrigerator for 30 minutes. To serve, add the beet rounds and the scamorza strips and drizzle with the remaining dressing.

Zucchini with lemon

Zucchine al limone

Preparation time: 1 hr
(including marinating)
Cooking time: 15 mins
Serves 4

1 pound 5 ounces zucchini,
    cut into thick strips
1 sprig tarragon, chopped
1 sprig flat-leaf parsley,
    chopped
4 basil leaves, chopped
4 borage leaves, chopped
olive oil, for drizzling
juice of 1 lemon, strained
salt and pepper

Steam the zucchini over a pan of boiling water for about 15 minutes. Let cool slightly, then place on a serving dish. Sprinkle the herbs on top. Drizzle with olive oil, season with salt and pepper to taste, and sprinkle with the lemon juice. Toss, set aside in a cool place for the flavors to mingle, then serve.

/ Light lunches and suppers /

Anchovy fritters

Frittelle di mucco

Preparation time: 20 mins
Cooking time: 20 mins
Serves 6

2½ pounds baby anchovies
    or snapper, cleaned
4 eggs
generous ¾ cup all-purpose
    flour, plus extra for
    dusting
⅔ cup grated Parmesan cheese
1 bunch flat-leaf parsley,
    finely chopped
1 clove garlic, finely
    chopped
2 ounces wild fennel, finely
    chopped (optional)
vegetable oil, for
    deep-frying
salt and pepper

Put the anchovies, eggs, flour, cheese, parsley, garlic, and fennel, if using, into a bowl, season with salt and pepper, and use a fork to blend to a soft mixture. Shape into balls with 2 tablespoons and dust with flour. Heat the oil in a deep-fryer to 350–375°F, or until a cube of day-old bread browns in 30 seconds. Add the fritters carefully, in batches, and fry for a few minutes until golden brown all over. Remove with a slotted spoon and drain on paper towels. Serve immediately.

Note: The Sicilian word *mucco*, meaning "baby anchovies", is thought to derive from the Arabic word *sumuk*, meaning "fish," and is used in the coastal regions of Sicily.

Squid with potatoes and Swiss chard

Calamari all'inzimino

Preparation time: 30 mins
Cooking time: 45 mins
Serves 4

¼ cup olive oil
2 cloves garlic
4 potatoes, cut into wedges
1 pound 2 ounces cleaned
    squid (see p.265), cut
    into strips
scant ½ cup dry white wine
7 ounces Swiss chard, stalks
    removed
1 tablespoon chopped flat-
    leaf parsley
1 tablespoon chopped oregano
salt and pepper

Heat the oil in a heavy pan. Add the garlic cloves and cook over low heat, stirring frequently, for a few minutes, until lightly browned, then remove and discard them. Add the potatoes to the pan and cook, stirring occasionally, for 10 minutes. Add the squid, season with salt, increase the heat to medium-high, and cook for a few minutes. Add the wine and cook until the alcohol has evaporated. Reduce the heat, pour in scant 1 cup water, cover, and simmer for 20–25 minutes.

Meanwhile, cut the Swiss chard into strips. Stir it into the pan, sprinkle with the parsley and oregano, and season with salt and pepper. Cook for another 5 minutes, then remove from the heat. Serve lukewarm.

Asparagus and shrimp salad

Insalata di asparagi e gamberi

Preparation time: 30 mins
Cooking time: 30 mins
Serves 6

1 lemon
2¼ pounds green asparagus,
    trimmed
5 eggs
14 ounces uncooked shrimp
scant 1 cup sunflower
    or olive oil, or
    a combination
1 tablespoon chopped
    flat-leaf parsley
salt and pepper

Halve the lemon and squeeze the juice from one
half. Cut a slice off the remaining half. Fill
a small bowl with water, twist the lemon slice
over the bowl, and then add it to the water.
Cut off the asparagus tips and put them into
the bowl. Cut the tender part of the stalks
into small pieces and cook them in salted boiling
water for 5-10 minutes, until they are nearly
tender. Drain the tips, add them to the pan, and
cook for another 5-10 minutes. Drain, refresh
in cold water, drain again, and put the asparagus
into a salad bowl.

Bring a small pan of water to a boil, add a pinch
of salt, and place 2 of the eggs in the pan.
Cook for 8 minutes over high heat, then drain and
cool under cold running water. Meanwhile, cook
the shrimp in another pan of boiling water for
10 minutes. Drain, peel, and add them to the
salad bowl. Shell and slice the hard-cooked eggs.

To make the mayonnaise, separate the remaining
eggs and put the yolks in a bowl. Season with
a pinch each of salt and of pepper, then add the
oil, a drop at a time, whisking constantly. As
soon as the mixture begins to thicken, whisk in
a little of the lemon juice.

Continue adding the oil in a steady stream,
whisking constantly and alternating with the
remaining lemon juice. Add the mayonnaise to the
salad bowl and gently toss the mixture. Garnish
with slices of hard-cooked egg and sprinkle with
chopped parsley.

Tangy herring and Belgian endive salad

Insalata piccante di aringhe e indivia

Preparation time: 1¼ hrs
(including soaking)
Serves 4

2 herrings, filleted, with
    roes reserved
2 tablespoons olive oil
2 tablespoons white-wine
    vinegar
¼ teaspoon anchovy paste
¼ teaspoon hot mustard
1 onion, finely chopped
1 sprig basil, finely chopped
1 sprig flat-leaf parsley,
    finely chopped
1 head Belgian endive,
    separated into leaves
¼ cup light cream
¼ cup plain yogurt
salt

Put the herring roes into a bowl of cold water and let them soak for 1 hour. Drain well, transfer to a bowl, and beat with a wooden spoon until creamy, then stir in the olive oil, vinegar, anchovy paste, and mustard. Stir in the onion, basil, and parsley. Line a salad bowl with the Belgian endive leaves, put the herring fillets on top, and dress with the herring roe cream. Combine the cream, yogurt, and a pinch of salt in a bowl and pour the mixture over the herrings. Serve immediately.

Hake with green sauce

Nasello con salsa verde

Preparation time: 10 mins
Cooking time: 10 mins
Serves 4

2 tablespoons olive oil,
    plus extra for brushing
4 hake steaks
1 onion, chopped
1 sprig flat-leaf parsley,
    chopped
1 celery stalk, chopped,
    plus a few leaves
juice of 1 lemon, strained
salt and pepper

Preheat the oven to 400°F. Brush an ovenproof dish with oil, put the fish in it, and bake for about 10 minutes, or until just cooked through. Meanwhile, heat the olive oil in a pan, add the onion, and cook over low heat, stirring occasionally, for 5 minutes, until softened. Season with salt and pepper, remove from the heat, and keep warm. Stir in the parsley, chopped celery and celery leaves, and lemon juice. Serve the hake with this green sauce.

Huss with green tomatoes

Palombo con pomodori verdi

Preparation time: 15 mins
Cooking time: 30 mins
Serves 4

4 huss fillets
3-4 green tomatoes, peeled,
    seeded, and diced
1 onion, thinly sliced
1 tablespoon chopped oregano
olive oil, for drizzling
1 cup fresh bread crumbs
salt and pepper

Preheat the oven to 350°F. Put the fish in an ovenproof dish, season with salt and pepper, top with the tomatoes, onion, and oregano, and drizzle with olive oil. Sprinkle the bread crumbs on top, cover with aluminum foil, and bake for 30 minutes. Serve hot.

Mixed fish carpaccio

Carpaccio di pesce misto

Preparation time: 40 mins
(including chilling)
Serves 4

14 ounces swordfish fillet,
    thinly sliced
9 ounces salmon fillet,
    thinly sliced
scant ½ cup olive oil
½ clove garlic, finely
    chopped
1 sprig flat-leaf parsley,
    chopped
1 sprig thyme, chopped
dash of brandy
salt and pepper

For the garnish

11 ounces baby spinach,
    coarse stalks removed
2 teaspoons Dijon mustard
scant ⅓ cup olive oil
salt

Arrange alternating slices of swordfish and salmon on a serving dish, cover, and chill in the refrigerator for 20 minutes.

Meanwhile, whisk together the olive oil, garlic, parsley, thyme, and brandy in a bowl and season with salt and pepper. To make the garnish, put the spinach into a bowl. In another bowl, whisk together the mustard, olive oil, and a pinch of salt, then pour the dressing over the spinach and toss. A few minutes before serving, drizzle the fish carpaccio with the herb sauce and arrange the spinach around it.

Sardines marinara

Sardine alla marinara

Preparation time: 30 mins
Cooking time: 30 mins
Serves 4

olive oil, for brushing and
    drizzling
1¾ pounds sardines, scaled,
    cleaned, and boned
3 sprigs rosemary, chopped
1 clove garlic, chopped
1 pinch dried oregano
1 tablespoon white-wine
    vinegar
salt

Lightly brush a heavy pan with olive oil. Make
2 layers of the sardines in the pan with the
rosemary and garlic between them. Sprinkle with
the oregano, season with salt, and drizzle
generously with olive oil. Cook over medium-low
heat for 15 minutes. Sprinkle with the vinegar
and continue to cook until the flesh flakes
easily. Remove from the heat and let cool. Serve
the sardines cold.

Mackerel tartare
with chives and yogurt

Tartare di sgombro all'erba
cipollina e yogurt

Preparation time: 15 mins
Serves 4

8 smoked mackerel fillets,
    skinned and flaked
2 cups plain yogurt
juice of 2 lemons, strained
1 bunch chives, finely
    chopped
8 slices white bread
salt and pepper
salad of lettuce and green
    tomatoes, to serve

Put the smoked mackerel into a bowl and mash
it with a fork. Combine the yogurt, lemon juice,
and chives in another bowl. Add the mackerel,
mix well, and season with salt and pepper,
if necessary.

Toast the bread and spread each slice with
a little of the mackerel mixture. Arrange
on a serving dish and serve with a salad of
lettuce and green tomatoes.

Swordfish carpaccio with caper sauce

Carpaccio di pesce spada alla salsa di capperi

Preparation time: 45 mins
(including chilling)
Cooking time: 25–30 mins
Serves 4

4 potatoes
14 ounces swordfish fillet,
    very thinly sliced
1 bunch arugula, separated
    into leaves
olive oil, for drizzling
salt and pepper

For the sauce

3 teaspoons capers preserved
    in salt, rinsed
    and drained
1–1¼ cups olive oil
juice of 2 lemons, strained

Cook the potatoes in a pan of salted boiling water for 25–30 minutes, until they are tender, then drain, peel them, and cut them into wedges. Let cool. To make the sauce, put the capers into a bowl, pour in water to cover, and let them soak for 15 minutes.

Drain the capers, squeeze out any excess liquid, and chop finely. Put them into a sauceboat and add olive oil and lemon juice to taste. Arrange the fish slices in concentric circles on a serving dish, season with salt and pepper, and pour the sauce over them. Chill in the refrigerator for 30 minutes. To serve, garnish with the arugula and potato wedges, drizzle with olive oil, and season with salt and pepper.

Sardines with wild fennel

Sardine con finocchietto

Preparation time: 20 mins
Cooking time: 20 mins
Serves 4

2 tablespoons olive oil
1 clove garlic, chopped
2¼ pounds sardines, scaled
    and cleaned
2 teaspoons fennel seeds
⅜ cup white wine
salt and pepper

Preheat the oven to 350°F. Heat the oil in a flameproof, heavy casserole pan. Add the garlic and cook over low heat, stirring frequently, for 2 minutes. Put the sardines in layers on top, season with salt and pepper, sprinkle with the fennel seeds, and pour over the white wine. Transfer to the oven and bake for 15–20 minutes, until the flesh flakes easily. Serve immediately.

/ Light lunches and suppers /

swordfish carpaccio with caper sauce

Mackerel
with green beans

Sgombri ai fagiolini

Preparation time: 20 mins
Cooking time: 30 mins
Serves 4

5 tablespoons olive oil
1 onion, sliced
1 carrot, chopped
1 sprig flat-leaf parsley,
    chopped
1 sprig thyme, chopped
5 ounces green beans, trimmed
1 tomato, peeled, seeded, and
    chopped
2 tablespoons rinsed and
    drained capers preserved
    in salt
4 mackerel, cleaned
all-purpose flour, for dusting
salt and pepper

Heat 2 tablespoons olive oil in a pan, add the onion, carrot, parsley, and thyme, and cook over low heat, stirring occasionally, for 5 minutes. Add the beans and cook, stirring frequently, for 15 minutes. Add the tomato and capers, season with salt and pepper, and cook for another 5 minutes. Meanwhile, dust the mackerel with flour, shaking off the excess. Heat the remaining olive oil in a skillet, add the mackerel, and cook on both sides until golden brown and the flesh flakes easily with a fork, about 20–25 minutes. Remove them from the skillet with a slotted spoon, add to the pan of vegetables, and cook for another 5 minutes. Taste and adjust the seasoning if necessary, then serve.

Mackerel with red
currants

Sgombri ai ribes

Preparation time: 20 mins
Cooking time: 30 mins
Serves 4

4 mackerel, cleaned
3 cups red currants
2 tablespoons butter
1 onion, chopped
1 clove garlic
scant 1 cup dry white wine
1 teaspoon sugar
salt and pepper

Preheat the oven to 350°F. Make 2 or 3 cuts in each side of the mackerel with a sharp knife and put them into an ovenproof dish. Crush 2¼ cups of the red currants in a bowl and strain the juice into another bowl.

Melt the butter in a shallow pan. Add the onion and garlic clove and cook over low heat, stirring occasionally, for 10 minutes. Pour in the white wine and red currant juice, stir in the sugar, and season with salt and pepper. Bring just to a boil, then pour the mixture over the fish. Bake for 10 minutes, then add the remaining red currants and bake for another 10 minutes. Serve immediately, straight from the dish.

/ Light lunches and suppers /

Smoked trout
with melon

Trota affumicata al melone

Preparation time: 30 mins

Serves 4

5 small white onions
1¼ cups plain yogurt
2 tablespoons heavy cream
1 tablespoon white-wine
    vinegar
4 smoked trout fillets
1 small melon, peeled,
    seeded, and thinly sliced
½ cucumber, thinly sliced
    into rounds
salt and pepper

Thinly slice 4 of the onions and chop the fifth.
Pour the yogurt into a salad bowl and stir in the
chopped onion, cream, and vinegar, season with
salt and pepper, and add the onion slices. Put
a fish fillet on each of 4 individual plates, add
a few slices of melon, and spoon 2–3 tablespoons
of the sauce over the top. Garnish with the
cucumber and serve.

Spicy salad of chicken,
truffle, and corn salad

Insalata piccante di pollo,
tartufo e songino

Preparation time: 40 mins

Cooking time: 15 mins

Serves 4

¼ cup olive oil, plus extra
    for drizzling
3 skinless, boneless chicken
    breasts
11 ounces corn salad
1 small black truffle, shaved
salt and pepper

For the sauce

1 tablespoon anchovy paste
3–4 tablespoons olive oil
juice of ½–1 lemon, strained

Heat the oil in a shallow pan. Add the chicken
and cook over medium-low heat, turning
occasionally, for 15 minutes, until cooked
through. Remove the chicken from the pan and cut
it into thin strips. Make a layer of corn salad
in a serving dish, drizzle with oil, season
lightly with salt and pepper, and toss gently.
Put the strips of chicken on the salad and
sprinkle with the truffle shavings.

To make the sauce, mash the anchovy paste in a
bowl with a fork. Gradually drizzle in the oil,
mix well, then stir in lemon juice to taste. Pour
the sauce over the chicken and truffle and serve
without tossing the salad.

Red snapper with tomatoes

Filetto di triglia e pomodorini

Preparation time: 20 mins

Cooking time: 25 mins

Serves 4

4 red snapper, filleted
2 tablespoons olive oil
13 ounces small tomatoes,
    peeled, seeded, and
    quartered
salt

For the tomato sauce

1 tablespoon olive oil
1 clove garlic
5 ounces small tomatoes,
    chopped
3 basil leaves, finely
    chopped
salt

For the quenelles

scant 1 cup pitted black
    olives
¼–⅓ cup olive oil

To make the tomato sauce, heat the oil in a small
shallow pan. Add the garlic clove and cook over
low heat, stirring frequently, for a few minutes,
until lightly browned, then remove and discard
it. Add the tomatoes and simmer, stirring
occasionally, for 15–20 minutes, until reduced
by half.

Meanwhile, make the quenelles. Put the olives
into a small food processor or blender
and process, adding enough oil to make a soft
mixture. Scoop out small quantities of the
mixture and use 2 teaspoons to shape them into
quenelles, or neat ovals. Transfer the tomato
sauce to a blender and process until smooth, then
pass through a strainer into a bowl. Stir in the
basil and season with salt.

Carefully remove any pin bones from the fish
with tweezers and season lightly with salt. Heat
the oil in a skillet. Add the fish, skin side
down, and cook over medium-high heat, shaking the
pan, for 3 minutes. Carefully turn the fillets
with a spatula and cook for 1 minute more. Pour
the tomato sauce into a warm serving dish,
put the fish on top, and garnish with the tomato
quarters and black olive quenelles.
Serve immediately.

Sweet-and-sour meatballs

Polpettine in agrodolce

Preparation time: 25 mins
Cooking time: 30 mins
Serves 6

5 slices white bread
    (about 5 ounces),
    crusts removed
generous ⅓ cup milk
11 ounces ground beef
11 ounces ground veal
generous 1 cup grated
    Parmesan cheese
2 eggs
1 tablespoon finely chopped
    flat-leaf parsley
olive oil, for frying
generous ½ cup superfine
    sugar
⅔ cup white-wine vinegar
salt and pepper

Tear the bread into pieces and put it into
a bowl. Pour in the milk and let the bread soak
for 10 minutes, then remove and squeeze out any
excess liquid. Put the bread into a bowl with the
beef, veal, cheese, eggs, and parsley and mix
well until thoroughly combined, adding a little
milk if the mixture is too stiff. Form small
pieces of the mixture into round meatballs
between the palms of your hands, then flatten
them slightly.

Heat the oil in a large skillet. Add the
meatballs, in batches if necessary, and cook over
medium heat, turning occasionally, for about
15 minutes, until browned all over. Remove with
a slotted spoon and drain on paper towels.

Put the sugar into a heavy pan and heat gently,
stirring occasionally, until it has melted, then
boil, without stirring, until golden brown.
Carefully pour in the vinegar, then add the
meatballs and cook them for a few minutes. Remove
the pan from the heat. Lift out the meatballs
with a spoon and arrange in a pyramid shape on a
warmed serving dish. Pour the remaining sweet-
and-sour sauce over them and serve immediately.

Note: There are many sweet-and-sour dishes like
this one in Sicilian cooking. This is a tradition
that dates back to Roman times and is also
influenced by Arab cuisine.

Summer Entertaining

Feste d'estate

For many Italians, summer is the season
for gathering around the table to
eat with family and friends, and many of
the classic Italian summer dishes are
perfect for a celebration. The days are
longer and more relaxed, and preparing
and eating food together is an important
part of the vacation season. The dishes
are colorful, appetizing, and a little
different from the usual fare, and they
sometimes include unusual combinations
of ingredients. For example, the
abundance of seasonal fruit and flowers
is not only used to create wonderful
desserts and ice creams, but also
in fragrant savory dishes, such as roast
quail with grapes or calendula risotto.

Delicious summer canapés and appetizers,
such as crostini and bruschetta, are
ideal served with drinks, and simple
but smart first courses include risottos
made with fresh vegetables and fruit,
as well as light and tasty summer soups.
The main course is often brought to the
table on a large platter, forming a
marvelous centerpiece for the meal, such
as a Cacciucco, the traditional fish
stew from Livorno in Tuscany, or the
classic favorite Vitello tonnato,
a dish of cold roast veal in tuna and
caper sauce.

Canapés and appetizers

Pear and fontina puffs
Sfogliatine di pere e fontina

Preparation time: 30 mins
Cooking time: 15 mins
Serves 4

3 medium-ripe Bartlett pears
9 ounces ready-made puff
    pastry dough, thawed
    if frozen
all-purpose flour, for
    dusting
5 ounces fontina cheese,
    sliced
2 egg yolks, lightly beaten
pepper

Preheat the oven to 400°F. Peel, core, and thinly slice the pears. Roll out the dough on a lightly floured counter, cut it into 3¼-inch strips, and then into squares. In the middle of half the squares, put 2 slices of pear, season with pepper, and put 2 slices of fontina on top. Brush the edges with a little water, then cover with the remaining dough squares, sealing the edges well. Brush with the beaten egg yolk and decorate the surface by scoring lines with the tip of a knife. Put the squares onto a baking sheet, and bake for 15 minutes.

Mushroom and caper crostini
Crostini con funghi e capperi

Preparation time: 15 mins
Cooking time: 30 mins
Serves 6

3 tablespoons olive oil
scant 4½ cups chopped or
    sliced porcini mushrooms
1 clove garlic, finely
    chopped
½ tablespoon chopped marjoram
generous ⅓ cup vegetable
    stock
1 tablespoon capers preserved
    in salt, rinsed, drained,
    and chopped
1 tablespoon chopped flat-
    leaf parsley
1 large baguette, sliced
salt and pepper

Heat the oil in a small skillet. Add the porcini, garlic, and marjoram and cook, stirring frequently, over medium heat for 20 minutes, gradually adding the stock. Add the capers and parsley, season with salt and pepper, and cook until all the liquid has evaporated.

Meanwhile, preheat the broiler, put the baguette slices on a baking sheet, and toast them on both sides. Spread the mushroom mixture on the toast and serve immediately.

Baby artichoke canapés

Canapé di carciofini

Preparation time: 10 mins

Serves 4

4 tablespoons butter
anchovy paste, to taste
4 slices white bread, crusts
    removed and cut in half
4 baby artichokes in oil,
    drained and quartered
2 teaspoons mayonnaise

Beat the butter with a little anchovy paste in a bowl until combined, then spread on the slices of bread. Put the baby artichokes in the middle of the slices and garnish with mayonnaise. Arrange on a serving dish and serve immediately.

Photograph p.202

Lobster canapés

Canapé di aragosta

Preparation time: 15 mins

Serves 4

5 tablespoons mayonnaise
1 tablespoon brandy
1–2 teaspoons ketchup
4 slices whole-wheat bread,
    crusts removed
1 small, cooked lobster tail,
    shelled and cut
    into 8 slices
8 small sprigs thyme

Combine the mayonnaise, brandy, and ketchup in a bowl. Cut the slices of bread in half and spread with the mayonnaise mixture. Put a slice of lobster in the middle of each one and garnish with a sprig of thyme.

Bruschetta with tomato

Bruschetta al pomodoro

Preparation time: 10 mins

Cooking time: 5–8 mins

Serves 4

8 slices rustic bread
4 cloves garlic, halved
6–8 ripe tomatoes, diced
extra-virgin olive oil,
    for drizzling
salt and pepper

Toast the slices of bread on both sides under the broiler or on a barbecue. Rub them all over with the garlic while they are still hot and put back under the broiler for a moment. Arrange the tomatoes on the slices of toast, season with salt and pepper, and drizzle with olive oil. Serve immediately.

Photograph p.203

Baby artichoke canapés (p.201)

bruschetta with tomato (p.201)

Cheese crackers

Gallettine al formaggio

Preparation time: 30 mins
Cooking time: 45 mins
Serves 6

2¼ pounds potatoes
1¼ cups all-purpose flour,
    plus extra for dusting
scant ½ cup (1 stick) butter,
    softened
3 ounces Gorgonzola cheese
6 slices medium-sharp cheese,
    such as provolone
1 egg yolk, lightly beaten
salt

Cook the potatoes in a large pan of salted boiling water for 20–30 minutes, until soft but not falling apart. Preheat the oven to 350°F. Drain, peel, and mash the potatoes, then turn them onto a counter. Add the flour and half the butter and knead to a smooth dough. Roll out the dough on a lightly floured counter to make a round ¼ inch thick.

Beat the Gorgonzola with the remaining butter in a bowl until smooth. Cut out triangles from the dough and cut the cheese slices to fit. Put a cheese triangle on half the dough triangles, top each with a little of the Gorgonzola mixture, and cover with the remaining dough triangles, pressing the edges to seal.

Brush the tops of the crackers with egg yolk. Put the crackers on a baking sheet and bake for about 15 minutes, or until golden brown. Serve warm or cold.

Bottarga crostini

Crostini di bottarga

Preparation time: 15 mins
Cooking time: 5 mins
Serves 6

1 baguette, sliced diagonally
butter, for spreading
1 piece (3½ ounces) smoked
    bottarga, thinly sliced
    diagonally
1 celery stalk, cut into
    ¾-inch lengths

Preheat the oven to 350°F. Put the bread in the oven and toast for 5 minutes, then remove and spread thinly with butter.

Put a slice of bottarga on each one, arrange the crostini on a serving dish, garnish with a piece of celery, and serve immediately.

Note: Grated and flavored with a drizzle of oil, bottarga (pressed dried striped mullet or tuna roe) is also delicious spread on bread.

Sardine barquettes

Barchette di sardine

Preparation time: 10 mins

Serves 4

4 radishes
4 lettuce leaves
4 canned sardines, drained
4 dill pickles, drained
⅔ cup mayonnaise
4 slices white bread, crusts
    removed
butter, for spreading

Holding a radish by the stalk, cut off the root and make V-shaped notches from the center outward all the way around. Repeat with the remaining radishes, then place them in a bowl of ice water until they open out like flowers. Put the lettuce leaves, concave sides uppermost, on a serving plate. Open out each sardine like a book and pull out the backbones, snipping with kitchen scissors at the tail ends. Close the sardines and put one on each lettuce leaf.

Starting ½ inch from one end, thinly slice each dill pickle lengthwise, then gently spread out into a fan shape. Put a pickle fan on each lettuce leaf. Drain the radishes and put one on each lettuce leaf.

Spoon the mayonnaise into a pastry bag fitted with a small star tip and garnish the lettuce leaves with stars. Spread the slices of bread with a little butter on one side, carefully top each slice with a filled lettuce leaf, arrange on a serving dish, and serve.

Ham mousse canapés

Canapé con mousse di prosciutto

Preparation time: 10 mins

Serves 4

3 tablespoons butter
generous ½ cup chopped ham
8 slices white bread, crusts
    removed
8 green olives, pitted and
    sliced

Beat the butter in a bowl until soft and creamy, then mix in the ham. Spread the slices of bread on one side with the mixture, cut into triangles, and garnish with slices of olive. Arrange on a dish and serve.

Sausage and stracchino crostini

Crostini con salsiccia e stracchino

Preparation time: 15 mins
Cooking time: 15 mins
Serves 6

3 Italian sausages
5 ounces stracchino or other
    mild soft cheese
1 tablespoon fennel seeds
6 slices rustic bread
salt

Preheat the oven to 350°F. Skin the sausages and break up the meat in a bowl with a fork. Mash the cheese in a another bowl to soften, then stir it into the sausage meat and add the fennel seeds. Season with salt to taste and beat the mixture until creamy.

Spread the mixture on the slices of bread. Put them onto a baking sheet and bake for 15 minutes. Transfer the crostini to a serving dish and serve immediately.

Tuscan crostini

Crostini toscani

Preparation time: 10 mins
Cooking time: 10–12 mins
Serves 4

4 slices Tuscan or other
    rustic bread
4 canned anchovy fillets,
    drained
2 tomatoes, sliced
1 pearl onion, chopped
1 tablespoon chopped basil
olive oil, for drizzling
salt

Preheat the oven to 350°F and preheat the broiler. Toast the bread on both sides under the broiler until golden.

Put an anchovy fillet, a slice of tomato, and a little chopped onion and basil on each slice. Drizzle with olive oil and season with salt. Put the toasts on a baking sheet and heat in the oven for a few minutes, then serve.

Photograph p.208

Summer stuffed peppers

Peperoni ripieni d'estate

Preparation time: 50 mins
(including salting)
Cooking time: 1 hr
Serves 6

1 eggplant, diced
2 salted anchovies,
    with heads removed,
    cleaned, and filleted,
    then soaked in cold water
    for 10 mins and drained
2 tablespoons olive oil,
    plus extra for brushing
5 ounces Gruyère cheese,
    diced
scant 1 cup olives, pitted
    and thinly sliced
¾ cup chopped flat-leaf
    parsley
6 basil leaves, chopped
3 tomatoes, peeled, seeded,
    and chopped
2 potatoes, diced
1 tablespoon capers, rinsed
    and drained
pinch of dried oregano
6 green bell peppers
salt and pepper

Put the eggplant cubes in a colander, sprinkle with salt, and let drain for 30 minutes. Meanwhile, chop the anchovy fillets.

Preheat the oven to 350°F. Brush an ovenproof dish with oil. Put the Gruyère, olives, parsley, basil, tomatoes, and potatoes into a large bowl. Rinse the eggplant, pat dry with paper towels, and add to the bowl with the anchovies, capers, and oregano. Season with salt and pepper and mix well.

Remove the stalks from the bell peppers and cut off and reserve the tops. Remove the seeds and membranes using a small sharp knife and a teaspoon.

Fill the bell peppers with the stuffing mixture, drizzle a teaspoon of olive oil into each, replace the tops, and secure them with a toothpick if necessary. Place the bell peppers in the prepared dish and bake for 1 hour. Serve hot or cold.

Photograph p.209

Speck and apple cream crostini

Crostini montanari con speck e crema di mele

Preparation time: 20 mins
Serves 6

1 green apple
2 tablespoons grated
    horseradish
juice of 1 lemon, strained
scant ½ cup low-fat plain yogurt
⅓ cup heavy cream
1 baguette, sliced diagonally
7 ounces cooked sliced speck
    or bacon
salt and pepper

Peel, core, and finely chop the apple, put it into a bowl, and stir in the horseradish, then beat in lemon juice to taste until the mixture is creamy. Stir in the yogurt, then stir in the cream and season with salt and pepper to taste. Spread the mixture evenly on the slices of bread, lay a slice of speck over each, and serve.

Tuscan crostini (p.206)

summer stuffed peppers (p.207)

Panzarotti

Panzarotti

Preparation time: 3¾ hrs
(including rising)
Cooking time: 8–10 mins
Serves 4

generous 1 cup ricotta cheese
scant 1 cup diced ham
4–5 firm red cherry
    tomatoes, peeled and
    diced
olive oil, for deep-frying
salt and pepper

For the dough

4½ cups all-purpose flour,
    preferably Italian
    type 00, plus extra
    for dusting
1 ounce fresh yeast
1 cup lukewarm water
salt

To make the dough, sift the flour with a pinch of salt into a mound on a counter and make a well in the center. Mash the yeast in the water with a fork until smooth and pour it into the well. Gradually incorporate the flour with your fingers, then knead well until smooth and elastic. Shape the dough into a ball, put it into a bowl, cover with a dish towel, and let rise in a warm place for about 2–3 hours, until almost doubled in size.

Combine the ricotta and ham in a bowl and season with salt and pepper. Divide the dough into 8 pieces and roll out each piece on a lightly floured counter into a fairly thick sheet. Spoon the ricotta mixture onto the middle of each sheet and top with the diced tomatoes. Fold the dough over the top and crimp the edges to seal.

Heat the oil in a deep-fryer to 350–375°F, or until a cube of bread browns in 30 seconds. Add the panzarotti, in batches if necessary, and deep-fry for 8–10 minutes, until golden brown all over. Remove with a slotted spoon, drain on paper towels, and serve immediately.

Piquant avocados

Avocado piccanti

Preparation time: 10 mins
Serves 4

2 ripe avocados
6 black olives, pitted
    and sliced
1 tablespoon capers preserved
    in salt, rinsed and drained
2–3 canned anchovy fillets,
    drained and chopped
generous ⅓ cup olive oil
juice of 1 lemon, strained

Halve the avocados, remove the pits, and carefully scoop out the flesh without piercing the skin. Reserve the skins. Dice the flesh, put it into a bowl, and add the olives, capers, and anchovies. Whisk together the olive oil and lemon juice in a small bowl, pour it over the avocado mixture, and toss lightly. Spoon the mixture into the avocado skins and serve.

Avocado with cheese

Avocado con formaggio

Preparation time: 20 mins
Serves 4

2 ripe avocados
juice of 1 lemon, strained
scant 1 cup pitted black
    olives
¼ cup mild, soft cheese, such
    as stracchino or quark
1 large pinch paprika
olive oil, for drizzling
salt and pepper
sprigs of curly parsley,
    to garnish

Halve and pit the avocados, then drizzle the flesh with the lemon juice. Chop half the olives and put them into a bowl with the cheese and paprika. Drizzle with olive oil and season with salt and pepper. Mix well and divide among the hollows in the avocado halves. Chill in the refrigerator until ready to serve. Arrange the avocado halves on a serving dish and garnish with the remaining olives and a little curly parsley.

Avocado with potato cream

Crema di patate e avocado

Preparation time: 20 mins
Cooking time: 1 hr
Serves 6

6 potatoes, with their skins
4 cups milk
3½ ounces stracchino or other
    mild, soft cheese
2 eggs
2 avocados
salt and pepper

Cook the potatoes in a large pan of salted boiling water for 25–30 minutes, until tender. Drain, peel, and mash them in a bowl. Pour the milk into a pan and heat gently, but do not let it boil. Remove the pan from the heat.

Beat the cheese with the eggs in a bowl, then beat in the warm milk. Gradually add the mashed potato, a little at a time, and season with salt and pepper. Transfer the mixture to a pan and cook over low heat, stirring occasionally, until thickened. Do not let the mixture come to a boil. Let cool.

Meanwhile, peel, pit, and dice the avocados, then sprinkle them over the bottom of a serving dish. Spoon the potato cream on top and serve.

Warm figs with mascarpone

Fichi caldi al mascarpone

Preparation time: 10 mins
Cooking time: 8 mins
Serves 6

12 figs, halved lengthwise
⅔ cup mascarpone cheese
⅔ cup grated Parmesan cheese
balsamic vinegar, for
    brushing

Preheat the oven to 475°F and line a baking sheet with aluminum foil. Put the figs, cut sides uppermost, on the prepared baking sheet. Combine the mascarpone and Parmesan in a bowl, put a teaspoon of the mixture onto each fig half, and brush lightly with the balsamic vinegar. Bake for 8 minutes. Transfer the figs to a serving dish and serve warm.

Goat cheese bavarois

Bavarese di caprini

Preparation time:
3½–4½ hrs
(including setting)
Serves 4

2 ounces gelatin leaves
scant ½ cup heavy cream
4 ounces goat cheese
olive oil, for drizzling
    and brushing
1¼ teaspoons white-wine
    vinegar
2 egg whites
10 radishes, thinly sliced
    into rounds
1 bunch arugula, shredded
2 tomatoes, peeled, seeded,
    and sliced
2 celery stalks, chopped
salt and pepper

Put the gelatin leaves into a bowl of cold water and let soak for 5 minutes, then squeeze out the liquid and put them into a small heatproof bowl with the cream. Set the bowl over a pan of barely simmering water and heat until the gelatin has dissolved, then remove from the heat. Put the cheese into a bowl and mash it with a fork, slowly drizzling over a little olive oil. Add 1 teaspoon of the vinegar and whisk until the mixture is light and foamy. Add the cream mixture to the bowl and whisk again.

In a separate bowl, whisk the egg whites to stiff peaks, then fold them into the cheese mixture and season with salt and pepper. Lightly brush 4 small molds with olive oil and divide the mixture among them. Cover and let stand in the refrigerator to set for 3–4 hours. Turn out the cheese molds onto the middle of a serving dish and cover them with the radish slices and shredded arugula. Garnish with the tomatoes on one side and the celery on the other. Drizzle with olive oil and the remaining vinegar, season with salt and pepper, and serve immediately.

Watermelon with shrimp

Cocomero e gamberi

Preparation time: 2½ hrs
(including chilling)
Serves 4

1 small watermelon
scant 1 cup brandy
11 ounces cooked, peeled
    shrimp
scant 1 cup mayonnaise
4 mint leaves, chopped
1¼ cups pitted and halved
    small green olives
salt and pepper

Halve the watermelon, scoop out the flesh, and
seed it, reserving the shells. Using a melon
baller, make balls from the flesh and put them
into a bowl. Season the watermelon shells
with salt and pepper, pour in the brandy, and
chill in the refrigerator for 2 hours.

Just before serving, combine the shrimp,
mayonnaise, mint leaves, and olives in a bowl.
Make alternating layers of watermelon balls
and the shrimp mixture in the watermelon shells
until all the ingredients have been used.

Melon skewers

Spiedini di melone

Preparation time: 10 mins
Serves 6

1 small melon
5 ounces sliced ham, cut
    into cubes
5 ounces cherry tomatoes
12 firm figs, cut into cubes
4 slices bread, toasted and
    cut into cubes

Halve the melons, scoop out and discard the
seeds, and scoop out the flesh, reserving
the shells. Cut the flesh into cubes. Thread
12 skewers with alternating melon cubes, ham
cubes, whole tomatoes, fig cubes, and cubes
of toast.

Arrange the melon shells upside down on a serving
dish, insert the skewers, and serve.

Stuffed eggplants
with vegetables

Melanzane ripiene alle verdure

Preparation time: 50 mins
(including cooling)
Cooking time: 35 mins
Serves 4

6 eggplants
3 tablespoons olive oil,
    plus extra for brushing
1 onion, chopped
3 red bell peppers, seeded
    and chopped
1 celery stalk, chopped
4 ripe tomatoes, diced
3 eggs, lightly beaten
⅔ cup grated Parmesan cheese
salt and pepper

Halve the eggplants lengthwise and scoop out
the flesh with a teaspoon. Reserve the shells and
chop the flesh. Preheat the oven to 350°F. Heat
the olive oil in a shallow pan. Add the onion and
cook over low heat, stirring occasionally, for
5 minutes, or until softened. Add the chopped
eggplant, bell peppers, celery, and tomatoes,
season with salt and pepper, and cook, stirring
occasionally, for 15 minutes.

Meanwhile, brush an ovenproof dish with oil. Turn
off the heat under the pan and pour the beaten
eggs over the mixture, stirring until creamy.
Fill the eggplant shells with the mixture, put
them into the prepared dish, sprinkle with the
cheese, and bake for 15 minutes. Remove from the
oven and let cool before serving.

Buffalo
mozzarella caprese

Caprese di mozzarella di bufala

Preparation time: 5 mins
Serves 4

11 ounces buffalo mozzarella
    cheese
3–4 tomatoes, peeled,
    seeded, and sliced
8 basil leaves
olive oil, for drizzling
salt

Drain the mozzarella and cut into ⅛-inch
slices. Arrange the mozzarella and tomato slices
alternately in concentric rings on a serving
dish. Sprinkle with the basil leaves, drizzle
with olive oil, and season with salt. Keep in
a cool place until ready to serve.

/ Summer entertaining /

Eggplant
and mozzarella rounds

Dischetti di melanzane e mozzarella

Preparation time: 45 mins
(including draining)
Cooking time: 55 mins
Serves 4

3 eggplants, cut into
    ½-inch rounds
5 tablespoons olive oil
4¼ ounces mozzarella, sliced
salt

For the tomato sauce

9 ounces canned chopped
    tomatoes
1 pinch sugar
2 cloves garlic
2 tablespoons olive oil
salt

First, make the tomato sauce. Put the tomatoes, sugar, and garlic into a pan and season with salt, then cover and cook over very low heat for 20 minutes. Remove and discard the garlic, mash the tomatoes with a wooden spoon, and return to the heat for another 15 minutes.

Meanwhile, put the eggplant slices into a colander, sprinkle with salt, and let drain for 30 minutes, then rinse and pat dry with paper towels. Remove the pan of tomato sauce from the heat and let cool, then stir in the olive oil.

Preheat the oven to 350°F. Line a baking sheet with parchment paper. Heat the olive oil in a skillet. Add the eggplant slices, in batches if necessary, and fry, turning once, for 10 minutes, until they are a light golden brown. Remove with a slotted spoon and drain on paper towels. Put a slice of mozzarella on each slice of eggplant and top with a teaspoon of tomato sauce.

Put the rounds on the prepared baking sheet and bake for 5-10 minutes, until the cheese has melted. Serve warm, although they are also excellent cold. Leftover tomato sauce may be frozen for future use.

Roast bell peppers

Peperoni arrosto

Preparation time: 1¼ hrs
(including standing)
Cooking time: 1 hr
Serves 4

4 bell peppers
3 cloves garlic, halved
12 basil leaves
olive oil, for drizzling
salt and pepper

Preheat the oven to 350°F. Line a roasting pan with aluminum foil. Prick the bell peppers with a fork, place in the pan, and roast for 1 hour. Remove from the oven, wrap in aluminum foil, and let cool. Peel and halve the bell peppers and let drain, cut side down, on paper towels.

Remove the seeds and membranes, then cut the bell peppers into ⅜-inch strips and arrange in layers on a fairly deep serving dish, sprinkling each layer with garlic and basil and seasoning with salt and pepper. Drizzle with olive oil and let stand in a cool place for 1 hour before serving.

Tomato sherbet

Sorbetto al pomodoro

Preparation time: 45 mins
(including freezing)
Serves 16

scant 4 cups tomato juice
2½ cups vodka
5 tablespoons freshly
    squeezed lemon juice
6 drops Tabasco, or to taste
6 drops Worcestershire sauce,
    or to taste
1 egg white, lightly beaten
basil leaves, to garnish
salt

Combine the tomato juice, vodka, lemon juice, Tabasco, and Worcestershire sauce, adding more sauce, if you like. Stir in the egg white and season with salt.

Transfer the mixture to an ice-cream maker and freeze for 30 minutes, or according to the manufacturer's directions. To serve, divide the sherbet among individual bowls and garnish with the basil leaves.

Tomato mousse

Mousse di pomodoro

Preparation time: 2½ hrs
(including chilling)
Serves 6

8 ripe tomatoes, peeled,
    halved, and seeded
1 tablespoon snipped chives
1 clove garlic, finely chopped
scant 1 cup mayonnaise
⅔ cup low-fat plain yogurt
scant ½ cup heavy cream
salt and pepper
basil leaves, to garnish

Sprinkle the insides of the tomatoes with salt
and turn upside down on paper towels to drain.
Put them into a food processor or blender and
process to a puree, then transfer to a large bowl.

Stir in the chives and garlic. Gently stir in the
mayonnaise, followed by the yogurt and cream,
and season with salt and pepper to taste. Divide
the mixture among 6 individual dishes and chill
in the refrigerator for at least 2 hours. Serve
garnished with basil leaves.

Photograph p.222

Tomatoes with robiola

Pomodori con robiola

Preparation time:
1 hr 20 mins
(including draining)
Serves 4

4 round tomatoes, halved
3½ ounces robiola
    cheese, diced
2 ounces mild Gorgonzola
    cheese, crumbled
2 tablespoons butter,
    softened
4 plum tomatoes,
    peeled and chopped
1 pinch paprika
4 chives, snipped
2 tablespoons vodka
salt and pepper

Scoop out the seeds and some of the flesh from
the halved tomatoes, sprinkle the shells with
salt, and turn them upside down on paper towels
to drain for 1 hour.

Put the robiola, Gorgonzola, and butter in a
bowl, season with salt and pepper, and beat until
smooth and combined. Add the plum tomatoes,
paprika, and chives, mix well, and sprinkle with
the vodka. Fill the tomato halves with the
mixture, arrange them on a serving dish, and keep
in a cool place until ready to serve.

Photograph p.223

Tomato mousse (p.221)

Baked ricotta with sun-dried tomato pesto

Ricotta del pastore infornata con pesto di pomodori secchi

Preparation time: 20 mins
Cooking time: 10 mins
Serves 6

butter, for greasing
all-purpose flour, for
    dusting
2⅔ cups very fresh sheep's
    milk ricotta
2 heaping tablespoons chopped
    mixed flat-leaf parsley,
    basil, marjoram, and
    thyme
11 ounces sun-dried tomatoes
    in oil
1 cup pitted black olives
1 cup shelled pistachio nuts
11 ounces ripe plum tomatoes,
    peeled, seeded, and
    chopped
olive oil, for drizzling
4 basil leaves, torn
6 slices of rustic bread,
    lightly toasted
salt and pepper

Preheat the oven to 400°F. Grease and dust with flour 6 individual dariole molds or other small ovenproof molds. Combine the ricotta and herbs and season with salt and pepper to taste. Divide the mixture among the molds, put them on a baking sheet, and bake for 10 minutes.

Meanwhile, chop together the sun-dried tomatoes, olives, and pistachios. Put the fresh tomatoes into a bowl, season with salt, drizzle with olive oil, and sprinkle with the basil leaves.

Put the toasted bread on individual plates, turn the baked ricotta out onto them, and spoon the sun-dried tomato pesto on one side and the chopped tomatoes on the other side. Drizzle with olive oil and serve.

Mixed vegetable ring

Anello freddo di verdure miste

Preparation time: 1 hr
(including standing
and cooling)
Cooking time: 1 hr
Serves 4

2 yellow bell peppers
4 eggplants, thinly sliced
    lengthwise
4 zucchini, thinly sliced
    lengthwise
2 white onions, thinly sliced
    into rings
olive oil, for drizzling
butter, for greasing
2 eggs
3 sprigs basil, chopped
salt and pepper
halved cherry tomatoes and
    basil leaves, to garnish
    (optional)

Preheat the oven to 450°F. Put the bell peppers on a baking sheet, and roast, turning occasionally, for 25–30 minutes, until they are blistered and charred. Remove from the oven, put into a plastic bag, and tie the top.

Preheat the broiler. When the bell peppers are cool enough to handle, peel off the skins, remove and discard the seeds, and dice the flesh. Meanwhile, spread out the eggplants, zucchini, and onions on a baking sheet, drizzle with olive oil, season with salt and pepper, and broil for a few minutes.

Generously grease a ring mold with butter and line it with alternating slices of eggplants and zucchini, letting the slices overlap the sides. Dice the remaining slices and sprinkle the onion rings and bell peppers evenly into the mold.

Beat the eggs with the basil in a bowl, season with salt and pepper, and pour the mixture into the mold. Fold the overlapping vegetable slices over the top, put the mold on a baking sheet, and bake for 35 minutes.

Remove the mold from the oven and let stand for 5 minutes, then turn out onto a serving dish and let cool completely before serving. Garnish with halved cherry tomatoes and basil leaves, if you like.

Fried zucchini flowers

Fiori di zucchine fritti

Preparation time: 1¼ hrs
(including standing)
Cooking time: 15 mins
Serves 4

scant 1 cup all-purpose flour
2 tablespoons olive oil
5 tablespoons dry white wine
1 egg, separated
vegetable oil, for
    deep-frying
12 zucchini flowers, trimmed
salt and pepper

Combine the flour, oil, wine, and egg yolk
in a bowl and season with salt and pepper.
Add ⅔-1 cup warm water to make a fairly runny,
smooth batter. Let stand for 1 hour.

Whisk the egg white to stiff peaks in a grease-
free bowl and fold gently into the batter.
Heat the vegetable oil in a deep-fryer or heavy
pan to 350–375°F, or until a cube of day-old
bread browns in 30 seconds.

Dip the flowers in the batter, shake off the
excess, and fry in the hot oil in batches until
they are golden. Remove with a slotted spoon
and drain on paper towels. Sprinkle with salt
and serve immediately.

Scamorza carpaccio

Carpaccio di scamorza

Preparation time: 15 mins
Serves 4

3 tablespoons olive oil
juice of ½ lemon, strained
1 sprig mint, chopped
14 ounces scamorza cheese,
    sliced
1 cucumber, thinly sliced
salt and pepper
green bean salad, to serve
    (optional)

First, make the dressing. Whisk together the
olive oil, lemon juice, and mint in a bowl
and season with salt and pepper. Spread out
the slices of cheese on a serving dish, add the
slices of cucumber, and drizzle with the
dressing. Serve immediately, with a green bean
salad, if you like.

/ Summer entertaining /

Zucchini and mozzarella tartare with tarragon

Tartare di zucchine
e mozzarella al dragoncello

Preparation time: 45 mins
(including chilling)
Serves 4

14 ounces mozzarella, diced
7 ounces cooked ham, in a
    single thick slice, diced
6 small zucchini, diced
4 palm hearts, diced
olive oil, for drizzling
½ bunch tarragon, chopped
salt

Put the mozzarella, ham, zucchini, and palm
hearts into a large salad bowl and drizzle
generously with olive oil. Season with salt and
sprinkle with the tarragon. Toss lightly, then
divide the mixture among 4 ramekins, pressing
down firmly. Cover and chill in the refrigerator
for 30 minutes. Turn out onto individual plates
and serve immediately.

Figs Russian style

Fichi alla russa

Preparation time: 30 mins
Serves 4

12 ripe black figs
4 tablespoons butter,
    softened
1½ tablespoons pink Malossol
    caviar or salmon roe
    (keta)
juice of 1 lemon, strained

Halve the figs and scoop out the flesh with
a teaspoon, leaving a little in the bottom.
Beat the butter with the roe until well combined,
then stir in the scooped-out fruit flesh. Put
the fig shells on a bed of crushed ice. Spoon
the fig mixture into a small pastry bag and use
it to fill the shells. Drizzle with the lemon
juice and serve immediately.

Note: This sophisticated antipasto should be
prepared just before serving, and should not be
stored in the refrigerator.

Raw anchovies
with citrus fruit

Alici crude agli agrumi

Preparation time: 1¼ hrs
(including marinating)
Serves 6

4 lemons
4 oranges
1 pound 5 ounces small
   anchovies, filleted
⅜ cup olive oil
1 fresh red chile, seeded and
   finely chopped
2 tablespoons chopped
   flat-leaf parsley
salt and pepper

Squeeze the juice from 3 lemons and from
3 oranges. Rinse the anchovy fillets, pat them
dry with paper towels, and put them in a
nonmetallic dish in a single layer. Strain
the lemon juice over them and let marinate for
1 hour.

Drain the fish well, removing all the dark
liquid which will have accumulated, and arrange
them in a sunburst pattern in a serving dish.
Whisk together the oil, orange juice, and chile
in a small bowl and season with salt and
pepper. Pour the dressing over the fish. Cut
3 slices each from the remaining orange and
lemon, leaving their rinds intact, then cut out
small triangles from each slice, and arrange
them on top of the anchovies. Sprinkle with the
parsley and serve.

Anchovies
with wild fennel

Alici al finocchietto

Preparation time: 3¼ hrs
(including marinating)
Serves 4

1 pound 5 ounces fresh
   anchovies
juice of 5 lemons, strained
1¼ tablespoons chopped
   wild fennel
11 ounces mixed salad greens
1 cucumber, seeded and thinly
   sliced
4 tomatoes, peeled, seeded,
   and coarsely chopped
2 tablespoons olive oil
salt

To fillet the anchovies, remove the heads and cut
off the tails. Open out each anchovy like a book,
putting it on a cutting board with the skin
side uppermost. Press all along the backbone with
your thumb, then turn over and remove the bones,
snipping them with scissors at the tail ends.
Rinse the anchovies, pat dry, and put them into
a nonmetallic dish in a single layer. Drizzle
with 1 cup of the lemon juice and sprinkle
with 1 tablespoon of the fennel. Let marinate in
the refrigerator for 3 hours.

→

Make a bed of salad greens on a serving dish.
Drain the anchovies and add them to the dish
with the cucumber slices. Put the tomatoes into
a food processor or blender and process to a
puree. Transfer to a bowl and whisk in the olive
oil and the remaining lemon juice and fennel,
and season with salt. Pour dressing over the
anchovies and serve.

Note: Wild fennel is one of the most typical
aromatic plants in Mediterranean cooking.
The Sicilian variety, in particular, is an
essential ingredient in pasta with sardines.
If wild fennel is not available, the fronds
from cultivated fennel can be substituted.

Salt cod carpaccio
Carpaccio di baccalà

Preparation time:
26–32 hrs (including
de-salting and marinating)
Serves 4

1½ pounds salt cod loin
juice of 2 lemons, strained
¾ cup olive oil
3 small cloves garlic,
    thinly sliced
6 black peppercorns,
    lightly crushed
2 tablespoons chopped borage
2 tablespoons snipped chives
7 ounces corn salad
balsamic vinegar,
    for drizzling
salt

Put the cod into a colander standing inside
a large bowl, add water to cover, and let soak,
changing the water several times, for 18–24
hours. Drain well, then slice crosswise as thinly
as possible and put the slices into a bowl.

Whisk together the lemon juice, olive oil,
garlic, peppercorns, and a pinch of salt in
another bowl and then drizzle the mixture
over the fish. Cover with plastic wrap and let
marinate overnight in the refrigerator.

To serve, drain the fish well, reserving the
marinade, and arrange on individual dishes.
Sprinkle with borage and chives, surround with
the corn salad, and drizzle with a few
drops of balsamic vinegar. Strain the marinade,
drizzle it over the cod, and serve the dish
very cold.

Marinated anchovies

Acciughe marinate

Preparation time: 3½ hrs
(including marinating)
Serves 4

1 pound 2 ounces small
   anchovies, cleaned
   and heads removed
1 sprig flat-leaf parsley
1 clove garlic
juice of 2 lemons, strained
olive oil, for drizzling
salt and pepper

Open out each anchovy like a book, putting it on a cutting board with the skin side uppermost. Press all along the backbone with your thumb, then turn over and remove the bones, snipping them with scissors at the tail ends. Arrange the opened-out fish like sun rays in a shallow dish.

Chop the parsley and garlic together and put the mixture into a small bowl. Add the lemon juice, season with salt and pepper, and mix well. Pour the marinade over the fish, cover with plastic wrap, and let marinate in the refrigerator for a few hours. Just before serving, uncover and drizzle with olive oil.

Photograph p.237

Endive with crab

Indivia belga con polpa di granchio

Preparation time: 15 mins
Serves 4

1–2 heads endive, separated
   into leaves
4 ounces canned crabmeat,
   drained
1 cup mayonnaise
2 tablespoons heavy cream
2 tablespoons ketchup
½ teaspoon Worcestershire
   sauce
1 teaspoon brandy

Arrange the endive leaves in concentric circles on a serving dish, using the smaller leaves for the inner circles. Pick over the crabmeat and remove any pieces of shell and cartilage.

Combine the mayonnaise and crabmeat in a bowl, then add the cream, ketchup, and Worcestershire sauce, sprinkle with the brandy, and stir gently. Put 1 tablespoon of the mixture into the concave part of each endive leaf. This dish makes a delicious antipasto.

/ Summer entertaining /

Citrons and mussels

Cedri ai peoci

Preparation time: 40 mins
Cooking time: 3-5 mins
Serves 4

3½ ounces canned tuna in
    oil, drained and flaked
scant ⅓ cup capers, rinsed,
    drained, and chopped
4 canned anchovy fillets,
    drained and chopped
1 hard-cooked egg yolk
1 cup olive oil
juice of ½ lemon, strained
2 large citrons
1 pound 2 ounces mussels
16 olives stuffed with
    pimientos
salt and pepper

Put the tuna, capers, and anchovies into a food processor, crumble in the egg yolk, and season with salt and pepper. Add 2–3 tablespoons olive oil to the food processor and process for a few seconds. Reserving 2–3 tablespoons, add the remaining oil to the food processor and process again.

Transfer the mixture to a bowl and stir in the lemon juice, then rinse the food processor. Halve the citrons and scoop out the flesh, discarding the seeds and reserving the citron skins. Coarsely chop the flesh, put it into the food processor, add the reserved olive oil, and process to a thick, foamy mixture. Stir into the tuna sauce.

Scrub the mussels under cold running water and remove the beards. Discard any with damaged shells and any that do not shut immediately when sharply tapped. Put them into a large skillet and cook over low heat for 3–5 minutes, until the shells have opened. Remove the pan from the heat and discard any mussels that remain shut.

Remove the mussels from the shells and thread them onto 8 wooden toothpicks, alternating with the olives. Put the citron shells on a serving dish, season with salt and pepper, and fill them with the tuna and citron foam. Insert 2 toothpicks into each shell, so that they stand up.

Serve immediately with any remaining tuna and citron foam and the remaining mussels on the side.

Note: Mussels (referred to as *peoci* in this recipe and also known in Italian as *cozze*, *muscoli*, or *mitili*) open up in a few minutes in a pan over a lively heat. Once their shells are open, they are ready. Discard any whose shells do not open.

Marinated swordfish

Pesce spada marinato

Preparation time: 2¼ hrs
(including marinating)
Serves 4

11 ounces swordfish, very
    thinly sliced
olive oil, for drizzling
juice of 2 lemons, strained
3½ ounces arugula, chopped
3½ ounces escarole, chopped
2 sprigs chervil, leaves only
salt and pepper
1 lemon, sliced, to garnish

Place the swordfish on a plate, drizzle with
olive oil and the lemon juice, and season
with salt and pepper. Cover and chill in the
refrigerator for about 2 hours.

Mix together the arugula, escarole, and chervil
in a bowl. Drain the slices of fish, reserving
the marinade, and arrange in a ring on a serving
dish, then put the salad greens in the center.
Spoon the marinade over the dish and garnish with
the lemon slices.

Rice and salmon ring

Anello di riso e salmone

Preparation time: 45 mins
(including soaking)
Cooking time: 8 mins
Serves 6

1 cup basmati rice, rinsed
    and soaked in cold water
    for 30 mins
15 black olives, pitted
7 ounces canned salmon,
    drained and flaked
14 ounces canned peas,
    drained and rinsed
7 ounces cherry tomatoes,
    cut into wedges
2 tablespoons capers
    preserved in salt,
    rinsed and drained
juice of 1 lemon, strained
1 sprig flat-leaf parsley,
    chopped
1 sprig basil, chopped
5 tablespoons olive oil
3½ ounces corn salad
1 tomato, cut into strips
salt and pepper

Drain the rice and cook it in a large pan of
salted boiling water for 8 minutes, or according
to package directions. Meanwhile, chop 10 of the
olives. Drain the rice well, rinse it under
cold running water, drain again thoroughly, and
transfer to a bowl.

Add the salmon, peas, cherry tomatoes, chopped
olives, capers, lemon juice, parsley, and basil.
Drizzle with the olive oil, season with salt and
pepper, and stir.

Put the rice mixture into a ring mold, pressing
it down well with the back of a spoon.
Make a bed of corn salad on a serving dish and
turn out the rice mold on top. Garnish with
strips of tomato and the remaining whole olives
and serve.

Marinated langoustines
Marinata di scampi

Preparation time: 1½ hrs
(including marinating)
Cooking time: 5 mins
Serves 4

½ red bell pepper, seeded
    and diced
4 tablespoons olive oil
juice of 1 lemon, strained
16 langoustines (Norwegian
    lobsters) or crayfish
1 sprig basil, chopped
1 sprig thyme, chopped
1¾ cups shredded lettuce
5 ounces baby zucchini,
    cut into thin strips
salt and pepper

Combine the red bell pepper, olive oil, and lemon juice in a large bowl and season with salt and pepper. Peel the langoustines, put them into another bowl, sprinkle with the basil and thyme, and let marinate for 1 hour in the refrigerator. Rinse the langoustines and steam them over a pan of boiling water for 5 minutes, then remove them from the pan.

Make a bed of lettuce on a serving dish and put the langoustines on top. Arrange the zucchini strips on top of the langoustines. Drizzle with the red bell pepper sauce and let stand for 5 minutes to let the flavors mingle, then serve.

Salmon tartare
Tartare di salmone

Preparation time: 50 mins
(including chilling and
standing)
Serves 4

1 pound 2 ounces salmon
    fillet, skinned
1 tablespoon white-wine
    vinegar
2 tablespoons snipped chives
juice of ½ lemon, strained
2-3 tablespoons olive oil
salt and pepper
strips of chive, to garnish

Put the salmon in the freezer for 30 minutes, then remove and dice it finely. Whisk together the vinegar, chives, lemon juice, and olive oil in a large bowl and season with salt and pepper. Add the salmon and let stand for 10 minutes to let the flavors mingle. Divide the mixture among 4 molds or ramekins and press it down firmly, then turn out onto 4 individual plates. Garnish with strips of chive and serve.

inated anchovies (p.232)

Sturgeon tartare

Tartare di storione

Preparation time: 50 mins
(including chilling)
Serves 4

9 ounces sturgeon fillet,
    skinned and finely
    chopped
1 shallot, finely chopped
1 tablespoon finely chopped
    chives
2 tablespoons capers, rinsed
    and finely chopped
olive oil, for drizzling
juice of 1 lemon, strained
2 tomatoes, peeled
    and diced
salt and pepper
toast triangles, to serve

Combine the fish, shallot, chives, and capers in
a bowl. Drizzle with olive oil, stir in the lemon
juice, and season with salt and pepper.

Transfer the mixture to a glass serving bowl and
garnish with the tomatoes. Cover and chill in
the refrigerator for 30 minutes. Serve with warm
toast triangles.

Langoustine cocktail

Cocktail di scampi

Preparation time: 20 mins
Cooking time: 5 mins
Serves 4

1 onion, quartered
1 carrot, cut into chunks
2¼ pounds langoustines
    (Norwegian lobsters)
    or crayfish
1 cup mayonnaise
scant 1 cup light cream
2 teaspoons Worcestershire
    sauce
1 teaspoon ketchup
dash of gin
dash of whiskey
1 tender lettuce, separated
    into leaves
salt

Fill a large pan halfway with water, add the
onion, carrot, and a pinch of salt, and bring
to a boil. Add the langoustines and cook
for 5 minutes, then drain, discarding the onion
and carrot. Peel them and set them aside. Whisk
together the mayonnaise, cream, Worcestershire
sauce, and ketchup in a bowl, drizzle with
the gin and whiskey, season with salt, and stir.
Line 4 bowls with lettuce leaves, divide the
langoustines among them, and cover with plenty of
the sauce. Keep in the refrigerator until ready
to serve.

Note: The cooking time for langoustines varies:
5 minutes after returning to a boil when added to
boiling water, 3 minutes after coming to a boil
if added to cold water.

Sardines with basil

Sardine al basilico

Preparation time: 24½ hrs
(including marinating)
Serves 4

24 sardines, scaled and
    cleaned
¼ cup olive oil
juice of 1 lemon, strained
2 red bell peppers, seeded
    and diced
10 black olives, pitted
    and chopped
8 basil leaves
salt and pepper

For the sauce

1 egg yolk
1 tablespoon white-wine
    vinegar
3 canned anchovy fillets,
    drained
5 basil leaves

Cut off the heads from the sardines if this has
not already been done. Open out the fish like
a book and put them on a cutting board, flesh
side down. Press all along the backbones with
your thumb, then turn them over and lift out the
backbones, snipping them at the tail ends with
scissors. Rinse them, pat dry, and put them into
a shallow dish. Mix together the oil and lemon
juice in a bowl, season with salt and pepper, and
pour the mixture over the sardines. Cover with
plastic wrap and let marinate in the refrigerator
for 24 hours.

Drain the sardines, reserving the marinade,
and transfer them to a serving dish. To make
the sauce, put the egg yolk, vinegar, anchovies,
basil, and reserved marinade in a blender and
blend at a low speed. Garnish the sardines with
the red bell peppers, olives, and basil leaves,
pour the sauce over them, and serve.

Summer antipasto

Antipasto estivo

Preparation time: 25 mins
Cooking time: 10 mins
Serves 4

2 tomatoes, peeled and sliced
5 ounces mozzarella
    cheese, sliced
olive oil, for drizzling
2 sprigs basil
2 red bell peppers
7 ounces canned tuna, drained
salt and pepper

Preheat the broiler. Arrange the tomato slices
in a ring on a serving dish and partly cover each
with a slice of mozzarella. Drizzle with olive
oil, season with salt and pepper, and sprinkle
with some of the basil leaves. Set aside in
a cool place. Broil the bell peppers, turning
frequently, for about 10 minutes, until blistered
and charred. Remove them with tongs and when cool
enough to handle, peel and halve them, remove
and discard the seeds, then cut the flesh into
diamonds and place on top of the mozzarella
slices. Spoon the tuna into the middle of the
ring, garnish with the remaining basil leaves,
and serve immediately.

Corn salad
and sturgeon

Insalata di songino a storione

Preparation time: 6¼ hrs
(including marinating)
Serves 4

9 ounces sturgeon fillet
scant 1 cup olive oil,
    plus extra for drizzling
3–4 tablespoons apple
    vinegar, plus extra
    for drizzling
6 green peppercorns
1 tablespoon snipped chives
2 bunches corn salad
salt
hot toast, to serve

Slice the sturgeon fillet very thinly. Pour the oil into a bowl, add the vinegar, green peppercorns, chives, and a large pinch of salt, and mix well. Put the slices of sturgeon into the bowl and let them marinate for at least 6 hours. To serve, spread out the corn salad on a serving dish, drizzle with a little oil and vinegar, and season with salt. Drain the slices of fish and put them on top. Serve immediately with hot toast.

Rolled bell pepper
with tuna

Peperoni arrotolati con il tonno

Preparation time: 40 mins
Cooking time: 10 mins
Serves 4

4 large red bell peppers
11 ounces canned tuna in
    olive oil, drained
10 black olives, pitted and
    coarsely chopped
1 tomato, peeled, seeded,
    and coarsely chopped
½ fresh red chile, seeded
    and coarsely chopped
4 basil leaves
juice of 1 lemon, strained
olive oil, for drizzling
salt

Holding the bell peppers with a long-handled fork, roast them over a naked flame until they are blistered and charred. Alternatively, halve them, place skin side uppermost on a baking sheet, and broil for about 10 minutes, until they are blistered and charred.

Remove from the heat and let cool, then peel off the skins, remove and discard the seeds, and cut the flesh of each bell pepper into 2–3 large strips. Put the tuna, olives, tomato, chile, and basil into a food processor or blender and process until combined.

Transfer the mixture to a bowl, add sufficient lemon juice to soften it, drizzle with a little olive oil, and season with salt. Spread each bell pepper strip with the tuna sauce, roll up, and secure with a wooden toothpick. Keep cool until ready to serve.

/ Summer entertaining /

Faux eggs

Uova finte

Preparation time: 4½ hrs
(including chilling)
Cooking time: 20 mins
Makes 16

12 ounces peeled, uncooked
    shrimp
15 clams, scrubbed
1 clove garlic
1 fresh chile, halved
    and seeded
¾ cup fish stock
¾ cup dry white wine
3 tablespoons peas
3 tablespoons small balls
    of carrot
2 hard-cooked eggs
1 teaspoon chopped flat-leaf
    parsley
4 cups dissolved gelatin
juice of 1 lemon juice,
    strained

To garnish

mixed salad greens
baby tomatoes

Soak the shrimp and clams in separate bowls of salted water for about 8 minutes, then drain. Put the garlic, chile, stock, and white wine into a pan and bring to a boil. Boil until reduced by a third. Add the shrimp and cook for 2 minutes, then add the clams and cook for another 2 minutes. Drain the seafood and shell the clams, discarding any that remain closed, along with the chile and garlic.

Cook the peas and carrots in lightly salted boiling water for 10–15 minutes, until tender, then drain. Let all the ingredients cool. Shell the hard-cooked eggs, then halve them and scoop out the yolks. Dice the egg whites and puree the egg yolks with a handheld mixer. Mix the yolks with the chopped parsley. Stir the lemon juice into the dissolved gelatin. Stand 16 empty eggshells in egg racks or egg cartons and use a teaspoon to fill them, alternating the shrimp, clams, peas, carrots, egg whites, and egg yolks. Do not press down on the mixture. Pour in the gelatin to fill the shells completely and chill in the refrigerator for at least 3 hours, until set.

To serve, shell the faux eggs very carefully and stand them up in the center of a serving dish. Garnish with salad greens and tomatoes cut in half or into flower shapes.

Note: This dish requires 16 empty eggshells. You may be able to find a gadget for neatly removing the tops of the shells in specialty cookware stores. Otherwise, use a sharp, pointed kitchen or craft knife to cut a small slice from the top of the shell. Pour the yolks and whites into a bowl to use later for another dish and carefully rinse the shells. Dry the outsides and let drain until required. This antipasto can also be made with honeydew melon, avocados, or fresh pineapple.

Bresaola and bell pepper involtini

Involtini di bresaola ai peperoni

Preparation time: 15 mins
Serves 4

2 red bell peppers preserved
   in olive oil, drained and
   cut into thin strips
2 tablespoons capers, rinsed
   and drained
7 ounces bresaola
juice of 1 lemon, strained
pepper

Put 2 bell pepper strips and a few capers on each slice of bresaola, roll up, and arrange on a serving dish. Drizzle the rolls with lemon juice and season lightly with pepper, then serve.

Note: Capers are the flower buds of a Mediterranean plant. The best ones are the small ones, because they have more flavor. Bresaola is a type of cured, air-dried beef, which is sold very thinly sliced. Prosciutto can be substituted if bresaola is not available.

Cipriani carpaccio

Carpaccio cipriani

Preparation time: 20 mins
Serves 6

1 pound 7 ounces sirloin of
   beef, cut into wafer-thin
   slices
2 egg yolks
scant 1 cup olive oil
1½ teaspoons lemon juice,
   strained
1–2 teaspoons Worcestershire
   sauce
3 tablespoons milk
salt and freshly ground white
   pepper

Arrange the slices of beef flat on a serving dish, cover with plastic wrap, and keep in the refrigerator until required.

To make the sauce, whisk the egg yolks with a pinch each of salt and of pepper in a bowl. Gradually drizzle in the oil, stirring constantly with a small whisk. Once the mixture begins to thicken, stir in ½ teaspoon of the lemon juice. Continue whisking in the oil in a slow, steady stream, until it has all been used.

Stir in the Worcestershire sauce, remaining lemon juice, and the milk, adjust the seasoning, and keep in the refrigerator until ready to serve.

To serve, dip a spoon into the sauce several times and drizzle it over the meat in a whirling pattern.

Beef tartare

Tartare

Preparation time: 20 mins

Serves 4

1 pound 2 ounces lean
    ground beef
4 egg yolks
2 canned anchovy fillets,
    drained and chopped
1 onion, thinly sliced
    into rings
1 tablespoon capers, rinsed
    and drained
1 tablespoon chopped flat-
    leaf parsley

To serve

olive oil
freshly squeezed lemon juice,
    strained
Dijon mustard (optional)
salt and pepper

Divide the ground beef among 4 individual plates,
shaping it into small mounds. Make a small hollow
in the top of each mound and put a raw egg yolk
into each.

Garnish with the anchovies, onion rings, capers,
and parsley. Serve with oil, lemon juice, salt,
and pepper on the side, so that each diner can
dress the meat according to taste and then, using
a fork, mix in the other ingredients. You can
also add a dash of Dijon mustard, if you like.

Photograph p.246

Carpaccio with radishes

Carpaccio con ravanelli

Preparation time: 15 mins

Serves 4

12 ounces lean beef, such as
    sirloin, very thinly
    sliced
4 radishes, thinly sliced
juice of 1 lemon, strained
extra-virgin olive oil, for
    drizzling
4–5 white peppercorns
3½ ounces Grana Padano
    cheese, shaved into
    flakes
salt

Spread out the slices of meat on a serving dish,
slightly overlapping, and arrange the radish
slices on top. Put the lemon juice, a drizzle
of oil, the peppercorns, and a pinch of salt into
a blender and process. Pour the dressing over
the beef and radishes, sprinkle with the cheese,
and serve.

Photograph p.247

Beef tartare (p.245)

Melon and ham

Prosciutto e melone

Preparation time: 10 mins
Serves 4

1 melon
8 slices prosciutto
8 butter curls
salt

If possible, store the melon in a cool place, but not the refrigerator, for a few hours before preparing.

Cut the melon into 8 wedges, scoop out the seeds, and cut off the rind. Sprinkle with salt and wrap each wedge in a slice of prosciutto.

Arrange on a round dish, garnish with the curls of butter, and serve immediately.

Ricotta and ham pâté

Pâté di ricotta e prosciutto cotto

Preparation time: 4¼ hrs
(including chilling)
Serves 6

1½ cups cooked, finely
    chopped ham
generous 1 cup ricotta
2 tablespoons pine nuts
scant ½ cup heavy cream
½ cup brandy
salt and pepper
warm whole-wheat bread
    croûtons, to serve

Combine the ham, ricotta, pine nuts, cream, and brandy in a bowl until soft and creamy, and season the mixture with salt and pepper.

Line a rectangular baking pan with plastic wrap and pour in the mixture, smoothing the surface with a spatula. Chill in the refrigerator for 4 hours.

Turn the pâté out onto a serving dish and serve with warm whole-wheat bread croûtons.

Note: The word ricotta comes from the Latin *recoctus*, meaning "cooked twice." It is the whey used to make cheese that is cooked twice.

Tenderloin of veal marinated with herbs

Filetto in conza

Preparation time: 24½ hrs
(including marinating)

Serves 6

1 pound 2 ounces veal
    tenderloin
1 sprig rosemary
8 sage leaves, chopped
8 basil leaves, chopped
1 onion, thinly sliced
thinly pared zest of 1 lemon,
    cut into strips
¼-⅜ cup olive oil
juice of 2 lemons, strained
salt and pepper

Cut the tenderloin into extremely thin slices and place in a layer in a bowl. Cover with a layer of rosemary needles, sage, basil, onion slices, and strips of lemon zest. Drizzle with olive oil and lemon juice and season with salt and pepper. Continue making alternate layers until all the ingredients are used, ending with a layer of herbs, onion, and lemon zest. Drizzle with a little more oil, cover the bowl with plastic wrap, and chill in the refrigerator for 24 hours.

Veal tartare with mustard and brandy sauce

Tartare di vitello alla salsa
di senape e cognac

Preparation time: 50 mins
(including standing)

Serves 4

1 pound 2 ounces veal
    tenderloin, finely diced
2 teaspoons Dijon mustard
pinch of cayenne pepper
juice of ½ lemon, strained
2 tablespoons brandy
2 tablespoons olive oil
4 tablespoons finely chopped
    flat-leaf parsley
2 tablespoons snipped chives
salt and pepper
sprigs of curly parsley
    and strands of chives,
    to garnish

Put the meat into a bowl, cover, and keep in the refrigerator until required. Combine the mustard, cayenne pepper, lemon juice, brandy, and olive oil in another bowl and season with salt and pepper.

Add the parsley and chives. Pour the sauce over the meat, stir, and let stand for 30 minutes to let the flavors mingle.

To serve, divide the mixture among 4 individual plates, shaping it into a small mound, and garnish with parsley and chives.

First courses

Cold cucumber and potato soup
Crema fredda di cetrioli e patate

Preparation time: 4 hrs
(including cooling and
chilling)
Cooking time: 30 mins
Serves 4

3 tablespoons olive oil
1 onion, chopped
2¼ cups chopped cucumbers
scant 1 cup chopped potatoes
½ cup chopped lettuce
3-4 pennyroyal or mint
   leaves, plus extra to
   garnish
2¼ cups hot vegetable stock
¼ cup heavy cream
salt and pepper

Heat the olive oil in a shallow pan. Add the
onion and cook over low heat, stirring
occasionally, for 5 minutes, or until softened.
Add the cucumbers, potatoes, lettuce, and
pennyroyal or mint leaves and cook, stirring
occasionally, for another 5 minutes.

Season with salt and pepper, pour in the hot
stock, and simmer for 15 minutes. Remove the pan
from the heat and ladle the mixture into a
food processor or blender. Process until smooth,
then return to a clean pan, add the cream, and
heat gently, stirring constantly, for 5 minutes.

Remove the pan from the heat and let cool, then
chill in the refrigerator for 3 hours. Transfer
the soup to a tureen, garnish with pennyroyal or
mint leaves, and serve.

Minestrone with pesto

Minestrone con il pesto

Preparation time: 40 mins
(including soaking)
Cooking time: 1 hr 10 mins
Serves 4–6

¼ cup dried mushrooms
¾ cup shelled fresh
    cannellini beans
1⅓ cups trimmed and halved
    green beans
3 tomatoes, peeled, seeded,
    and chopped
3 zucchini, diced
½ cabbage, shredded
1 eggplant, diced
3 tablespoons olive oil
¾ cup short pasta
salt
grated Parmesan cheese,
    to serve

For the pesto

25 basil leaves
scant ½ cup olive oil
⅓ cup pine nuts
⅓ cup grated Parmesan cheese
⅓ cup grated pecorino cheese
salt

Put the mushrooms into a small bowl, add warm water to cover, and let soak for 20 minutes, then drain, and squeeze out any excess liquid. Meanwhile, make the pesto. Put the basil, olive oil, pine nuts, and a pinch of salt in a blender and blend briefly at medium speed. Add the grated cheeses and blend again. Transfer to a small bowl, cover, and set aside.

Pour 8¾ cups water into a large pan and add a small pinch of salt. Add the cannellini beans, green beans, tomatoes, zucchini, cabbage, and eggplant. Chop the mushrooms and add them to the pan with the olive oil. Bring to a boil, then reduce the heat, cover, and simmer for 1 hour. Add the pasta and cook for another 8–10 minutes, or according to the package directions, until the pasta is tender. Remove the pan from the heat.

Stir in the pesto and serve warm or cold in individual bowls, offering the grated cheese separately. If the soup is to be served cold, instead of adding the oil before cooking the soup, add it just before serving.

Milanese minestrone

Minestrone alla milanese

Preparation time: 1¾ hrs
(including cooling)
Cooking time: 1½ hrs
Serves 4-6

1½ ounces lardo (Italian
    pork fat) or fatty bacon
½ clove garlic
4 onion rings
1 sprig flat-leaf parsley,
    finely chopped
1 celery stalk, finely
    chopped
¾ cup shelled fresh borlotti
    beans
3 tomatoes, peeled,
    seeded, and diced
3 carrots, diced
3 potatoes, diced
2 zucchini, diced
1 sprig sage, chopped
1 sprig basil, chopped
1¾ cups shelled peas
½ savoy cabbage, shredded
¼ cup long-grain rice
2 tablespoons olive oil
salt
grated Parmesan cheese,
    to serve

Finely chop the lardo or bacon with the garlic
and onion rings and put the mixture into a bowl.
Add the parsley and celery, mix well, and
transfer to a pan. Add the borlotti beans,
tomatoes, carrots, potatoes, zucchini, sage, and
basil. Pour in 8¾ cups water, season with salt,
and bring to a boil over medium-high heat.

Reduce the heat, cover, and simmer gently
for 1 hour. Add the peas and cabbage, re-cover
the pan, and simmer for another 15 minutes.
Add the rice and cook, stirring occasionally, for
another 15-18 minutes, until the rice is tender.
The minestrone must be fairly thick. Remove the
pan from the heat, stir in the olive oil, and let
cool. Serve cold with plenty of grated cheese.

Note: The typical Milanese minestrone is served
cold in summer. It should be cooled at room
temperature (never in the refrigerator) in
individual bowls lined with slices of bacon and
covered with a napkin.

Photograph p.255

Cream of pea soup

Crema di piselli

Preparation time: 25 mins
Cooking time: 35 mins
Serves 4

5¼ cups shelled peas
2 potatoes, diced
1 white onion, sliced
3 tablespoons olive oil, plus
    extra for drizzling
4 slices white bread, crusts
    removed
salt

Put the peas, potatoes, and onion in a pan, pour in 4 cups water, add a pinch of salt, and bring to a boil. Reduce the heat, cover, and simmer for 20–25 minutes, until the vegetables are tender. Remove the pan from the heat, reserve a ladleful of peas, and transfer the remaining mixture to a food processor or blender. Process until smooth, then return the soup to the pan and bring back to a boil. Stir in the reserved peas and season to taste with salt.

Meanwhile, heat the oil in a skillet. Cut the slices of bread in half, put them into the skillet and cook for a few minutes on each side, until they are golden. Divide the fried bread among 4 soup plates and ladle the soup over them. Drizzle with olive oil and serve immediately.

Bread soup with tomato

Pappa al pomodoro

Preparation time: 30 mins
Cooking time: 1 hr
Serves 4

1 tablespoon olive oil
11 ounces ripe tomatoes,
    peeled, seeded, and
    coarsely chopped
1 clove garlic, chopped
1 celery stalk, chopped
2 slices day-old rustic
    bread, cubed
6 basil leaves, chopped
¼ cup grated Parmesan cheese
salt and pepper

Put the olive oil, tomatoes, garlic, celery, and a pinch each of salt and pepper into a pan, add 5 cups water, and bring to a boil. Lower the heat and simmer for about 1 hour.

After about 30 minutes, stir in the bread and continue to simmer the soup over low heat. Remove the pan from the heat and let stand.

Ladle into a soup tureen, sprinkle with the basil and Parmesan, and serve.

Zucchini flower soup

Minestra ai fiori di zucchine

Preparation time: 20 mins
Cooking time: 20 mins
Serves 4

4 cups meat stock
2 tablespoons butter
1 tablespoon olive oil
1 onion, chopped
1 carrot, chopped
1 celery stalk, chopped
4 zucchini, finely diced
11 ounces zucchini flowers,
    cut into strips
1 cup very small pasta, such
    as ditalini
salt and pepper
grated Parmesan cheese, to
    serve

Bring the stock to a boil in a small pan. Heat the butter and olive oil in a large pan, add the onion, carrot, and celery, and cook over low heat, stirring occasionally, for 10 minutes. Add the zucchini and zucchini flowers and cook for 2 minutes, then pour in the hot stock. Bring to a boil, add the pasta, and cook for 5–6 minutes, or according to the package directions, until al dente.

Season with salt and pepper to taste, ladle into a soup tureen, and serve with Parmesan.

Hidden soup

Suppa quatta

Preparation time: 15 mins
Cooking time: 40 mins
Serves 6

1 pound 2 ounces dry rustic
    bread, cut into ¾-inch
    slices
11 ounces fresh caciotta or
    pecorino cheese, sliced
6¼ cups well-flavored meat
    stock
1–2 tablespoons chopped
    mixed aromatic herbs,
    such as parsley,
    marjoram, and thyme

Preheat the oven to 325°F. Make alternating layers of bread and cheese slices in a shallow ovenproof dish. Use the handle of a cooking spoon or a knitting needle to make deep holes in the layers so that they can absorb the stock easily.

Pour the stock over the top and sprinkle with the herbs. Bake for about 40 minutes, until the cheese starts to melt and a golden brown crust has formed on the top. Serve immediately.

Note: Quatta means "hidden": The soup is hidden under the cheese crust. It is delicious served lukewarm on summer evenings.

Asparagus risotto

Risotto con punte di asparagi

Preparation time: 10 mins
Cooking time: 35 mins
Serves 4

1 pound 2 ounces asparagus
    spears, trimmed
about 6¼ cups vegetable stock
5 tablespoons butter
3 tablespoons olive oil
½ onion, chopped
1¾ cups risotto rice
salt
grated Parmesan cheese, to
    serve

Cook the asparagus in a pan of salted boiling water
for 5-8 minutes, until it is tender, then drain
and cut off and reserve the tips. Chop the stems
and set aside. Bring the stock to a boil.
Meanwhile, melt 1 tablespoon of the butter in
a skillet, add the asparagus tips, and cook over
low heat, stirring occasionally, for 5 minutes,
then remove from the heat and set aside. Melt
2 tablespoons of the remaining butter with the
oil in a separate pan, add the onion, and cook
over low heat, stirring occasionally, for
5 minutes. Stir in the rice and cook, stirring,
until the rice is coated in butter, then add the
asparagus stems. Add a ladleful of the hot stock
and cook, stirring, until it has been absorbed.
Continue adding the stock, a ladleful at a time,
and stirring until each addition has been
absorbed. This will take 18-20 minutes. When the
rice is tender, stir in the remaining butter and
the asparagus tips. Serve with grated Parmesan.

Calendula risotto

Risotto alla calendula

Preparation time: 15 mins
Cooking time: 25 mins
Serves 4

about 6¼ cups vegetable stock
6 tablespoons butter
1 onion, finely chopped
2 cups risotto rice
1 ounce unsprayed calendula
    petals, shredded
2 cups thinly sliced white
    mushrooms
¾ cup grated Parmesan cheese
salt and pepper

Pour the stock into a large pan and bring to a
boil, then reduce the heat and simmer. Meanwhile,
melt half the butter in another large pan. Add
the onion and cook over low heat, stirring
occasionally, for 5 minutes, or until softened.
Add the rice and cook, stirring constantly, for a
few minutes, until all the grains are coated with
melted butter. Stir in a ladleful of the hot
stock and add the calendula petals and mushrooms.
Cook, stirring constantly, until all the liquid
has been absorbed. Continue adding the hot stock,
a ladleful at a time, and stirring constantly
until each addition has been absorbed. This will
take 18-20 minutes. Gently stir in the remaining
butter and grated Parmesan and serve immediately.

Photograph p.262

Strawberry risotto

Risotto alle fragole

Preparation time: 10 mins
Cooking time: 35 mins
Serves 4

4 cups vegetable stock
6 tablespoons butter
1 onion, finely chopped
1¼ cups risotto rice
1¾ cups dry white wine
2¾ cups hulled strawberries
1 cup heavy cream
salt and freshly ground white
    pepper

Pour the stock into a pan and bring to a boil, then reduce the heat and simmer.

Meanwhile, melt half the butter in another pan. Add the onion and cook over low heat, stirring occasionally, for 5 minutes, or until it is softened. Add the rice and cook, stirring, until all the grains are coated with melted butter.

Add the wine and cook for 5 minutes, or until the alcohol has evaporated. Add a ladleful of the hot stock to the rice and cook, stirring, until it has been absorbed. Continue adding the stock, a ladleful at a time, and stirring until each addition has been absorbed. This will take 18–20 minutes.

Meanwhile, set a few whole strawberries aside for the garnish and mash the remainder in a bowl. Ten minutes before the end of the cooking time, add the mashed strawberries to the risotto. When it is almost ready, gently stir in the cream and season with salt and pepper. Serve garnished with the reserved whole strawberries.

Photograph p.263

Calendula risotto (p.260)

strawberry risotto (p.261)

Blueberry risotto

Risotto ai mirtilli

Preparation time: 10 mins

Cooking time: 30 mins

Serves 4

5 cups vegetable stock
3 tablespoons butter
1 onion, finely chopped
1⅓ cups risotto rice
scant 1 cup white wine
1¼ cups blueberries
scant ½ cup heavy cream
grated Parmesan cheese,
    to serve

Pour the stock into a large pan and bring to a boil, then reduce the heat and simmer. Meanwhile, melt the butter in another pan. Add the onion and cook over low heat, stirring occasionally, for 5 minutes, until softened. Add the rice and cook, stirring constantly, for a few minutes until all the grains are coated with melted butter.

Add the wine and cook for 5 minutes, or until the alcohol has evaporated. Reserve 2 tablespoons of the blueberries and add the remainder. Stir in a ladleful of the hot stock and cook, stirring constantly, until all the liquid has been absorbed. Continue adding the hot stock, a ladleful at a time, and stirring constantly until each addition has been absorbed. This will take 18–20 minutes. Stir in the cream and transfer the risotto to a serving dish, garnishing it with the reserved blueberries. Serve the grated cheese separately.

Cold risotto with melon and speck

Risotto freddo al melone e speck

Preparation time: 45 mins
(including cooling)

Cooking time: 25 mins

Serves 16

8¾ cups chicken stock
2 small melons, chilled
3 tablespoons butter
1 large onion, finely
    chopped
5 cups Carnaroli or other
    risotto rice
2⅓ cups diced speck or bacon

To finish

scant ½ cup heavy cream
    or 3 tablespoons butter

Pour the stock into a large pan and bring to a boil, then reduce the heat and simmer. Meanwhile, halve the melons and scoop out the seeds. Make small balls from the flesh with a melon baller. Melt the butter in a pan. Add the onion and cook over low heat for 5 minutes, or until softened. Add the rice and cook, stirring constantly, until all the grains are coated with melted butter. Stir in a ladleful of the hot stock and cook, stirring constantly, until all the liquid has been absorbed. Continue adding the hot stock, a ladleful at a time, stirring until each addition has been absorbed. This will take 18–20 minutes. Remove the pan from the heat and stir in the cream or butter, then let cool slightly. Add the speck and melon and serve when almost cold.

/ Summer entertaining /

Seafood risotto

Risotto alla marinara

Preparation time: 1¼ hrs
Cooking time: 1 hr 5 mins
Serves 6

2 onions
1 carrot, cut into chunks
2 sprigs flat-leaf parsley
1 pound 2 ounces shrimp
1 pound 2 ounces mussels,
    scrubbed and cleaned
¾ cup olive oil
1 pound 2 ounces clams,
    scrubbed
1 squid, 9 ounces
1 cuttlefish, 9 ounces
2 cloves garlic
scant 1 cup dry white wine
1 fresh red chile, seeded and
    finely chopped
1 pound 2 ounces Carnaroli or
    other risotto rice
finely grated zest of 1 lemon
salt and pepper

Bring a pan of salted water to a boil. Cut 1 onion into quarters and add to the pan with the carrot, parsley, and shrimp and boil for 2–3 minutes. Remove the shrimp with a slotted spoon, reserving the cooking liquid, then peel the shrimp and set them aside. Strain the cooking liquid through a cheesecloth-lined strainer into a bowl. Discard any mussels with broken or damaged shells or that do not shut immediately when sharply tapped.

Put them into a large pan with 1 tablespoon of the oil, cover, and cook over high heat, shaking the pan occasionally, for 4–5 minutes, until the mussels have opened. Discard any that remain shut, remove the remainder from the shells, and put them into a bowl. Put the clams into a large pan, add 1 tablespoon of the remaining oil, cover, and cook over high heat, shaking the pan occasionally, for 3–5 minutes, until they have opened. Discard any that remain shut, remove the remainder from the shells, and put them into a bowl.

Rinse the squid, then pull the head and body apart (the innards will come away with the head). Cut off the tentacles and squeeze out the beak. Pull out the transparent quill from the body sac and remove any remaining membrane. Rinse the body sac well under cold running water and rub off the skin. Cut the body sac and tentacles into pieces and set aside. To clean the cuttlefish, cut off the tentacles just in front of the eyes, then remove, and discard the beak. Separate the tentacles and pull off the skin from each. Pull off the skin from the body sac, then cut down the center and remove the cuttlebone. Remove and discard the innards and the head. Wash the body sac and tentacles under cold running water and cut into pieces.

→

→ Heat scant ½ cup of the remaining oil in a skillet. Add the garlic cloves and cook over low heat, stirring frequently, for a few minutes, until they are lightly browned, then remove and discard them. Add the squid and cuttlefish to the skillet and cook, stirring frequently, for a few minutes, then add half the wine and cook for 5 minutes, or until the alcohol has evaporated. Season with salt and pepper, stir in the chile, and cook for another 10 minutes. Add the shrimp, mussels, and clams and remove the skillet from the heat. Pour the reserved cooking liquid into a pan and bring to a boil, then reduce the heat and simmer.

Meanwhile, finely chop the remaining onion. Heat the remaining oil in a large shallow pan. Add the chopped onion and cook over low heat, stirring occasionally, for 5 minutes, or until softened. Add the rice and cook, stirring constantly, for 1 minute, until all the grains are coated with oil. Add the remaining wine and cook for another 5 minutes, or until the alcohol has evaporated.

Stir in a ladleful of the hot cooking liquid and cook, stirring constantly, until all the liquid has been absorbed. Continue adding the hot cooking liquid, a ladleful at a time, and stirring constantly until each addition has been absorbed. This will take 18-20 minutes. As soon as the rice is cooked, gently stir in the seafood and the grated lemon zest. Serve immediately.

Green bean timbale

Timballo di fagiolini

Preparation time: 30 mins
Cooking time: 1¼ hrs
Serves 4

1 pound 2 ounces green
   beans, trimmed
2 tablespoons butter,
   plus extra for greasing
1 tablespoon olive oil
1 pearl onion, chopped
1 celery stalk, chopped
1 carrot, chopped
¾ cup fresh white bread
   crumbs
2 eggs, separated
½ cup grated Parmesan cheese
2¼ cups Béchamel sauce
   (see Stuffed eggplants,
   p.171)
salt and pepper

Cook the beans in a pan of salted boiling water
for 8–10 minutes, until they are tender, then
drain. Melt the butter with the oil in a pan. Add
the onion, celery, and carrot and cook over low
heat, stirring occasionally, for 5 minutes,
or until softened. Add the beans and ⅔ cup hot
water, season with salt and pepper, and cook
until the liquid has been absorbed. Remove the
pan from the heat.

Preheat the oven to 400°F. Grease a high-sided
ovenproof mold with butter and sprinkle with the
bread crumbs. Whisk the egg whites to stiff
peaks in a separate bowl.

Stir the egg yolks and grated cheese into the
béchamel sauce, then fold in the egg whites.
Spread a layer of the béchamel mixture over the
inside of the prepared mold, tip in the beans,
and cover with remaining béchamel mixture.

Put the mold on a baking sheet and bake
for 45 minutes. Run a round-bladed knife around
the inside of the mold, invert onto a warmed
serving dish, and serve immediately.

Main courses

Fish stew
Cacciucco

Preparation time: 40 mins

Cooking time: 50 mins

Serves 4

2½ pounds mixed fish and
    seafood, such as
    monkfish, John Dory,
    red snapper, squid,
    cuttlefish, grouper,
    rascasse, and mackerel,
    cleaned
3 tablespoons olive oil
1 onion, chopped
1 clove garlic, finely
    chopped
11 ounces tomatoes, chopped
1 pinch cayenne pepper
1¾ cups dry white wine
fish stock, to taste
11 ounces shelled mussels
3 tablespoons chopped
    flat-leaf parsley
salt

To serve
----

4 slices rustic bread,
    toasted
1 clove garlic
cayenne pepper, for
    sprinkling

Cut the larger fish into even pieces, leaving the
small fish whole. Cut the squid and cuttlefish
into pieces. Heat the oil in a large pan. Add the
onion and garlic and cook over low heat, stirring
occasionally, for 5 minutes, until softened. Stir
in the tomatoes, season with salt, and cook for
2 minutes, then sprinkle with a pinch of cayenne
pepper and add the larger fish.

Drizzle with the wine and scant ½ cup hot water,
then cover and simmer for 30 minutes, gradually
adding the smaller fish. Remove the lid from the
pan and add sufficient water or fish stock to
produce a stew with a slightly liquid consistency,
and add the mussels to warm through.

Cook for another few minutes, then sprinkle with
the parsley. Taste and adjust the seasoning,
if necessary. To serve, rub the slices of toast
with the garlic and season with cayenne pepper.
Put the toast slices into the bottom of each
of 4 bowls, then ladle the fish stew over them.

Note: Cacciucco, one of a large number of fish
stews, is a specialty of Livorno. In Tuscany,
it means "hotchpotch" or "mixture." In Grosseto
and Arezzo, cacciucco is also made with garbanzo
beans or with meat.

Fritto misto with sage batter

Fritto misto di pesce alla salvia

Preparation time: 1½ hrs

Cooking time: 30–40 mins

Serves 16

2¼ pounds eggplants, thinly
    sliced into rounds
5½ pounds mussels, scrubbed
    and cleaned
generous ⅓ cup olive oil,
    plus extra for deep-
    frying
2 cloves garlic
5½ pounds clams, scrubbed
2¼ pounds shrimp
2¼ pounds squid
1 yellow bell pepper, seeded
    and cut into 1¼-inch
    squares
1 red bell pepper, seeded and
    cut into 1¼-inch squares
1 green bell pepper, seeded
    and cut into 1¼-inch
    squares
all-purpose flour, for
    dusting
2¼ pounds zucchini, sliced
    lengthwise
salt

For the batter

4½ cups all-purpose flour
4 eggs, separated
¾ cup dry white wine
1 tablespoon finely chopped
    sage
salt

Put the eggplant slices into a colander, sprinkle with salt, and let drain. Discard any mussels with damaged shells or that do not shut immediately when sharply tapped. Heat half the oil with a garlic clove in a large pan. Add the mussels, cover, and cook over high heat, shaking the pan occasionally, for 4–5 minutes, until the shells have opened. Remove with a slotted spoon, discarding any that remain shut. Remove the remainder from their shells.

Discard any clams with damaged or broken shells or that remain shut when sharply tapped. Heat the remaining oil with 1 garlic clove in another large pan. Add the clams, cover, and cook over high heat, shaking the pan occasionally, for 3–5 minutes, until the shells have opened. Remove the clams with a slotted spoon, discard any that remain shut, and remove the remainder from their shells.

Cook the shrimp in a large pan of salted boiling water for 2 minutes, then drain and peel them while they are still hot. Rinse the squid, then pull the head and body of each apart (the innards will come away with the head). Cut off the tentacles and squeeze out the beak. Pull out the transparent quill from the body sac and remove any remaining membrane. Rinse the body sacs well under cold running water and rub off the skin. Cut the body sacs into rings.

To make the batter, sift the flour and a pinch of salt into a bowl, then stir in the egg yolks and wine. In a separate bowl, whisk the egg whites to stiff peaks, then fold them into the batter with the sage.

→

→ Thread the clams and mussels onto skewers, using
4–5 shellfish for each skewer and alternating them
with pieces of bell pepper of different colors.
Rinse the eggplants and pat them dry. Heat the oil
in a deep-fryer to 350–375°F, or until a cube of
day-old bread browns in 30 seconds. Dust the squid
with flour and put the pieces into the oil.

Cook for 1–2 minutes, until golden brown and
crisp. Dip the skewers in the batter, drain
off the excess, and add to the hot oil. Fry for
a few minutes, until golden brown and crisp.
In turn, dip the shrimp, zucchini slices, and
eggplant slices in the batter, drain off the
excess, and deep-fry in the hot oil until golden
brown and crisp.

As the fried ingredients are ready, remove them
from the oil using a slotted spoon and drain
them on paper towels. Season them with salt and
put them onto a warmed serving dish. Keep warm
until all the ingredients are cooked, then serve.

Squid stuffed with shrimp

Calamari ripieni di gamberetti

Preparation time: 50 mins
(including cooling)
Cooking time: 20 mins
Serves 4

8 squid
2¼ cups dry white wine
2 bay leaves
11 ounces peeled shrimp
1 clove garlic, finely
    chopped
2 tablespoons chopped flat-
    leaf parsley
juice of 2 lemons, strained
scant ½ cup olive oil, plus
    extra for drizzling
salt and pepper
radicchio leaves, to garnish

Rinse the squid, then pull the head and body of
each apart (the innards will come away with the
head). Cut off the tentacles and squeeze out the
beak. Pull out the transparent quill from the
body sac and remove any remaining membrane. Rinse
the body sacs well under cold running water and
rub off the skin. Bring 4 cups water to a boil in
a large pan, add a large pinch of salt, the white
wine, and bay leaves. Bring back to a boil, add
the squid, and simmer for 20 minutes. Drain the
squid and let cool.

→

/ Summer entertaining /

Meanwhile, cook the shrimp in a pan of salted boiling water for 4–5 minutes, then remove from the heat and let cool in the liquid.

When cold, drain the shrimp and put them into a large bowl. Add the garlic, half the parsley, and 2 tablespoons of the lemon juice, drizzle generously with olive oil, season with pepper, and stir well.

Fill the squid sacs with the mixture and secure the opening with wooden toothpicks. Arrange the stuffed squid on a serving dish and garnish with the radicchio leaves. Whisk together the olive oil and the remaining lemon juice and parsley and season with salt and pepper. Pour the dressing over the squid and serve.

Note: The smallest squid are the best, because they are the tastiest and most tender.

Cuttlefish with peas
Seppie ai piselli

Preparation time: 20 mins
Cooking time: 1 hr 20 mins
Serves 4

4 tablespoons olive oil
1 clove garlic
1¾ pounds cuttlefish, cleaned and cut into strips
¾ cup dry white wine
6 cups shelled peas or canned peas, drained and rinsed
salt and pepper

Heat the oil and garlic in a pan until the garlic turns brown, then remove, and discard it. Add the cuttlefish to the pan, season with salt and pepper, stir well, and cook for a few minutes.

Add the wine and cook for 5 minutes, or until it has evaporated. Pour in water to almost cover the cuttlefish and bring to a boil. Reduce the heat, cover, and simmer for about 1 hour. Add the peas and cook for about 5–10 minutes, or until tender. Serve hot.

Fisherman's octopus

Polpi del marinaio

Preparation time: 4½ hrs
(including marinating)
Cooking time: 5 mins
Serves 6

2¼ pounds octopus, cleaned
1 clove garlic, crushed
1 onion, thinly sliced
olive oil, for drizzling
1 tomato, peeled, seeded,
    and chopped
5 tablespoons white wine
salt and pepper

Put the octopus into a heavy flameproof pan, preferably earthenware, add the garlic and onion, season with salt and pepper, and drizzle with olive oil.

Cover and cook over low heat for 1 hour. Add the tomato and wine and cook for another 1 hour, or until the octopus is tender.

Remove the octopus from the pan and cut it into pieces. Serve with the cooking juices, which should be fairly thick; if they are too thick, add a little lukewarm water.

Turbot with orange

Rombo all'arancia

Preparation time: 10 mins
Cooking time: 25 mins
Serves 4

2 oranges
1 tablespoon olive oil
4 turbot or halibut fillets
2 tablespoons superfine sugar
salt
orange segments, to garnish

Thinly pare the zest from 1 orange, avoiding any traces of bitter white pith, and chop finely. Squeeze the juice from the orange. Heat the olive oil in a shallow pan. Add the fish fillets, season with salt, and strain the orange juice over them. Cook over medium heat, turning occasionally, for 15 minutes.

Meanwhile, squeeze the juice from the remaining orange and strain it into a bowl. Pour 2 table-spoons water into a small pan, add the sugar and chopped orange zest, and heat gently for a few minutes, then stir in the remaining orange juice.

Pour the sauce over the fish and simmer for another 10 minutes. Transfer to a serving dish, garnish with orange segments, and serve immediately.

Fish couscous

Cuscus di pesce

Preparation time: 3½ hrs
(including drying)
Cooking time: 1½ hrs
Serves 4

3 cups couscous
   (see Note)
2 tablespoons olive oil,
   plus extra for drizzling
1 red onion, chopped
1 large clove garlic, finely
   chopped
1 celery stalk, chopped
2 tablespoons chopped
   flat-leaf parsley
3 tomatoes, peeled
   and chopped
2¼ pounds mixed fish and
   seafood, such as
   mackerel, rascasse,
   gurnard, conger eel,
   grouper, cuttlefish, or
   squid, cleaned and
   chopped
salt and pepper

Sprinkle the couscous into a large, shallow bowl, add a few drops of salted water, and knead with dampened fingers to obtain small and even grains. Drizzle lightly with olive oil, then sprinkle the grains over a clean dish towel, and let dry for at least 3 hours.

Heat the oil in a large pan. Add the onion, garlic, celery, and parsley and cook over low heat, stirring occasionally, for 5 minutes, or until the onion has softened. Stir in the tomatoes, then add the fish, pour in 6¼ cups boiling water, and season with salt and pepper. Cover and simmer for 30 minutes, then remove the pan from the heat. Lift the fish out of the pan, cover, and set aside.

Measure the cooking liquid, transferring one-third to a clean pan or a couscous pan (couscousier), and stir in 4 cups boiling water. Gather up the dish towel with the couscous inside and place it in a steamer basket or in the upper part of the couscous pan, and steam over low heat for at least 1 hour, until the couscous is tender. Spoon the couscous into the center of the serving dish and arrange the fish and sauce over and around it.

Note: Couscous originated in North Africa, where it was traditionally served with meat, but in Sicily it is often prepared with fish. This recipe calls for traditional couscous made with durum wheat semolina flour, and not the instant or partly cooked varieties.

Swordfish carpaccio with eggplant caviar

Carpaccio di spada con caviale di melanzane

Preparation time: 3½-4½ hrs
(including marinating)
Cooking time: 5 mins
Serves 6

juice of 2 lemons, strained
⅔ cup olive oil
pinch of dried oregano
1 swordfish fillet, 1 pound
    2 ounces, thinly sliced
salt and pepper

For the eggplant caviar

3 eggplants, sliced
juice of 1 lemon, strained
1 clove garlic
1 tablespoon chopped
    flat-leaf parsley
2 tomatoes, peeled, seeded,
    and chopped
2 tablespoons olive oil
salt

Combine the lemon juice, olive oil, and oregano in a large nonmetallic dish and season with salt and pepper. Add the swordfish slices to the dish, cover with plastic wrap, and let marinate in the refrigerator for 3–4 hours.

To make the eggplant caviar, blanch the eggplant slices in a pan of boiling water for 4 minutes. Remove with a slotted spoon, spread them out on a clean dish towel, and let cool.

Put the eggplant slices into a food processor and process to a puree, then add the lemon juice, garlic, parsley, tomatoes, and oil, process briefly to combine, and season with salt.

To serve, drain the swordfish slices and arrange them on a large serving dish, leaving the center of the dish empty. Strain the marinade and pour it over the fish. Spoon the eggplant caviar into the center of the dish and serve.

/ Summer entertaining /

Swordfish in a parcel

Ruota di pesce spada al cartoccio

Preparation time: 25 mins
Cooking time: 40 mins
Serves 6

1 swordfish fillet,
   3¼ pounds, no more than
   2½ inches thick
¾ cup olive oil
juice of 1 lemon, strained
1 fresh red chile, seeded and
   finely chopped
1 clove garlic, sliced
1 bunch of flat-leaf parsley,
   chopped
salt
curls of lemon zest,
   to garnish

Preheat the oven to 325°F and put a dish of water in the oven. Line a large ovenproof dish with aluminum foil, letting it overhang the sides. Pour half the oil and half the lemon juice over the aluminum foil, sprinkle with half the chile, half the garlic, and half the parsley, and season with salt.

Put the fish on top, pour over the remaining oil and lemon juice, sprinkle with the remaining chile, garlic, and parsley, and season with salt. Fold the aluminum foil over the fish and roast for 40 minutes (the dish of water in the oven helps to prevent the fish from drying out during cooking).

Remove the dish from the oven, unwrap the fish, and cut it into slices. Put them on a serving plate, garnish with curls of lemon zest, and serve.

Sea bream with fennel bulbs

Orata ai finocchi

Preparation time: 10 mins
Cooking time: 40 mins
Serves 4

4 fennel bulbs, trimmed
  and halved
1 sprig thyme
2¼ pounds giltheaded sea
  bream or porgy, fins
  trimmed, scaled, and cleaned
1 clove garlic
olive oil, for drizzling
juice of 2 lemons, strained
salt and pepper

Preheat the oven to 350°F. Cook the fennel in a pan of salted boiling water for 10 minutes, then drain. Put the thyme sprig in the cavity of the fish and season the cavity with salt and pepper.

Place the fish in an ovenproof dish, add the garlic, drizzle with olive oil, and season with salt and pepper. Arrange the fennel all around the fish and bake, turning halfway through cooking, for about 30 minutes. Drizzle the fish with the lemon juice and serve.

Piquant sea bream

Orata piccante

Preparation time: 20 mins
Cooking time: 30 mins
Serves 4

1 sea bream, 2¼ pounds,
  fins trimmed, scaled,
  and cleaned
2 sprigs sage, chopped
1 sprig rosemary, chopped
2 sprigs basil, chopped
1 clove garlic, chopped
2 tomatoes, sliced
5 tablespoons dry white wine
olive oil, for drizzling
salt and pepper

Preheat the oven to 400°F. Season the cavity of the fish with salt and pepper and make a cut in the back. Put the fish on a large sheet of parchment paper and cover with the herbs, garlic, and tomatoes.

Drizzle with the white wine and olive oil and season with salt and pepper. Fold in the sides of the parchment paper, put the parcel on a baking sheet, and bake for 30 minutes.

Salmon trout fillets
with lemon and gin

Filetti di trota salmonata al limone e gin

Preparation time: 2½ hrs
(including marinating)
Cooking time: 10 mins
Serves 4

2 pounds salmon trout fillets
generous ⅓ cup olive oil
juice of 3 lemons, strained
1 tablespoon chopped
    flat-leaf parsley
2 tablespoons butter
¼ cup gin
salt and pepper

Put the fish fillets in the bottom of a nonmetallic dish in a single layer. Whisk together the oil, lemon juice, and parsley in a bowl and season with salt. Pour the marinade over the fish, cover with plastic wrap, and let marinate in the refrigerator for 2 hours. Melt the butter in a large skillet. Add the fish fillets together with their marinade and cook over medium-high heat for 3 minutes on each side, or until the marinade has evaporated. Reduce the heat, pour in the gin, and carefully ignite it, standing well back. When the flames have died down, season with pepper and serve immediately.

Stuffed salmon trout
with almonds and yogurt

Trota salmonata ripiena di mandorle e yogurt

Preparation time: 20 mins
Cooking time: 30 mins
Serves 4

olive oil, for brushing
scant 1 cup chopped blanched
    almonds
⅔ cup plain yogurt
juice of 2 lemons, strained
1 pinch ground cumin
2 salmon trout, cleaned
salt and pepper

For the sauce

scant 1 cup chopped blanched
    almonds
scant 1 cup white wine
⅔ cup whole-milk plain yogurt
½ green bell pepper, seeded
    and cut into strips
salt and pepper

Preheat the oven to 400°F and brush a roasting pan with oil. Combine the almonds, yogurt, lemon juice, and cumin in a bowl, season with salt and pepper, and divide the mixture between the cavities of the fish. Brush the fish with oil, lay them in the roasting pan, and bake for 30 minutes, or until the flesh flakes easily.

Meanwhile, make the sauce. Combine the almonds, wine, and yogurt in a pan, season with salt and pepper, and simmer, stirring occasionally, for 10 minutes. Add the strips of green bell pepper and heat through. Transfer the fish to a serving dish, pour the sauce over them, and serve immediately.

Tuna tagliata with potatoes and honey sauce

Tagliata di tonno con patatine
e salsa al miele

Preparation time: 1 hr
(including cooling and
marinating)
Cooking time: 1 hr 10 mins
Serves 6

6 tuna steaks, 7 ounces each
3–4 lemon myrtle leaves
1 clove garlic, sliced
6 tablespoons olive oil, plus
    extra for drizzling
24 new potatoes
salt and pepper

For the sauce

scant 1 cup white-wine
    vinegar
4–5 tablespoons millefiori
    honey (see Note)
4 tomatoes, peeled, seeded,
    and diced
1 tablespoon chopped flat-
    leaf parsley
1 tablespoon snipped chives
2 tablespoons olive oil
2 tablespoons toasted pine
    nuts
salt and pepper

First make the sauce. Bring the vinegar to a boil in a small pan and cook until reduced by a quarter. Stir in 4 tablespoons of the honey and taste. Add more honey if necessary. Remove the pan from the heat and let cool. Put the tomatoes into a bowl, sprinkle with a little salt, a pinch of pepper, the parsley, and chives. Stir the cooled vinegar mixture into the tomatoes, then add the oil, and pine nuts. Taste and season with salt and pepper, if necessary, and let stand.

Preheat the oven to 400°F. Season the tuna steaks with salt and pepper and put them into a shallow dish. Add the myrtle leaves and garlic slices, drizzle with oil, and let marinate for 10 minutes.

Heat 3 tablespoons of the oil in a shallow pan, add the tuna, and cook over medium-high heat for 2 minutes on each side, or until the steaks are seared. Transfer them to an ovenproof dish and roast for 10 minutes. Remove from the oven and let stand in a warm place for 10 minutes.

Meanwhile, parboil the potatoes in a pan of salted boiling water for 10 minutes, then drain. Heat the remaining 3 tablespoons of oil in a skillet, add the potatoes, and cook over low heat, shaking the pan occasionally, for 10–15 minutes, until they are tender. Transfer the tuna to a serving dish, arrange the potatoes around it, and pour the sauce over the dish.

Note: *Millefiori* ("thousand-flower") honey is produced from many different flowers, which can change from year to year and from region to region. Consequently, each millefiori honey has a different flavor and aroma.

Herbed roast

Arrosto alle erbe

Preparation time: 30 mins
Cooking time: 1 hr 15 mins
Serves 6

1 boned and rolled loin or
    leg of veal, 2¼ pounds
4 tablespoons butter, diced
2 tablespoons olive oil, plus
    extra for drizzling
scant ½ cup dry white wine
1¼–1½ cups hot veal or beef
    stock
½ cup chopped mixed aromatic
    herbs, such as thyme,
    sage, rosemary, flat-leaf
    parsley, and mint
1 slice garlic, chopped
1 tablespoon Dijon mustard
dash of brandy
salt and pepper
herb sprigs, to garnish

Rub the meat with salt and pepper and put it into a shallow pan. Add the butter, drizzle with oil, and cook over medium heat, turning frequently, for 10 minutes, until golden brown on all sides. Pour in the wine and cook for 5 minutes, or until the alcohol has evaporated. Continue to cook, adding the hot stock as it evaporates, for 1 hour. Preheat the oven to 400°F. Combine the herbs, garlic, mustard, olive oil, and brandy in a bowl. Remove the veal from the pan and put it on a large sheet of aluminum foil. Cover it evenly with the herb mixture and wrap it, securing the edges. Put the parcel in a roasting pan and roast for 10 minutes. Remove the veal from the oven, unwrap, and carve it into fairly thick slices. Put the slices on a serving plate and garnish with herb sprigs. Strain the cooking juices into a gravy boat and serve immediately with the veal.

Duckling with peaches

Filetti d'anatra alle pesche

Preparation time: 40 mins
Cooking time: 1¾ hrs
Serves 4

1 duckling, 3 pounds
3 sage leaves
1 bay leaf
2 tablespoons butter
1 pound 2 ounces white
    peaches, peeled, pitted,
    and cut into quarters
1 pinch ground cinnamon
salt and pepper

Put the duckling into a flameproof casserole dish, add the sage and bay leaf, season with salt, and pour in water to cover. Bring to a boil, reduce the heat, cover, and simmer for 1½ hours. Lift out the duckling from the casserole and remove and discard the skin. Remove the bones and cut the meat into chunks. Return the meat to the casserole and cook over low heat for about 15 minutes, until the liquid has completely evaporated. Meanwhile, melt the butter in a shallow pan. Add the peaches and cook over low heat, stirring occasionally, for 5–10 minutes. Sprinkle with the cinnamon and add to the duckling. Taste and adjust the seasoning, if necessary, and remove the pan from the heat. Arrange the duck meat in the center of a serving dish, put the peach slices all around it, and serve immediately. This dish is also tasty when served cold.

Wild duck with figs

Filetti d'anatra selvatica con i fichi

Preparation time: 30 mins

Cooking time: 1 hr 20 mins

Serves 4

1 wild duck, cleaned, with
    liver reserved
2 tablespoons olive oil
1 bottle red wine
¼ cup brandy
juice of 1 lemon, strained
14 ounces figs
2 tablespoons butter
salt and pepper

Preheat the oven to 400°F. Season the cavity of the duck with salt and pepper and put the liver inside the cavity. Heat the olive oil in a roasting pan, add the duck, and pour the wine over it. Place in the oven and cook for 1 hour, or until the duck is tender. Remove the duck from the oven and divide it into pieces. Remove and discard the bones and cut the meat into thick slices. Set the meat aside and keep it warm.

Thinly slice the liver, then reduce the oven temperature to 350°F. Stir the brandy and lemon juice into the cooking juices in the roasting pan and add the slices of liver. Cut the figs into quarters, leaving the quarters joined at the stalk. Put them into an ovenproof dish, season with salt and pepper, add the butter, and bake for about 10 minutes.

Meanwhile, heat the sauce in the roasting pan over low heat. Remove the figs from the oven. Arrange the slices of duck on a warm serving dish, pour the sauce over them, and garnish with the hot figs. Serve immediately.

Simple capon galantine

Galantina semplice di cappone

Preparation time: 12 hrs
(including cooling and
standing)
Cooking time: 1 hr
Serves 8

⅓ ounce powdered or 3 leaves
    gelatin
2¼ cups clear vegetable or
    chicken stock
1 capon or large roasting
    chicken
2 carrots
11 ounces lean ground veal
generous ½ cup chopped ham
salt

Make up the gelatin with the stock according to the package directions, pour it into a shallow rectangular pan, and chill in the refrigerator until set. Put the capon, carrots, and a pinch of salt into a large pan, pour in water to cover, and bring to a boil. Reduce the heat and simmer for 15 minutes. Remove the pan from the heat and let the bird cool in the cooking water. Lift out the capon from the pan, reserving the cooking liquid, and carefully remove the skin, in one piece if possible, and reserve it.

Cut off the meat from the capon and chop it into small pieces. Combine the capon meat, veal, and ham in a bowl and season with salt. Shape the mixture into a meat loaf, wrap it in the reserved skin, and then in a piece of cheesecloth. Tie it up securely with trussing thread or kitchen string. Remove and discard the carrots from the reserved cooking liquid, add the parcel, and bring to a boil. Reduce the heat and simmer for 45 minutes. Remove the parcel from the pan, drain well, and transfer it to a plate. Put a cutting board on top, weighed down with 2–3 food cans so that the weight is evenly distributed. Let the galantine stand in the refrigerator overnight to cool and flatten.

Cut the gelatin into small cubes. Unwrap the galantine and slice thinly. Put the slices on a serving dish and garnish with the cubed gelatin.

Note: It is thought that the name galantine derives from an old French word galatine ("gelatin"), or from galine ("hen"). The same dish made with duck is called ballottine and is round in shape. Its flavor is stronger than the capon version because the flavor of duck meat is more intense.

Sweet-and-sour rabbit

Coniglio in agrodolce

Preparation time: 12 hrs
(including overnight
marinating)
Cooking time: 35 mins
Serves 6

1 rabbit, 3¼ pounds, cut
    into pieces
all-purpose flour, for
    dusting

For the marinade

1 celery stalk, coarsely
    chopped
1 carrot, coarsely chopped
1 onion, coarsely chopped
1 shallot, coarsely chopped
1 clove garlic, coarsely
    chopped
1 sprig rosemary, chopped
1 sprig sage, chopped
⅔ cup white-wine vinegar
6 black peppercorns

For the sweet-and-sour
sauce

3 tablespoons olive oil
2 shallots, finely chopped
1 onion, finely chopped
1 celery heart, chopped
1¼ cups green olives, pitted
    and chopped
¼ cup Pantelleria capers
2 tablespoons pine nuts
2 heaping tablespoons sugar
scant 1 cup white-wine
    vinegar
salt

Put the pieces of rabbit into a large dish
in a single layer. Combine all the marinade
ingredients in a bowl and pour the marinade
over the rabbit, turning to coat. Cover
with plastic wrap and let marinate in the
refrigerator overnight.

The next day, remove the rabbit from the
marinade, drain the pieces well, and pat them
dry. Dust with flour, shaking off any excess.
For the sauce, heat the oil in a large pan.
Add the shallots and onion and cook over low
heat, stirring occasionally, for 5 minutes,
until softened.

Add the pieces of rabbit, increase the heat to
medium, and cook, turning the rabbit occasionally,
for 8-10 minutes, until evenly browned. Add the
celery heart, season with salt, reduce the heat,
cover, and cook for 15 minutes.

If the mixture is too dry, drizzle with 5 tablespoons water. Add the olives, capers, and pine
nuts and cook for another few minutes, until the
rabbit is tender.

Stir in the sugar and vinegar and simmer for
another few minutes, then turn off the heat and
let the mixture cool in the pan. To serve,
arrange the meat on a serving dish and pour the
cooking juices over it.

Note: Rabbit meat, tender and easy to digest,
has a delicate flavor and is good when flavored
with the same herbs that the animal eats. Capers
grown in the volcanic soil of the island of
Pantelleria, off the Sicilian coast, are said
to among the best in the world.

Rabbit with bell peppers

Coniglio ai peperoni

Preparation time: 25 mins

Cooking time: 1 hr 20 mins

Serves 4

1 rabbit, cut into pieces

all-purpose flour, for
   dusting

4 tablespoons olive oil

1 sprig rosemary, chopped,
   plus extra to garnish

2 sprigs sage, chopped, plus
   extra to garnish

¾ cup white wine

1 onion, chopped

1 clove garlic, chopped

⅔ cup chicken stock

3 yellow bell peppers, seeded
   and cut into quarters

salt and pepper

Dust the pieces of rabbit with flour and shake
off the excess. Heat the oil in a large pan, add
the rabbit and herbs, and cook over medium heat,
turning occasionally, for about 10 minutes,
until browned all over. Pour in the white wine
and cook for 5 minutes, or until the alcohol
has evaporated. Add the onion and garlic, season
with salt and pepper, and pour in the stock.

Bring to a boil, then reduce the heat, cover, and
simmer, stirring occasionally, for 30 minutes.
Add the bell peppers, re-cover the pan, and
simmer for another 30 minutes, or until the
rabbit is tender. Before serving, sprinkle with
rosemary and sage.

Photograph p.296

Stuffed rabbit

Coniglio ripieno

Preparation time: 20 mins

Cooking time: 1¼ hrs

Serves 4-6

5 ounces ground veal

5 ounces ground pork

2¾ cups coarsely chopped
   white mushrooms

1 cup grated Parmesan cheese

2 eggs, lightly beaten

1 pinch freshly grated nutmeg

1 sprig thyme, chopped

1 sprig marjoram, chopped

1 rabbit, cleaned

3 tablespoons olive oil

scant 1 cup dry white wine

salt and pepper

Preheat the oven to 400°F. Combine the veal,
pork, mushrooms, cheese, and eggs in a large
bowl. Stir in the nutmeg, thyme, and marjoram
and season with salt and pepper. Stuff the cavity
of the rabbit with the mixture, sew it up
with trussing thread, and put the rabbit into
a roasting pan with the oil.

Set the pan over medium-high heat and cook for
a few minutes on both sides, then drizzle with
the wine and cook for 5 minutes, or until
the alcohol has evaporated. Transfer the roasting
pan to the oven and roast for 1 hour. Remove
the rabbit from the oven and let cool, then carve
into slices and serve.

Quails with white grapes

Quaglie all'uva bianca

Preparation time: 25 mins
Cooking time: 20 mins
Serves 4

8 quails
1 bunch seedless white
    grapes, peeled
8 slices bacon
2 tablespoons olive oil
2 tablespoons butter
¼ cup brandy
salt and pepper

Preheat the oven to 425°F. Season the quails with salt and pepper and put 2 grapes in the cavity of each. Wrap each bird in a slice of bacon and tie with kitchen string. Put them into a large roasting pan in a single layer, add the oil and butter, and roast for 10 minutes.

Remove the roasting pan from the oven, but do not switch the oven off. Pour the brandy over the birds and carefully ignite it. When the flames die down, add the remaining grapes and return the roasting pan to the oven for another 10 minutes. Arrange the quails in a circle on a serving dish, pour the grapes and gravy into the middle, and serve immediately.

Photograph p.297

Pheasant with fruit

Fagiano alla frutta

Preparation time: 20 mins
Cooking time: 1¼ hrs
Serves 4

1 pound 10 ounces mixed black
    and green grapes
4 tablespoons butter
1 pheasant, cleaned and
    trussed
juice of 3 oranges, strained
scant 1 cup dry white wine
½ cup brandy
20 walnuts, chopped
1 tablespoon all-purpose
    flour
grated zest of ½ orange
salt and pepper

To garnish

1 orange, sliced
1 small bunch grapes

Crush ⅓ cup of the grapes and strain the juice into a bowl. In a flameproof casserole, melt half the butter over medium heat. Add the pheasant and cook, turning occasionally, for 15 minutes, until it is evenly browned. Add the grape juice, orange juice, wine, and brandy, season with salt and pepper, reduce the heat, cover, and simmer for 30 minutes. Put the remaining grapes into a heatproof bowl, pour in boiling water to cover, and let soak for 1 minute, then drain and peel off the skins. Add the grapes and walnuts to the casserole, re-cover, and simmer for another 10 minutes. Lift out the bird from the casserole and cover loosely with aluminum foil. Add the remaining butter to the pan juices, stir in the flour, and bring to a boil, stirring constantly. Add the grated orange zest and remove from the heat. Garnish the pheasant with slices of orange and grapes and serve immediately, handing the sauce separately.

Rabbit with bell peppers   (p.294)

...ils with white grapes (p.295)

Pheasant with grapes

Fagiano all'uva

Preparation time: 15 mins
Cooking time: 45 mins
Serves 4

1 hen pheasant
2 ounces bacon
2 tablespoons butter
1 tablespoon olive oil
2¼ pounds black grapes
⅗ cup heavy cream
1 tablespoon brandy
salt and pepper

Season the cavity of the pheasant with salt and pepper, tie the legs of the bird together with string, and cover it with the bacon slices, tying them in place with string. Melt the butter with the oil in a large pan. Put the pheasant into the pan and cook over low heat, turning occasionally, for 10 minutes, or until it is golden brown all over.

Meanwhile, set aside a scant 2 cups of the grapes, squeeze the remaining grapes into a bowl, and stir in the cream and brandy. Pour the mixture over the pheasant, season with salt and pepper, cover, and cook gently for 15 minutes. Add the remaining grapes to the pan, re-cover, and simmer for another 15-20 minutes, until the pheasant is tender and cooked through.

Transfer the pheasant to a cutting board and cover loosely with aluminum foil. If the sauce needs thickening, return the pan to the heat and cook until it has reduced a little. Carve the pheasant and put the meat on a warmed serving dish. Spoon the sauce over it and surround it with the grapes. Serve immediately.

/ Summer entertaining /

Chicken, anchovy, and caper roulades

Involtini di pollo alle acciughe e capperi

Preparation time: 15 mins

Cooking time: 35–40 mins

Serves 4
---

4 salted anchovies, soaked in
   water and drained
4 skinless, boneless chicken
   breasts
3 tablespoons capers, rinsed
   and drained
2 tablespoons butter
1 tablespoon olive oil
1 onion, thinly sliced
¼ cup dry white wine
salt and pepper

Place the anchovies skin side up and press along the backbones with your thumb, then turn them over and remove the bones.

Lightly pound the chicken with a meat mallet. Divide the boned anchovies and capers among the chicken breasts, roll them up, and secure with toothpicks. Heat the butter and oil in a skillet, add the onion, and cook over low heat, stirring occasionally, for 5 minutes.

Add the roulades and cook, turning frequently, until they are browned all over. Season with salt and pepper, increase the heat to high, pour in the wine, and cook until it has reduced slightly. Lower the heat, cover, and simmer for 20 minutes. Transfer to a warm serving dish.

Photograph p.306

Chicken with grapes

Pollo all'uva

Preparation time: 15 mins
Cooking time: 1 hr 25 mins
Serves 16

juice of 6 lemons, strained
11 pounds chicken pieces
scant ½ cup butter
4 tablespoons olive oil
3–4 shallots, chopped
1 pound 2 ounces white
    grapes, halved and seeded
salt

To garnish

black and white grapes
grape leaves

Preheat the oven to 350°F. Pour the lemon juice into a dish and add the chicken pieces, a few at a time, turning to coat, then drain. Reserve the lemon juice.

Melt half the butter with the oil in a large roasting pan or flameproof casserole dish. Add the chicken pieces and cook over medium-low heat, turning occasionally, for 8–10 minutes, until lightly browned all over. Season with salt, cover, and transfer to the oven. Roast for about 1 hour, until the juices run clear when the thickest part of the chicken is pierced with point of a knife. Check during cooking and, if the chicken seems to be drying out, drizzle with the reserved lemon juice.

Melt the remaining butter in a shallow pan. Add the shallots and cook over low heat, stirring occasionally, for 5 minutes, or until softened. Add the halved grapes and cook over low heat, stirring occasionally, for another 5 minutes. To serve, arrange the chicken on a large serving dish, spoon the grape mixture over it, and drizzle with the cooking juices. Garnish with whole black and white grapes and a few grape leaves.

/ Summer entertaining /

Pork meat loaf with vegetables

Polpettone di maiale alle verdure

Preparation time: 30 mins
Cooking time: 55 mins
Serves 4

2 bread rolls
11 ounces savoy cabbage,
    cored
1 pound 2 ounces spinach,
    coarse stalks removed
14 ounces Swiss chard, stalks
    removed
14 ounces ground pork
2 eggs yolks
all-purpose flour, for
    dusting
4 cups chicken stock
olive oil, for drizzling
juice of 1 lemon, strained
salt and pepper

Tear the rolls into pieces, put them into a bowl, pour in 6 tablespoons water, and let soak for 10 minutes, then drain and squeeze out.

Meanwhile, set aside 5 cabbage leaves. Pour 8¾ cups water into a large pan, bring to a boil, and blanch the remaining cabbage, the spinach, and the Swiss chard for a few minutes to soften them, then drain, reserving the cooking water, and chop the blanched greens.

Return the cooking water to the pan, bring it back to a boil, and blanch the reserved cabbage leaves briefly to soften them, then drain, and set them aside to cool. Put the pork, soaked bread, greens, egg yolks, and a pinch of salt and pepper into a bowl and mix well.

Lay out the whole cabbage leaves on a clean dish towel, letting them overlap slightly. Spoon the filling evenly onto the leaves and roll up carefully to form a meat loaf. Tie the ends with kitchen string. Dust the meat loaf with flour and put it into a flameproof casserole, pour in the stock to cover, and bring to a boil. Reduce the heat, cover, and simmer for 45 minutes. Remove the meat loaf from the casserole and let it cool.

Once cold, slice the meat loaf, put the slices onto a serving dish, drizzle with olive oil and lemon juice to taste, and serve.

Tenderloin of beef
with fava beans

Filetto con le fave

Preparation time: 20 mins
Cooking time: 25–30 mins
Serves 4

scant 1 cup shelled
    fava beans
8 thick slices beef
    tenderloin
all-purpose flour, for
    dusting
3 tablespoons olive oil
juice of ½ lemon
scant ½ cup dry white wine
1½ ounces speck or bacon,
    cut into strips
salt

Cook the fava beans in a pan of salted boiling water for 5–10 minutes, until tender, then drain. Pop the beans out of their skins with a thumb and index finger. Dust the slices of beef with flour, shaking off the excess. Heat the oil in a skillet, add the slices of beef, and cook over medium-high heat, turning once, until lightly browned and cooked to your liking. Sprinkle with the lemon juice and wine and cook for a few minutes until the alcohol has evaporated. Add the fava beans and strips of speck, mix carefully, and cook for another 5 minutes. Serve immediately.

Photograph p.307

Broiled veal chops
with grapefruit

Costolette grigliate al pompelmo

Preparation time: 50 mins
(including marinating)
Cooking time: 10 mins
Serves 4

juice of 2 grapefruits,
    strained
4 veal chops, trimmed
    of fat
3 tablespoons pink
    peppercorns, crushed
2 tablespoons olive oil, plus
    extra for drizzling
1 sprig mint, chopped
1¾ shredded lettuce
salt

Drizzle half the grapefruit juice over the chops in a nonmetallic dish. Sprinkle with 2 tablespoons of the peppercorns and let marinate for 30 minutes. Preheat the broiler. Drain the chops, put them on the broiler rack, and drizzle with olive oil.

Cook for about 5 minutes on each side, until golden brown. Remove the meat and season with salt. Whisk together the remaining grapefruit juice, 2 tablespoons of the olive oil, and the remaining peppercorns in a bowl, season with a pinch of salt, and stir in the chopped mint. Make a bed of lettuce on a serving dish and put the chops on top. Serve immediately, handing the sauce separately.

Summer veal

Carne estiva

Preparation time: 1 hr
(including cooling and
marinating)
Cooking time: 2 hrs
Serves 6

1 celery stalk
1 carrot
1 onion
1 veal round, 2¼ pounds
¾ cup capers, rinsed and
    drained
scant ½ cup olive oil
juice of 4 lemons, strained
salt

Bring a pan of water to a boil with the celery,
carrot, and onion. Tie the veal neatly with kitchen
string, add to the pan, and simmer for 2 hours.

Remove the pan from the heat and let the meat
cool in its stock. Drain the veal, untie,
and carve very thinly. Arrange the slices on a
serving dish and sprinkle with the capers.

Whisk together the oil and lemon juice in
a bowl, season with salt, and pour the dressing
over the meat. Let marinate for 30 minutes,
then serve.

Veal meat loaf

Polpettone di vitello

Preparation time: 25 mins
Cooking time: 1 hr 20 mins
Serves 4

1 pound 2 ounces ground
    veal tenderloin
generous ⅓ cup chopped ham
2 eggs, lightly beaten
1 pinch freshly grated nutmeg
all-purpose flour, for
    dusting
4 tablespoons butter
2 tablespoons olive oil
1 onion, chopped
1 carrot, chopped
1 celery stalk, chopped
1 teaspoon tomato paste
salt and pepper

Combine the veal, ham, eggs, and nutmeg in
a bowl and season with salt and pepper. Shape the
mixture into a ball, dust with flour, and pat
into an elongated oval. Melt the butter with the
oil in a shallow pan. Add the onion, carrot, and
celery and cook over low heat, stirring
occasionally, for 5 minutes, or until they are
softened. Put the meat loaf into the pan,
increase the heat to medium, and cook, turning
occasionally, for 10–15 minutes, until it is
evenly browned on all sides.

Mix the tomato paste with ¼ cup warm water in a
small bowl and add to the pan, stirring. Reduce
the heat, cover, and simmer gently for 1 hour.
Lift out the meat loaf from the pan and let stand
for 10 minutes. Cut into fairly thick slices,
put them on a serving dish, and drizzle with the
cooking juices. Serve immediately.

Chicken, anchovy, and caper roulades (p.299)

tenderloin of beef with fava beans (p.304)

Veal roulades in aspic

Involtini di vitello in gelatina

Preparation time: 4 hrs
(including setting)
Cooking time: 35 mins
Serves 6

1 slice bread, crusts removed
5 ounces ground beef
1⅓ cup chopped prosciutto
1⅗ grated Parmesan cheese
1 egg, plus 1 egg yolk
1 pound 2 ounces veal steaks
2 tablespoons butter
4 tablespoons olive oil
4–5 sage leaves
scant 1 cup dry white wine
⅔ cup veal stock or water
¾ ounce powdered or
    4½ leaves gelatin
salt and pepper

Tear the bread into pieces, put it into a bowl, add water to cover, and let soak for 10 minutes, then drain and squeeze out. Combine the beef, bread, prosciutto, and grated cheese in a bowl. Stir in the egg and egg yolk and season with salt and pepper. Pound the veal steaks with a meat mallet until they are thin and even and divide the filling among them. Roll them up and tie with kitchen string.

Melt the butter with the oil in a pan, add the sage leaves, and cook for a few minutes, then remove and discard the sage leaves. Add the roulades to the pan and cook, turning frequently, until they are browned all over. Pour in all but 1 tablespoon of the wine and cook for 5 minutes, or until the alcohol has evaporated. Pour in the stock or water and simmer for 15 minutes. Add 2–3 tablespoons water to dilute the cooking juices, increase the heat, and cook for another 1 minute. Remove the pan from the heat and transfer the roulades to a serving dish.

Prepare the gelatin according to the package directions, with the reserved white wine, making up the liquid to 4 cups with water. Pour it over the roulades until they are completely covered. Let cool, then chill in the refrigerator for a few hours until the gelatin is set.

Photograph p.310

Vitello tonnato

Vitello tonnato

Preparation time: 3¼ hrs
(including cooling and
standing)
Cooking time: 2 hrs
Serves 6

1 veal round, 1¾ pounds
1 carrot
1 onion
1 celery stalk
1 tablespoon white-wine
   vinegar
1 tablespoon olive oil
salt

For the sauce

7 ounces canned tuna in oil,
   drained
3 canned anchovy fillets in
   oil, drained
2 tablespoons capers, rinsed
   and drained
2 hard-cooked egg yolks
3 tablespoons olive oil
juice of 1 lemon, strained

Tie the veal neatly with kitchen string. Bring
a pan of salted water to a boil and add the veal,
carrot, onion, celery, vinegar, and olive oil.
Cover and simmer over a low heat for 2 hours, or
until the meat is tender. Remove the pan from the
heat and let the veal cool in the stock.

For the sauce, put the tuna, anchovy fillets,
capers, and egg yolks through a mincer, or
process in a food processor. Stir in the olive
oil, 2–3 tablespoons of the stock, and the
lemon juice.

Untie the meat, carve into slices, and place on a
serving dish. Spoon the sauce over the slices and
let stand for a few hours for the flavors to
mingle before serving.

Note: Vitello tonnato, or *vitel tonné* as it is
also known, is a dish of French origin that dates
back to the eighteenth century. It has since
become, with a few changes, a typical dish of the
cuisine of Piedmont.

Photograph p.311

Veal roulades in aspic (p.308)

Desserts

Dolci

The abundance of seasonal fruit and flowers in summer, from the early cherries in May to the fragrant roses and succulent plums, apricots, and other fruit with pits in late August and September, contribute to a delicious and tempting range of Italian summer desserts. In hot weather, a simple, lightly chilled fruit salad is often the the most appealing dessert, especially with a little sweet wine poured over it, and perhaps infused with fresh mint leaves.

However, there are many other summer desserts, such as mousses, gelatins, cakes, tarts, and charlottes, which can provide a splendid finale to a summer dinner. They can function equally well as a *merenda*, or afternoon snack, or even as a tasty brunch dish.

It is important to choose fruit carefully, checking that it is ripe by pressing gently and checking for a full and pleasant aroma. It is best not to store most fruit in the refrigerator, and to eat it at its peak of ripeness.

Melon and
watermelon aspic

Aspic di anguria e melone

Preparation time: 11 hrs
(including setting)
Cooking time: 25 mins
Serves 8

2 small watermelons
4 cantaloupe melons

For the syrup

2½ ounces gelatin leaves
2 cups superfine sugar

For the sauce

½ cantaloupe melon, seeded
1 cup superfine sugar
⅓ cup sparkling wine

Halve the watermelons and cantaloupes and remove discard the seeds. Reserve some flesh of each type of melon to make balls for decoration. Put the remaining watermelon flesh in a food processor or blender and process to a puree, then transfer to a bowl.

Put the remaining cantaloupe melon flesh in a food processor or blender and process to a puree, then transfer to a separate bowl.

To make the syrup, put the gelatin leaves into a bowl of cold water and let stand for 5 minutes to soften. Pour 3½ cups water into a pan, stir in the sugar, and bring to a boil, continuing to stir until all the sugar has dissolved. Boil, without stirring, for 5 minutes, then squeeze out the gelatin and mix it into the syrup.

Divide the syrup between the bowls of melon puree, mixing it in well. Pour half the cantaloupe mixture into a large gelatin mold and chill in the refrigerator for about 1 hour, or until it is just set.

Add the watermelon mixture to the mold, return to the refrigerator, and chill for about 1 hour, or until it is just set. Add the remaining cantaloupe mixture to the mold, return to the refrigerator, and chill overnight until completely set.

To make the sauce, scoop out the melon flesh, put it into a food processor or blender, and process to a puree. Pass the puree through a strainer into a bowl. Pour scant 1 cup water into a pan, add the sugar, and bring to a boil, stirring until the sugar has dissolved. Boil, without stirring, until the mixture has turned a light golden color, then remove from the heat and stir in the sparkling wine and half the melon puree.

/ Desserts /

Using a melon baller, make watermelon and cantaloupe balls from the reserved fruit.

Briefly dip the bottom of the mold in hot water and turn the watermelon and melon aspic out onto a serving dish. Decorate with the melon balls and serve with the sauce.

Apricot cake
Torta di albicocche

Preparation time: 35 mins
Cooking time: 1 hr
Serves 4

generous 1 cup (2 sticks)
    butter, plus extra
    for greasing
3¾ cups all-purpose flour,
    plus extra for dusting
1¾ pounds apricots
1¼ cups superfine sugar
4 eggs, lightly beaten
2 teaspoons baking powder
⅓ cup chopped pistachio nuts

Preheat the oven to 375°F. Grease and flour a 9-inch cake pan. Put the apricots into a bowl, pour in boiling water to cover, and let stand for 15 seconds, then drain. Peel off the skins, halve, and remove the pits, then cut each half into 2 pieces.

Beat together the butter and sugar in a bowl until creamy, then fold in the eggs, one at a time.

Sift the flour over the mixture and stir in, then stir in the apricots. Dissolve the baking powder in a little lukewarm water and add to the mixture.

Pour the batter into the prepared pan, sprinkle with the pistachios, and bake for about 1 hour, until risen and golden. Let stand in the pan for 5 minutes, then transfer to a wire rack to cool.

Photograph p.322

Apricot gratin

Albicocche al gratin

Preparation time: 15 mins

Cooking time: 15 mins

Serves 4–6

6 tablespoons butter
generous ½ cup sugar
12 apricots, halved
    and pitted
generous ½ cup apricot
    liqueur

Preheat the broiler. Melt the butter and sugar in a flameproof dish, stirring well. Add the apricots and cook over low heat for 10 minutes, but do not let them disintegrate. Pour in scant ½ cup of the liqueur and cook until the alcohol has evaporated, then put the dish under the broiler and cook until golden brown. Remove the dish from the broiler. Heat the remaining liqueur in a small pan or metal ladle, pour it over the apricots, and carefully ignite it, standing well back. Let stand until the flames have died down. Serve the apricots warm.

Note: This recipe can also be prepared with 6 fine-skinned peaches.

Ricotta and apricot cream

Crema di ricotta e albicocche

Preparation time: 10 mins

Serves 4

scant 1 cup ricotta cheese
4 tablespoons vanilla sugar
⅓ cup apricot jam
scant ½ cup heavy cream

Beat the ricotta with the sugar and jam in a bowl. Whip the cream to stiff peaks in another bowl, then fold it into the ricotta mixture. Divide the mixture among 4 individual dishes and chill in the refrigerator until ready to serve.

Apricot parcels

Fagottini di albicocche

Preparation time: 50 mins

Cooking time: 30 mins

Serves 6

2¼ pounds potatoes
1¾ cups all-purpose flour,
    sifted
2 eggs, lightly beaten
1 pound 2 ounces apricots
about 12 sugar cubes
4 tablespoons butter
1 cup fresh white bread
    crumbs
1 tablespoon sugar
1 teaspoon ground cinnamon
confectioners' sugar, for
    dusting
salt

Cook the potatoes in salted boiling water for 25–30 minutes, until tender. Drain, peel, and pass them through a strainer into a bowl. Add the flour, eggs, and a pinch of salt and knead until thoroughly combined. Pit each apricot without fully separating the two halves and put a sugar cube into each cavity. Roll out the dough on a lightly floured counter and cut out rounds that are twice the size of the apricots. Wrap each apricot in a dough round to make small balls, sealing well at the edges.

Bring a pan of water to a boil, then add a pinch of salt. Add the apricots and cook for 3 minutes. Remove with a slotted spoon and drain well. Melt the butter in a small skillet. Add the bread crumbs and cook over low heat, stirring frequently, for a few minutes, until golden brown. Stir in the sugar and cinnamon, remove the skillet from the heat, let cool slightly, and roll the apricot balls in the mixture. Dust with confectioners' sugar and serve.

Apricot cream

Crema di albicocche

Preparation time: 1½ hrs
(including cooling)

Cooking time: 15 mins

Serves 6

1 pound 5 ounces apricots,
    peeled, pitted, and
    chopped
scant 1 cup superfine sugar
2 gelatin leaves
1¼ cups light cream
1–2 ice cubes, crushed
1 egg white

Put the apricots and ⅔ cup of the sugar in a pan and cook over low heat, stirring frequently, until tender. Meanwhile, fill a small bowl with water, add the gelatin, and let soak. Put the apricots into a food processor and process to a puree, then transfer into a bowl. Drain and squeeze out the gelatin, stir it into the puree while it is still hot, then chill in the refrigerator. Mix together the cream and ice cubes and beat well. Set a heatproof bowl over a pan of barely simmering water, add the egg white and the remaining sugar, and whisk until firm and foamy. Remove from the heat and let cool. Combine the 3 mixtures and divide among individual dishes.

Orange nests with cream

Cestini di arance con crema

Preparation time: 4 hrs
(including cooling and
chilling)
Cooking time: 25 mins
Serves 4

4 oranges
⅗–1 cup milk
3 egg yolks
⅔ cup superfine sugar
¼ cup all-purpose flour
2 tablespoons orange liqueur

Cut a slice off the tops of the oranges and scoop out the flesh and juice into a bowl with a teaspoon. Reserve the "shells." Put the flesh and juice into a strainer set over a measuring cup and extract from it as much liquid as possible by pressing down with the back of a spoon. Add enough milk so that there is 2¼ cups liquid.

Beat the egg yolks with the sugar in a bowl until pale and fluffy, then sift the flour over the bowl and fold into the eggs. Gradually, stir in the orange juice mixture. Pour the mixture into a pan and cook over low heat, stirring constantly with a wooden spoon, for 20–25 minutes, until the mixture is thick enough to coat the back of the spoon.

Remove the pan from the heat and let cool. Stir the liqueur into the mixture and divide it among the orange shells. Cover with plastic wrap and chill in the refrigerator for about 3 hours, until set.

Borage flower fritters

Frittelle ai fiori di borragine

Preparation time: 20 mins
Cooking time: 10 mins
Serves 4

7 ounces borage flowers
3 tablespoons all-purpose
    flour
1 egg yolk
⅖ cup milk
extra-virgin olive oil,
    for deep-frying
salt

Rinse the flowers and let dry on a clean dish towel. Sift the flour with a pinch of salt into a bowl and stir in the egg yolk and enough milk to produce the consistency of heavy cream. Pour oil into a high-sided pan to a depth of about 2 inches. Heat the oil to 350–375°F, or until a cube of day-old bread browns in 30 seconds. Dip the flowers into the batter and drain off the excess, then place them carefully into the hot oil, in batches, and cook for about 2 minutes, or until golden. Remove with a slotted spoon and drain on paper towels. Serve immediately.

Photograph p.323

Fruit fritters
with champagne

Frittelle di frutta allo Champagne

Preparation time: 1½ hrs
(including standing)
Cooking time: 40 mins
Serves 8

1 pineapple
4 apples
2 bananas
oil, for deep-frying
½ cup confectioners' sugar

For the batter

1¼ cups all-purpose flour
1 egg
scant ½ cup sweet champagne
2 egg whites

For the sauce

3 cups raspberries
2 tablespoons confectioners'
    sugar
2 tablespoons kirsch

To make the batter, sift the flour into a bowl,
break the egg into the middle, and pour in half
the champagne. Whisk well until smooth, then stir
in the remaining champagne. Cover and let stand
in a cool place for 1 hour.

To make the sauce, crush the raspberries in
a bowl, then stir in the confectioners' sugar and
kirsch. Strain into another bowl and keep cool.
Peel and core the pineapple, then cut it into
½-inch slices. Peel and core the apples, then cut
them into ½-inch rounds. Peel the bananas and
cut into ¾-inch slices.

Whisk the egg whites to stiff peaks and fold into
the batter. Heat the oil in a high-sided pan
to 350–375°F, or until a cube of bread browns in
30 seconds. Dip a few pieces of fruit at a time
into the batter, drain, and fry in the hot oil
until golden brown. Remove with a slotted spoon
and drain on paper towels.

When all the fritters are ready, put them on
a serving dish and sprinkle with the
confectioners' sugar. Serve immediately, offering
the sauce separately.

Apricot cake (p.315)

rage flower fritters (p.320)

Semolina with cherries

Semolino alle ciliegie

Preparation time: 20 mins
Cooking time: 1 hr
Serves 6

1 cup sweet white wine
⅔ cup semolina
butter, for greasing
2 eggs, plus 1 egg white
generous ½ cup superfine
    sugar
1 pound 2 ounces cherries,
    pitted
½ cup blanched almonds,
    chopped

Pour the wine and 2¼ cups water into a pan and bring to a boil. Sprinkle in the semolina and cook, stirring constantly, for 15 minutes. Remove from the heat and let cool.

Preheat the oven to 400°F and grease a mold with butter. When the semolina is cold, beat in the eggs, one at a time, then stir in the sugar, cherries, and almonds. In a separate bowl, whisk the egg white until stiff and fold it into the semolina mixture.

Pour the mixture into the prepared mold, stand the mold in a roasting pan, and pour in hot water to come about halfway up the sides. Bake for 45 minutes. Remove the mold from the oven and let cool to room temperature before turning the dessert out onto a serving dish.

Note: Italy is one of the world's leading growers of cherries. This delicious fruit, with its countless varieties, has been grown in Mediterranean countries for 3,000 years. The ancient Egyptians were the first to cultivate them.

Cherry compote

Zuppa di ciliegie

Preparation time: 30 mins
Cooking time: 30 mins
Serves 4

4 tablespoons butter
1 pound 10 ounces cherries,
    pitted
½ cup superfine sugar
½ bottle red wine
1 teaspoon ground cinnamon
1 tablespoon cornstarch
1 tablespoon kirsch

Melt the butter in a pan over medium heat.
Add the cherries, stir well to coat them in the
butter, and cook for 3–4 minutes. Add the sugar
and stir until it has dissolved, then remove the
pan from the heat.

Pour the wine into another pan, add the cinnamon,
and bring to a boil over low heat. Pour in
the cherries, with their cooking liquid, and cook
for another 5–6 minutes, stirring constantly.
Remove the cherries with a slotted spoon and
divide them among individual bowls.

Mix the cornstarch and the kirsch into a paste
in a small bowl, then add to the pan and cook,
stirring constantly, over low heat until
thickened. Pour the mixture into the bowls over
the cherries and serve warm or cold.

Photograph p.326

Figs with cream

Fichi alla crema

Preparation time: 2½ hrs
(including chilling)
Serves 4

8 white figs
scant ¼ cup superfine sugar
rum, for drizzling
scant 1 cup heavy cream

Peel the figs, being careful not to break them.
Make a series of cuts almost all the way through
each fig to create a star shape and put them
into a dish. Sprinkle with the sugar, drizzle
with rum, and chill in the refrigerator for
2 hours.

Whisk the cream until stiff. Transfer the figs to
a round serving dish using a slotted spoon. Put
several spoonfuls of cream in the middle of each
and spoon a little of their juices on top.

Photograph p.327

Cherry compote (p.325)

Cherry tart

Torta di ciliege

Preparation time: 1½ hrs
(including resting)

Cooking time: 45 mins

Serves 6–8

¾ cup superfine sugar
1 egg
2 egg yolks
grated zest of ½ lemon
⅔ cup unsalted butter,
    softened and diced, plus
    extra for greasing
1¾ cups all-purpose flour,
    sifted, plus extra for
    dusting
salt

For the filling

1 cup milk
½ vanilla bean, slit
2 egg yolks
⅓ cup superfine sugar
¼ cup all-purpose flour,
    sifted
1½ tablespoons unsalted
    butter
9 ounces black cherries,
    pitted
2 tablespoons brandy

To make the dough, beat together the sugar, egg, one of the egg yolks, the lemon zest, and a pinch of salt in a bowl until pale and fluffy. Beat in the butter, a little at a time, then stir in the flour. Turn the mixture out onto a counter and knead gently, then shape into a ball and let rest in a cool place for 30 minutes. Lightly beat the remaining egg yolk in a small bowl.

To make the filling, put the milk and vanilla bean in a pan and bring just to a boil, then remove from the heat. Beat together the egg yolks with ¼ cup of the sugar and stir in the flour. Remove the vanilla bean from the milk and add the milk to the mixture in a thin continuous trickle, stirring constantly. Pour the mixture into a pan and bring to a boil over low heat, stirring constantly.

Remove the pan from the heat and place the butter on top, then spread it gently with a knife blade to prevent a skin from forming. Let cool. Put the cherries into a pan, sprinkle with the remaining sugar, add the brandy, and bring to a boil over low heat, then simmer for 10 minutes.

Meanwhile, preheat the oven to 400°F. Grease a tart pan with butter. Roll out two-thirds of the dough on a lightly floured counter and use it to line the prepared pan. Pour in the cooled custard and spread the cherries evenly on top. Roll out the remaining dough into a round the same size as the pan and place over the filling.

Crimp the edges well to seal, brush with the beaten egg yolk, score with a fork, and pierce with the point of a knife. Bake for 45 minutes, then let cool in the pan before serving.

Rice and cherry cake

Torta di riso e ciliegie

Preparation time: 25 mins
Cooking time: 1 hr 20 mins
Serves 8

1½ pounds cherries, pitted
¾ cup superfine sugar, plus
    extra for sprinkling
scant ½ cup red wine
½ cinnamon stick
cups milk
thinly pared zest of ½ lemon
1½ cups arborio or other
    short-grain rice
butter, for greasing
fresh white bread crumbs,
    for sprinkling
½ teaspoon ground cloves
2 tablespoons brandy
2½ tablespoons finely chopped
    candied citron peel
2 eggs, lightly beaten
¼ ounce peach-flavored
    gelatin
salt

Put the cherries, ½ cup of the sugar, the wine, and cinnamon in a pan and simmer until the juice has thickened, then remove the pan from the heat. Preheat the oven to 325°F. In another large pan, bring the milk to a boil with the lemon zest and a pinch of salt, add the rice, and cook for 15 minutes.

Grease a rectangular cake pan with butter and sprinkle it with bread crumbs and sugar. Remove the pan of rice from the heat. Remove and discard the lemon zest and stir in the cloves, brandy, citron peel, eggs, and the cherries with their syrup. Pour the mixture into the prepared cake pan and bake for 35 minutes, until a wooden skewer inserted into the center of the cake comes out clean.

Meanwhile, make up the gelatin according to the package directions and let cool. Remove the cake from the oven and let cool in the pan. Turn it out onto a serving dish, glaze with the gelatin, cut into slices and serve.

Figs with rum

Fichi al rum

Preparation time: 10 mins
Cooking time: 3–4 mins
Serves 4

1½ cups rum
2–3 tablespoons heavy cream
12 ripe figs, halved
3 tablespoons granulated
    or brown sugar
fresh fig leaves, to decorate

Pour the rum into a bowl, add the cream, and stir well. Put the figs, cut sides uppermost, on the grill over the hottest part of a lit barbecue or under a broiler, sprinkle with the sugar, and drizzle with a little of the rum mixture. Cook for 3–4 minutes, drizzling with the rum mixture several times and raising the barbecue grill 2 or 3 times. Arrange the figs on a serving dish, decorate with fresh fig leaves, and serve warm or cold.

Watermelon crowns

Corone di anguria

Preparation time: 1 hr
(including freezing)
Serves 10

1 watermelon, 4½ pounds
2 cups superfine sugar
juice of 1 lemon, strained
1 egg white
3 ounces semisweet chocolate,
    coarsely chopped
1 small melon, such as
    charentais or ogen,
    peeled, seeded, and
    thinly sliced

Halve the watermelon horizontally and slice
3 rounds from it, ¾ inch thick. From the
rounds, cut out ¾ inch of the zest every
1½ inches to create a serrated edge. Chill the
rounds in the refrigerator. Peel and seed the
remaining watermelon flesh, put it into a food
processor or blender, add 1¾ cups of the sugar
and the lemon juice, and process to a puree.
Transfer the mixture to an ice-cream maker and
freeze for 20 minutes, or according to the
manufacturer's directions.

Meanwhile, whisk the egg white in a bowl to stiff
peaks, then fold in the chocolate. When the ice
cream starts to thicken, fold the egg white
mixture into it. To serve, put a watermelon round
on a serving dish, and place a scoop of ice cream
on top. Put another watermelon round on top of
the ice cream, and cover with more scoops of ice
cream. Put the third watermelon round on top,
cover with scoops of ice cream, and arrange the
melon slices between them.

Baked figs with wild strawberry sauce

Fichi al forno con salsa di fragoline
di bosco

Preparation time: 15 mins
Cooking time: 6-8 mins
Serves 4

8 figs
2 tablespoons butter, diced
2 tablespoons sugar
⅖ cup rum
1¾ cups hulled wild
    strawberries
scant 1 cup heavy cream

Preheat the oven to 350°F. Halve the figs
crosswise and put them on a sheet of parchment
paper. Dot with the butter, sprinkle with the
sugar, and drizzle with the rum. Fold over the
parchment paper, seal the edges, and put the
parcel on a baking sheet. Bake for 6-8 minutes.
Set aside a few strawberries for decoration and
put the rest into a food processor or blender.
Add the cream and process to combine. Remove
the parcel from the oven, divide the figs among
individual bowls, top them with strawberry
cream, decorate with the reserved strawberries,
and serve.

/ Desserts /

Spiced figs

Fichi alle spezie

Preparation time: 2 hrs
(including cooling)
Cooking time: 20 mins
Serves 6

1 teaspoon ground cinnamon
1 teaspoon ground coriander
1 teaspoon ground ginger
2 cloves
½ cup superfine sugar
thinly pared zest of 1
    orange, cut into strips
12 ripe figs

Put the cinnamon, coriander, ginger, cloves, sugar, and orange zest into a pan and mix well. Pour in 2¼ cups water and bring to a boil, stirring until the sugar has dissolved. Boil, without stirring, for 10 minutes. Put the figs into the pan and cook for 3–4 minutes without bringing the syrup back to a boil. Remove the pan from the heat and let the figs cool in the syrup. When they are cold, drain, reserving the syrup, and put the figs into a glass bowl. Return the syrup to medium heat and simmer until reduced by half. Remove and discard the cloves and pour the syrup over the figs to cover. Let cool before serving.

Note: Coriander is a plant from the anise and cumin family. The leaves, known as cilantro, are used in cooking and the bitter-tasting seeds are ground and used as a spice.

Elderflower fritters

Frittelle di fiori di sambuco

Preparation time: 20 mins
Cooking time: 10–15 mins
Serves 4

generous 1 cup all-purpose
    flour
3 eggs, separated
1 tablespoon milk
2 tablespoons butter, melted
3 tablespoons white wine
1 tablespoon honey
olive oil, for deep-frying
12–16 elderflower heads
superfine sugar, for
    sprinkling
ground cinnamon,
    for sprinkling

Sift the flour into a bowl, add the egg yolks and milk, and beat well. Stir in the melted butter, wine, and honey. Whisk the egg whites to stiff peaks in a separate bowl, then fold them into the mixture. Heat the oil in a deep-fryer to 350–375°F, or until a cube of bread browns in 30 seconds.

Holding the flower heads by the stems, dip them into the batter a few at a time, drain off the excess, and add to the hot oil. Cook for a few minutes, until they are golden brown. Remove and drain on paper towels. Transfer to a serving plate, sprinkle with sugar and cinnamon, and serve immediately.

Orange blossom zabaglione

Zabaglione di fiori d'arancio

Preparation time: 1¼ hrs
(including steeping)
Cooking time: 6–8 mins
Serves 4

scant 1 cup sweet white wine
juice of ½ lemon, strained
12 orange blossoms
3 egg yolks
⅓ cup superfine sugar

Combine the wine and lemon juice in a bowl, add
the orange blossoms, and steep for 1 hour, then
strain the liquid into another bowl.

Beat the egg yolks with the sugar in a heatproof
bowl until frothy, then add the wine mixture.
Set the bowl over a pan of barely simmering water
and cook, whisking constantly, for 6–8 minutes,
until thickened. Pour into dishes and
serve immediately.

Cream cheese heart

Cuori di formaggio

Preparation time: 8¼ hrs
(including chilling)
Serves 4

scant 1 cup mascarpone cheese
scant 1 cup crumbled ricotta
    cheese
3½ ounces robiola cheese,
    crumbled
scant ½ cup heavy cream
4½ cups hulled strawberries
confectioners' sugar, for
    dusting

Put the mascarpone into a large bowl and stir
well with a wooden spoon, then add the ricotta,
robiola, and cream. Stir well until the mixture
is light and puffy. Line a heart-shaped mold
with a large piece of cheesecloth, pour in the
cheese mixture, and chill in the refrigerator
for at least 8 hours, until it is set. Chill the
strawberries in the refrigerator.

To serve, turn out the cheese heart onto
a serving dish, decorate with lines of
strawberries, and dust with confectioners' sugar.

Minted
strawberry salad

Insalata di fragole alla menta

Preparation time:

4¼–5¼ hrs

(including steeping)

Serves 4–6

2¼ cups Asti Spumante
   or other sparkling white
   wine
20 mint leaves
2 tablespoons white-wine
   vinegar
2¼ pounds strawberries
¾ cup superfine sugar

Pour the wine into a large bowl, add 12 of the
mint leaves, and let stand in a cool place for
3–4 hours. Pour the vinegar into a large
bowl of cold water, add the strawberries, without
hulling them, and rinse well. Drain on paper
towels, hull the strawberries, and cut any larger
ones in half. Put them into a salad bowl, add the
sugar, and stir gently. Remove the mint leaves
from the wine and discard.

Pour the wine over the strawberries, cover,
and let stand in a cool place, but not in
the refrigerator, for 1 hour, to let the
flavors mingle. Just before serving, finely
chop the remaining mint and sprinkle it over
the strawberries.

Strawberries in
pink cream

Fragole alla crema rosa

Preparation time:

2¼–3¼ hrs

(including chilling)

Serves 6

2¼ pounds strawberries,
   hulled
1 cup heavy cream
1¼ cups confectioners' sugar

Put half the strawberries into a blender and
blend to a puree. Transfer the puree into a bowl
and stir in the cream and sugar. Put the
remaining strawberries into a large dish, or
divide them among individual dishes, and spoon
the pink cream over them. Chill in the
refrigerator for 2–3 hours before serving.

Strawberry dessert

Dolce di fragola

Preparation time: 30 mins
Cooking time: 40 mins
Serves 6

scant ¾ cup raspberry jelly
3½ cups strawberries, hulled
¼ cup sugar
grated zest of 1 lemon

For the sponge cake

unsalted butter, for greasing
¾ cup all-purpose flour, plus
    extra for dusting
6 eggs, separated
¾ cup superfine sugar
¾ cup potato flour

First, make the sponge cake. Preheat the oven to 350°F. Grease a cake pan with butter and dust lightly with flour. Beat the egg yolks with the sugar in a bowl until pale and fluffy. Whisk the egg whites to stiff peaks, then gently fold into the egg yolk mixture. Sift in the 2 flours, adding a little at a time. Spoon the mixture into the prepared pan and smooth the surface. Bake for about 40 minutes. Remove from the oven and let cool in the pan, then turn out. To make the strawberry topping, put the jelly into a small pan, add 3 tablespoons water, and heat gently, stirring occasionally, until syrupy, then remove from the heat. Put the strawberries into a bowl, sprinkle with the sugar and grated lemon zest, and spoon onto the sponge cake. Spoon the raspberry syrup over them and let cool before serving.

Photograph p.338

Strawberry tart

Crostata di fragole

Preparation time: 1 hr
(including cooling)
Cooking time: 20 mins
Serves 6

butter, for greasing
1 pound 2 ounces prepared
    puff pastry dough
all-purpose flour, for
    dusting
scant ¾ cup strawberry jelly
1 cup heavy cream
2¼ pounds strawberries,
    hulled

Preheat the oven to 400°F and grease a cake pan with butter. Roll out the dough on a lightly floured counter and use to line the prepared pan so that it comes part way up the sides. Prick the bottom all over with a fork, line with parchment paper, and fill halfway with uncooked rice or beans. Put the pan on a baking sheet and bake for 20 minutes. Remove the pan from the oven and remove the rice or beans and parchment paper, then let cool. Remove the pastry shell from the pan and put it onto a serving plate. Reserve one-quarter of the jelly and spread the cooled pastry shell with the remainder. Whip the cream to stiff peaks in a separate bowl, then spoon it over the jelly. Arrange the strawberries on top. Dilute the remaining jelly with a little warm water in a bowl and let cool, then pour it over the strawberries.

/ Desserts /

Fruits of the forest tart

Crostata ai frutti di bosco

Preparation time: 2 hrs
(including cooling)
Cooking time: 1 hr
Serves 16

For the crème pâtissière

2¼ cups milk
½ cup superfine sugar
3 egg yolks
grated zest of 1 lemon
¾ cup cornstarch
2 tablespoons rum

For the pastry dough

5¼ cups all-purpose flour,
    plus extra for dusting
generous 1¼ cups (1⅝ sticks)
    butter cut into pieces,
    plus extra for greasing
1¼ cups superfine sugar
grated zest of 2 lemons
6 egg yolks

For the decoration

2 cups blackberries
2 cups wild strawberries
1⅓ cups raspberries
2 cups blueberries
2 cups red currants, or equal
    quantities red currants
    and white currants
confectioners' sugar, for
    dusting (optional)

To make the crème pâtissière, pour the milk into a pan and stir in the sugar, egg yolks, lemon zest, and cornstarch. Cook over medium heat, stirring constantly with a wooden spatula. As soon as it comes to a boil, beat the mixture vigorously, boil for a few more seconds, then pour into a bowl and add the rum. Continue stirring until the mixture has cooled completely.

Preheat the oven to 325°F. To make the pastry dough, sift the flour into a bowl and rub in the butter with your fingertips until the mixture resembles bread crumbs. Stir in the sugar, lemon zest, and egg yolks and knead together to form a smooth dough. Alternatively, combine all the ingredients and beat with an electric mixer fitted with dough hooks.

Cut off one-quarter of the dough, wrap in plastic wrap, and set aside. Grease a 16-inch round, ¾-inch deep tart pan with butter. Roll out the larger piece of dough on a lightly floured counter and use it to line the prepared pan. Prick the base, line it with parchment paper, and fill it with dry rice or dried beans. Bake for about 30 minutes, removing and discarding the paper and rice 10 minutes before the end of the cooking time. Remove the tart from the oven and let cool.

Once the tart shell is cool, preheat the oven to 325°F. Spread the crème pâtissière evenly over the bottom of the cooled tart. Roll out the remaining dough into strips and lay them over the tart in the pattern of your choice. Bake for about 30 minutes, until the strips of pastry are golden brown. Remove the tart from the oven and let cool. Once the tart has cooled, arrange the forest fruits on the surface between the pastry strips. Dust with confectioners' sugar, if desired.

Photograph p.339

Strawberry dessert (p.336)

Fruit salad

Macedonia

Preparation time: 3-4 hrs
(including soaking time)
Serves 6

2¼ pounds mixed fresh fruit
juice of 1 lemon, strained
¼ cup maraschino liqueur
¼ cup slivered almonds
¾ cup superfine sugar
vanilla or lemon ice cream,
    to serve

There should be equal quantities of each type of fruit. Prepare the fruit, peeling and coring as necessary, and cut it into cubes. Put it into a large dish, sprinkle with the lemon juice, maraschino liqueur, almonds, and sugar and stir well. Let stand in a cool place for a few hours to soak up the flavors before serving. Serve with ice cream.

Mixed fruit in wild strawberry coulis

Misto di frutta in salsa di fragoline

Preparation time: 40 mins
(including chilling)
Serves 4

4½ cups hulled wild
    strawberries
juice of 1 lemon, strained
3 tablespoons superfine sugar
1 small melon
6 apricots, peeled, pitted,
    and cut into wedges
2 peaches, peeled, pitted,
    and cut into wedges
1¼ cups blackberries
1¾ cups strawberries
2 kiwifruits, peeled and
    chopped

Put the wild strawberries, lemon juice, and sugar into a blender and process. Halve the melon, remove and discard the seeds, and, using a melon baller, scoop out small balls from the flesh. Put all the fruit into a large bowl, pour the wild strawberry coulis over it, and chill in the refrigerator for 20 minutes before serving.

Crown of red fruits in aspic

Corona di frutti rossi in gelatina

Preparation time: 12 hrs
(including cooling and
setting)
Cooking time: 10-15 mins
Serves 8

1¼ cups superfine sugar
2¼ pounds prepared mixed
    red fruit, such as
    strawberries,
    raspberries, cherries,
    and red currants
7 gelatin leaves
juice of 1 lemon, strained
2 tablespoons kirsch
mint leaves, to decorate

Put the sugar into a pan, pour in scant ½ cup water, and bring to a boil, stirring until the sugar has dissolved. Add the cherries, reduce the heat, and simmer for 10 minutes. Remove the pan from the heat, strain the syrup into a bowl, and let cool.

Put the gelatin leaves into a bowl of cold water and let soak for 5 minutes, or until softened. Squeeze out the gelatin, add to the cherry syrup, mix well to dissolve, and let cool completely.

Put the mixed fruit, including the cherries, into a bowl, pour the syrup over it, and add the lemon juice and kirsch. Stir gently to avoid breaking up the fruit. Dampen a ring mold with very cold water, drain, and pour in the fruit mixture. Cover with plastic wrap and chill overnight in the refrigerator.

To serve, remove the plastic wrap, run a dampened knife blade around the side of the mold, briefly dip the bottom into warm water, and turn out the mold onto a serving dish. Decorate with mint leaves and serve.

Fruit pudding in aspic

Budino di frutta in gelatina

Preparation time: 12 hrs
(including chilling)
Cooking time: 25 mins
Serves 6

juice of 2¼ pounds oranges,
    strained
juice of 2 lemons, strained
scant 1 cup superfine sugar
1 tablespoon powdered gelatin
4½ cups strawberries
1 small melon

Pour the orange juice and lemon juice into a pan,
add the sugar, and dissolve over low heat,
stirring constantly. Sprinkle the gelatin over
it and stir to dissolve. As soon as the liquid
starts to boil, remove from the heat and strain
into a clean pan. Put the strawberries into a
food processor or blender and process to a puree,
then stir them into the orange juice mixture.
Reheat gently, then remove from the heat and let
cool. Pour the mixture into a ring mold and chill
overnight in the refrigerator.

Halve the melon and scoop out and discard the
seeds. Using a melon baller, make as many small
balls as possible from the flesh. Briefly dip the
bottom of the mold in hot water and turn out the
dessert onto a serving dish. Fill the center with
the melon balls and serve.

Rice with fruit

Riso alla frutta

Preparation time: 1¾ hrs
(including cooling and
chilling)
Cooking time: 20 mins
Serves 4

1 cup long-grain rice
1 strip lemon zest
2¼ cups strawberries, hulled
6 apricots, peeled, pitted
    and chopped
4 kiwifruits, peeled and
    diced
1 melon, peeled, seeded, and
    diced
2¼ cups red currants
juice of 1 lemon, strained
½ cup superfine sugar
½ cup toasted pistachio nuts
salt

Cook the rice in a pan of lightly salted boiling
water with a piece of lemon zest for 15 minutes,
or according to package directions, until it
is tender. Drain and let cool, then transfer
to a large bowl. Add the strawberries, apricots,
kiwifruits, melon flesh, and half the red
currants and stir gently.

Pour the lemon juice and scant ½ cup water into
a small pan, add the sugar, and heat gently,
stirring until the sugar has dissolved. Remove
the pan from the heat and let cool, then pour the
mixture over the rice.

Stir, sprinkle with the remaining red currants
and the pistachios, and chill in the refrigerator
for 30 minutes before serving.

Raspberries
with cream in wafers

Lamponi alla crema in cialda

Preparation time: 40 mins
(including cooling)
Cooking time: 5-6 mins
Serves 4

⅔ cup heavy cream
5 tablespoons creamy plain
    yogurt
1 tablespoon kirsch
generous 1 cup raspberries
1 tablespoon confectioners'
    sugar, sifted

For the wafers

2 tablespoons butter,
    softened
⅓ cup confectioners' sugar,
    sifted, plus extra
    for dusting
2 tablespoons honey
⅓ cup all-purpose flour,
    sifted
1 pinch ground cinnamon
1 pinch freshly grated nutmeg
1 pinch ground cloves
1 egg white

Preheat the oven to 400°F and line a baking sheet with parchment paper. To make the wafers, beat the butter with the confectioners' sugar, then gradually beat in the honey, a little at a time, with the flour and the spices.

In a separate bowl, whisk the egg white to stiff peaks and fold it into the mixture. Spoon the mixture into 4 rounds on the prepared baking sheet, spacing them well apart.

Bake for 5-6 minutes, until golden. Remove the baking sheet from the oven, then lift the wafers, one at a time, with a spatula and rest each on a small upturned bowl so that they form a curved shape as they cool. Dust them with confectioners' sugar. To make the cream, whisk the cream to stiff peaks, then gently stir in the yogurt and kirsch.

When the wafers are cold and set, carefully remove them from the bowls and put them, hollow sides uppermost, on individual plates. Divide the cream among the wafers, top with the raspberries, sprinkle with the confectioners' sugar, and serve.

Fresh fruit in aspic

Frutta fresca in gelatina

Preparation time: 12½ hrs
(including cooling and
chilling)

Cooking time: 20 mins

Serves 6

3 gelatin leaves
1 bottle sweet white wine
½ cup superfine sugar
2 kiwifruits, peeled
  and chopped
2 clementines, peeled
  and chopped
12 raspberries
1 apple, peeled, cored,
  and chopped
1 banana, peeled and chopped
1 pear, peeled, cored, and
  chopped
2 mint leaves, chopped

Put the gelatin into a bowl of cold water and let soak for 5 minutes, until softened. Pour the wine into a pan and heat gently. Squeeze out the gelatin, add to the pan with the sugar, and stir until both the gelatin and the sugar have dissolved. Remove the pan from the heat and let cool, then chill overnight in the refrigerator.

Arrange all the fruit in a large bowl, carefully alternating the colors in order to create an attractive effect, and chill in the refrigerator for 3–4 hours.

Just before serving, pour the wine aspic into the bowl (it must have a semiliquid consistency). Sprinkle with the mint and serve.

Fruits of the forest bavarois

Bavarese ai frutti di bosco

Preparation time:

6¾–8¾ hrs

(including chilling)

Serves 8

¾ ounce leaf gelatin

1¾ cups wild strawberries

3½ cups blackberries

¼ cup white wine

4½ cups strawberries

2 tablespoons freshly
squeezed lemon juice,
strained

1½ cups confectioners' sugar

2¼ cups heavy cream, plus
extra to decorate
(optional)

To decorate

1 sprig lemon balm
strawberries
wild strawberries
blackberries

Put the gelatin into a bowl of cold water and let stand for 5 minutes to soften. Rinse the wild strawberries and blackberries with the white wine and pat dry. Put the strawberries and wild strawberries into a blender and process to a puree, then transfer to a large bowl.

Put the blackberries into a blender and process to a puree, then pass through a fine nylon strainer into the same bowl. Stir in the lemon juice and confectioners' sugar. Squeeze out the gelatin and put it into a heatproof bowl set over a pan of barely simmering water until it has dissolved completely. Gently stir it into the fruit puree.

Whisk the cream to stiff peaks in another bowl, then fold it into the fruit mixture. Pour into a mold, cover with plastic wrap, and chill in the refrigerator for 6–8 hours, or preferably overnight, until set.

To serve, briefly dip the bottom of the mold into hot water and turn out the bavarois onto a serving dish. Decorate with the lemon balm leaves and fruit and, if you like, with whipped cream.

Note: A bavarois, or Bavarian cream, is a simple dessert usually made with seasonal fruit added to a base of cream. It has the consistency of a custard cooked in a mold with the freshness of a summer dessert.

Forest fruit
gratin with zabaglione

Gratin di frutti di bosco all zabaione

Preparation time: 20 mins
Cooking time: 30 mins
Serves 4

1 pound 2 ounces mixed
    berries, such as
    strawberries,
    blackberries,
    raspberries, and
    blueberries
3 egg yolks
⅓ cup superfine sugar
2 tablespoons Grand Marnier
finely grated zest of ½ lemon

Cut any large berries in half and spread out the fruit on the bottom of a flameproof dish, or alternatively divide it among 4 individual flameproof dishes. Preheat the broiler. Beat the egg yolks with the sugar and Grand Marnier in a heatproof bowl. Set the bowl over a pan of barely simmering water and cook, whisking constantly, for 8–10 minutes, until thickened. Do not let the mixture boil. Remove the bowl from the heat, stir in the grated lemon zest, and pour the zabaglione over the fruit. Put the dish under the broiler and cook until golden brown. Serve warm or cold.

Photograph p.350

Melon balls with mint-
flavored yogurt

Palline di melone allo yogurt profumato
alla menta

Preparation time: 2¼–3¼ hrs
(including standing
and chilling)
Serves 6–8

scant 2 cups Greek yogurt
4 teaspoons honey
2 sprigs mint, chopped
2 melons

Combine the yogurt, honey, and mint in a bowl, then let stand in the refrigerator for 2–3 hours. Halve the melons, remove and discard the seeds, and scoop out as many balls of the flesh as possible with a melon baller. Mix the melon balls with the yogurt sauce and pour the mixture into a large glass bowl. Chill in the refrigerator for 10 minutes before serving.

Photograph p.351

/ Desserts /

Lime pudding

Budino al lime

Preparation time: 20 mins
Cooking time: 1 hr 10 mins
Serves 4–6

5 eggs
1 cup superfine sugar
scant ½ cup lime juice
thinly pared lime zest,
    shredded, to decorate

For the caramel

½ cup superfine sugar

To make the caramel, put the sugar into a pan
and stir in 5 tablespoons hot water to dissolve
the sugar. Cook over low heat, without stirring,
until golden. Carefully pour the caramel into
a mold and tilt to coat the sides of the mold
evenly as the caramel cools.

Beat the eggs with the sugar in a bowl until
light and frothy, then stir in the lime juice.
Pour the mixture into the caramel-lined mold and
cover with parchment paper. Cook in a pan of
barely simmering water for 1 hour.

Remove the mold from the heat and let cool.
To serve, turn out the pudding onto a serving
dish and decorate with the lime zest.

Almond blossom cake

Torta ai fiori di mandorlo

Preparation time: 15 mins
Cooking time: 30 mins
Serves 6

butter, for greasing
3 cups self-rising flour,
    plus extra for dusting
1 teaspoon baking powder
generous ¾ cup superfine
    sugar
½ cup chopped blanched
    almonds
2 tablespoons unsprayed
    almond blossoms
4 eggs, lightly beaten
4–5 tablespoons strawberry
    jam
1¼ cups strawberries, halved

Preheat the oven to 400°F and grease a baking
sheet with butter. Sift together the flour and
baking powder into a bowl and stir in the sugar,
almonds, and almond blossom. Add the eggs and
mix well. Turn out onto a lightly floured counter
and roll out to form a sheet. Carefully transfer
to the prepared baking sheet and bake for
about 30 minutes.

Let cool on the baking sheet, then transfer to
a plate and spread the surface with strawberry
jam. Arrange the strawberry halves on top.

Forest fruit gratin with zabaglione (p.348)

melon balls with mint-flavored yogurt (p.348)

Apple cake

Torta di mele

Preparation time: 1 hr
(including cooling)
Cooking time: 30-40 mins
Serves 6-8

6 tablespoons butter,
    softened, plus extra for
    greasing
2¾ cups self-rising flour,
    plus extra for dusting
3 eggs
¾ cup superfine sugar
1 teaspoon baking powder
3 apples, peeled, cored,
    and cut into even pieces
whipped cream, to serve

Preheat the oven to 350°F. Grease and flour a 9-inch cake pan, tipping out the excess. Beat the eggs with the sugar in a bowl until pale and fluffy. Beat in the softened butter until thoroughly combined. Sift together the flour and baking powder over the mixture and gently fold in. Gently fold in the apples.

Pour the mixture into the prepared pan, smooth the surface, and bake for 30-40 minutes, until a skewer inserted into the center of the cake comes out clean. Remove the cake from the oven and let cool, then turn out and serve with whipped cream. Alternatively, serve the cake while it is still warm.

Watermelon gelo

Gelo di melone

Preparation time:
4½-6½ hrs (including
cooling and chilling)
Cooking time: 5 mins
Serves 6

¾ cup arrowroot
generous ½ cup superfine
    sugar
4 cups watermelon juice
3½ ounces zuccata (candied
    pumpkin), diced
2 ounces semisweet chocolate
jasmine flowers, to garnish

Combine the arrowroot and sugar in a pan and gradually stir in the watermelon juice. Set over low heat and bring to a boil, stirring constantly. Cook for a few minutes until the mixture has thickened, stir in the zuccata, and remove from the heat. Divide the mixture among 6 small, plain bowls and let cool. Meanwhile, cut the chocolate into very small pieces to resemble watermelon seeds. Put 5-6 pieces into the mixture in each bowl, then chill in the refrigerator for 4-6 hours. To serve, briefly dip the bottoms of the bowls in warm water and turn them out onto a serving dish garnished with fresh jasmine flowers. Alternatively, serve in the bowls.

Note: This is a traditional dish for the Feast of the Assumption on August 15, both in Palermo and western Sicily. A good watermelon gelo should be transparent, a fine pink-tinged ruby color, and must melt in the mouth.

Photograph p.354

/ Desserts /

Melon surprise

Melone sorpresa

Preparation time: 2½ hrs
(including chilling)
Serves 6

1 large melon, halved and
    seeded
2 cups raspberries
12 ounces seedless
    white grapes
3 peaches, peeled, pitted,
    and diced
4 tablespoons superfine sugar
5 tablespoons sweet liqueur,
    such as maraschino

Scoop out balls of the melon flesh using a melon baller and place in a bowl. Reserve the half-melon shells. Add the raspberries, grapes, and peaches to the melon balls and sprinkle with the sugar and liqueur. Divide the fruit salad between the melon shells and chill in the refrigerator for at least 2 hours before serving.

Photograph p.355

Melon with cold coconut cream

Melone con crema fredda al cocco

Preparation time: 1 hr
(including cooling)
Cooking time: 45 mins
Serves 4

3⅗ cups dry unsweetened
    coconut
½ cup brown sugar
grated zest and juice of
    1 large lime
⅓ cup potato flour
5 tablespoons rum
2 cantaloupe or ogen melons
4 tablespoons plain yogurt
salt

Put the dry unsweetened coconut, sugar, grated lime zest, and a pinch of salt into a large pan, pour in 6¼ cups water, and cook over low heat, stirring occasionally, for about 30 minutes. Remove from the heat and strain into a clean pan. Mix the potato flour with 2 tablespoons water in a small bowl and stir into the coconut mixture. Set over low heat, drizzle with the rum, and simmer to let the alcohol evaporate.

Continue to cook, stirring constantly, for 15 minutes, or until the mixture has thickened. Stir in the lime juice, remove from the heat, and let cool. Halve the melons and remove and discard the seeds. Using a melon baller, scoop out as many balls as possible from the flesh, being careful not to pierce the skins. Stir the yogurt and the melon balls into the cooled coconut cream. Divide the mixture among the melon shells and serve.

Watermelon gelo (p.352)

...lon surprise (p.353)

Melon cups

Coppette di meloni

Preparation time: 50 mins
(including cooling time)
Serves 4

4 small cantaloupe
    or Charentais melons
1 small white melon,
    peeled, seeded,
    and cut into cubes
2 large slices watermelon,
    peeled, seeded, and
    cut into cubes
scant ½ cup superfine sugar
½ cup port
mint leaves, to decorate

Cut a slice from the top of each of the
cantaloupe or Charentais melons, scoop out the
flesh, being careful not to pierce the skins, and
put the half-melon shells in the refrigerator.
Cut the flesh into cubes and put it into a large
bowl. Add the white melon, watermelon, sugar, and
port, stir well, and chill in the refrigerator
for 30 minutes. To serve, divide the melon
salad among the melon shells and decorate with
mint leaves.

Melon with blackberries

Melone alle more

Preparation time: 20 mins
Serves 4

1 melon
4½ cups blackberries
¾ tablespoon port
confectioners' sugar, for
    sprinkling

Cut off a slice from the top of the melon and
scoop out the seeds with a tablespoon. Using a
melon baller, scoop out balls of the flesh.
Put them into a bowl, add the blackberries and
port, sprinkle with confectioners' sugar, and mix
carefully. Cover with plastic wrap and chill in
the refrigerator until ready to serve. To serve,
sprinkle 4 glass dishes with confectioners' sugar
and divide the melon-and-blackberry mixture
among them.

Blackberry tart

Crostata di more

Preparation time:
1 hr 40 mins
(including chilling)
Cooking time: 25–40 mins
Serves 6

unsalted butter, for greasing
all-purpose flour, for
    dusting
2¼ pounds blackberries
¾ cup raspberry jam

For the flaky pie dough

1¾ cups all-purpose flour,
    plus extra for dusting
⅓ cup superfine sugar
scant ½ cup unsalted butter,
    softened and cut into
    pieces
2 egg yolks
2 teaspoons grated lemon zest
salt

For the crème pâtissière

4 egg yolks
½ cup superfine sugar
¼ cup all-purpose flour
2¼ cups milk
a few drops of vanilla
    extract or 1 teaspoon
    grated lemon zest

First, make the pie dough. Sift the flour and sugar together into a mound, make a well in the center, and add the butter, egg yolks, lemon zest, and a pinch of salt. Mix thoroughly and knead briefly. Wrap the dough in plastic wrap and chill in the refrigerator for 1 hour.

Meanwhile, to make the crème pâtissière, beat the egg yolks with the sugar in a pan until pale and fluffy. Gradually stir in the flour until evenly mixed. Bring the milk just to boiling point in another pan and add the vanilla or lemon zest, then remove the pan from the heat. Gradually add the hot milk to the egg yolk mixture, then cook over low heat, stirring constantly, for 3–4 minutes, until it is thickened. Pour the custard into a bowl and let cool, stirring occasionally to prevent a skin from forming.

To make the tart, preheat the oven to 350°F. Grease a tart pan with butter. Roll out the dough to a round on a lightly floured counter, use it to line the prepared pan, and prick the bottom with a fork. Make sure the crème pâtissière has cooled, then pour it into the tart shell and bake for 35–40 minutes.

Meanwhile, set aside about 3–4 cups of the blackberries for decoration and put the remainder in a food processor. Process to a puree, transfer to a bowl, and stir in the raspberry jam, diluting the mixture with a little water if necessary (although the mixture should be thick).

Remove the tart from the oven and let cool. Spread the puree evenly over the tart, then cover with the reserved blackberries.

Blueberry cream

Crema ai mirtilli

Preparation time: 1 hr
(including cooling)
Cooking time: 25 mins
Serves 4

2¼ cups milk
1 teaspoon vanilla sugar
4 egg yolks
generous ½ cup superfine
    sugar

For the blueberries

1 tablespoon superfine sugar
1¾ cups blueberries

To make the custard, pour the milk into a pan, stir in the vanilla sugar, and bring just to a boil, then remove the pan from the heat. Beat the egg yolks with the superfine sugar in a bowl until thoroughly combined. Gradually whisk in the warm milk. Pour the mixture back into the pan, return to very low heat, and cook, stirring constantly, until thickened. Do not let the custard boil. Remove the pan from the heat and let cool.

To cook the blueberries, pour 2 tablespoons water into a small pan and stir in the sugar. Heat gently, stirring until the sugar has dissolved, then add the blueberries, increase the heat to medium, and simmer for 15 minutes. Remove the pan from the heat and let cool. Pour the custard into individual bowls. Spoon the blueberries over the custard and serve.

Blueberry rice pudding

Riso dolce ai mirtilli

Preparation time: 1¼ hrs
(including cooling)
Cooking time: 20 mins
Serves 4

2¼ cups milk
1¼ cups Vialone Nano or other
    risotto rice
1¾ cups blueberries
4 tablespoons superfine sugar
1 pinch ground cinnamon
½ teaspoon vanilla extract
finely grated zest of 1 lemon
1 cup heavy cream

Pour the milk into a large pan and bring just to a boil. Add the rice and simmer, stirring occasionally, for 20 minutes, until the liquid has been completely absorbed. If the rice seems too chewy, add a little warm water and cook for another few minutes. Transfer the rice to a bowl and stir in the blueberries, stirring until the rice is colored. Stir in the sugar, a little at a time, then stir in the cinnamon, vanilla, grated lemon zest, and half the cream. Pour the mixture into a mold or into individual bowls and let cool.

Whisk the remaining cream to stiff peaks. Turn out the rice pudding onto a serving dish, if using a mold, and serve, handing the whipped cream separately.

/ Desserts /

Stuffed peaches

Pesche ripiene

Preparation time: 20 mins
Cooking time: 1 hr
Serves 4

2 tablespoons unsalted
    butter, plus extra for
    greasing
5 yellow peaches
¼ cup superfine sugar
4 amaretti cookies, crushed
2 egg yolks
¼ cup unsweetened cocoa
    powder

Preheat the oven to 325°F. Grease an ovenproof
dish with butter. Peel, halve, pit, and chop one
of the peaches and put it into a bowl. Halve and
pit the remaining peaches. Scoop out a little
flesh from the cavity of each and add it to the
bowl. Stir in the sugar, amaretti, egg yolks, and
unsweetened cocoa powder. Divide the mixture
among the cavities of the peach halves, piling it
up into a dome. Dot each dome with the butter,
place the peaches in the prepared dish, and bake
for 1 hour. Serve hot.

Photograph p.360

Peach aspic

Aspic di pesche

Preparation time: 2½ hrs
(including chilling)
Cooking time: 20 mins
Serves 4

3 leaves gelatin
3 ripe yellow peaches, pitted
    and cut into eighths
½ cup amaretto or
    other liqueur
1 cup superfine sugar
scant 1 cup chopped candied
    fruit (optional)

Put the gelatin leaves into a small bowl of cold
water to cover and let soak for 10 minutes.
Meanwhile, put the peaches into a bowl, sprinkle
with the liqueur, and chill in the refrigerator.
Pour 2¼ cups of water into a small pan, add the
sugar, and bring to a boil, stirring until the
sugar has dissolved. Squeeze out the gelatin and
add it to the pan, then add the water from the
bowl. Bring to a boil, stirring to dissolve
the gelatin, then remove the pan from the heat.
Stir in ⅔ cup of the candied fruit, if using,
and let stand for 5 minutes. Pour one-third
of the mixture into a glass bowl and chill for
30 minutes, until it is beginning to set.

Remove the bowl from the refrigerator, arrange
half the peach slices on the gelatin, cover
with half the remaining liquid, and return to the
refrigerator for 30 minutes. Repeat with
the remaining peaches and liquid, return to the
refrigerator, and chill for 1 hour, until set. To
serve, turn out onto a serving dish and decorate
with the remaining candied fruit, if using.

Photograph p.361

Stuffed peaches (p.359)

Peaches with strawberries

Pesche con le fragole

Preparation time: 3-4 hrs
(including standing)
Serves 4

6 yellow peaches
2 tablespoons superfine sugar
2¾ cups hulled strawberries
3 tablespoons strawberry jam
2-3 tablespoons sweet
    white wine

Put the peaches into a bowl, pour in boiling water to cover, and let stand for a few minutes, then drain. Peel and halve the peaches and remove the pits, then put the peach halves on a serving dish, cut sides facing upward. Sprinkle them with the sugar and fill them with the strawberries. Combine the jam and wine in a small bowl and pour over the strawberries. Let stand in a cool place for a few hours before serving.

Pear and plum parcels

Fagottini di pere e prugne

Preparation time: 1½ hrs
(including soaking
and resting)
Cooking time: 45 mins
Serves 6

24 plums
generous 1 cup freshly brewed
    tea, cooled
1¾ cups all-purpose flour,
    plus extra for dusting
2 tablespoons olive oil
scant ½ cup butter, softened
3 tablespoons superfine sugar
2 tablespoons brandy
6 pears
1 egg yolk, beaten with
    1 teaspoon water
salt

Put the plums into a bowl, pour in the tea, and let stand for 1 hour. Meanwhile, sift together the flour and a pinch of salt into a mound on a counter and make a well in the center. Add the olive oil to the well and gradually incorporate the flour. Knead lightly, gradually blending in the butter. Add just enough water to make a soft, elastic dough. Shape the dough into a ball and cover, letting it rest in a cool place for 30 minutes.

Preheat the oven to 300°F. Drain the plums and pit them. Put them into a food processor or blender, add the sugar and brandy, and process until smooth. Peel and core the pears, leaving the stalks attached and keeping them whole. Fill the cavity of each pear with the plum mixture.

Line a baking sheet with parchment paper, roll out the dough on a lightly floured counter, and cut it into 6 squares. Wrap each pear in a dough square, making sure that only the stalk is protruding. Seal the edges well and brush with the egg yolk glaze. Put the parcels on the prepared baking sheet and bake for 45 minutes, until golden brown. Remove from the oven and let cool before serving.

/ Desserts /

Peaches with summer zabaglione

Pesche allo zabaione estivo

Preparation time: 20 mins
Cooking time: 25 mins
Serves 6

1¼ cups superfine sugar
9 medium-ripe white peaches, peeled, halved, and pitted
8 egg yolks
½ cup dry white wine
1 tablespoon kirsch
1¾ cups hulled wild strawberries
confectioners' sugar, for sprinkling

Pour scant 1 cup water into a pan, stir in ¾ cup of the sugar, add the peaches, and cook over low heat for 15 minutes, until the peaches are soft. Remove with a slotted spoon and let cool.

To make the zabaglione, beat the egg yolks with the remaining sugar in a heatproof bowl until pale. Add the wine, set the bowl over a pan of barely simmering water, and cook, whisking constantly, for 6–8 minutes, until the mixture is frothy and coats the back of a spoon. Do not let the mixture boil. Remove the zabaglione from the heat and stir in the kirsch.

Pour a few spoonfuls of zabaglione onto the bottom of 6 individual bowls, put the peaches on top, and spoon the remaining zabaglione over them. Divide the strawberries among the bowls, sprinkle with confectioners' sugar, and keep cool until ready to serve.

Broiled nectarines

Pesche noce alla griglia

Preparation time: 30 mins
Cooking time: 30 mins
Serves 4

4 large nectarines, halved and pitted
½ vanilla bean
½ cinnamon stick
2 tablespoons superfine sugar
3 tablespoons amaretto liqueur
2 kiwifruits, peeled and sliced

Preheat the oven to 375°F and preheat the broiler. Line a baking sheet with parchment paper. Put the nectarines, cut sides facing downward, on the prepared baking sheet and cook under the broiler for 10–15 minutes, until they are lightly browned.

Meanwhile, scrape the seeds from the vanilla bean into a mortar, add the cinnamon and sugar, and grind with a pestle. Transfer the nectarines to an ovenproof dish, cut sides facing upward. Sprinkle with the sugar mixture and spoon a little liqueur into the middle of each. Bake for 10–15 minutes. Serve warm or cold, decorated with kiwi slices.

Plums with cream and ice cream

Prugne con gelato alla panna

Preparation time: 15 mins

Cooking time: 20 mins

Serves 4

1 pound 2 ounces plums
scant ½ cup superfine sugar
2 tablespoons vanilla sugar
1 cup heavy cream
1 teaspoon confectioners'
    sugar
banana or zabaglione ice
    cream, to serve
4 cherries, to decorate
    (optional)

Blanch the plums in a large pan of boiling water for 2–3 minutes. Drain, peel, halve, and pit the plums. Put them into a dish, sprinkle with the superfine sugar, and vanilla sugar stir, and let stand. Meanwhile, whisk the cream in a bowl until soft peaks form, add the confectioners' sugar, and whisk until stiff. Spoon the mixture into a pastry bag fitted with a small star tip. Put a few scoops of ice cream into the bottoms of 4 small glass bowls and top with the plums. Decorate with the cream and the cherries, if using.

Plums with almonds

Prugne alle mandorle

Preparation time: 15 mins

Cooking time: 15 mins

Serves 4

8 plums, halved and pitted
¼ cup superfine sugar
scant ½ cup finely chopped
    blanched almonds

Pour about 2¼ cups water into the base of a steamer and bring to a boil. Sprinkle the plums with the sugar, put them into the steamer basket, set it over the base, cover, and cook for 10 minutes. Remove the pan from the heat, transfer the plums to a serving dish, and sprinkle with the almonds. Let cool before serving.

Plums in wine

Prugne al vino

Preparation time: 20 mins

Cooking time: 20 mins

Serves 6

3 cups sweet rosé wine
1 cinnamon stick
generous ½ cup superfine
    sugar
thinly pared zest of ½ lemon,
    finely chopped
2¼ pounds plums, pitted

Pour the wine into a medium pan, add the cinnamon, sugar, and lemon zest and gradually bring to a boil, stirring until the sugar has dissolved. Add the plums, bring back to a boil, and simmer for 10 minutes. Pour the mixture into a heatproof glass dish and let cool, then remove the cinnamon stick. Keep the dessert in the refrigerator until ready to serve.

Photograph p.370

Flambéed plums

Prugne flambé

Preparation time: 2½ hrs
(including chilling)
Serves 4

1 pound 5 ounces mixed red
   and green plums
⅗ cup heavy cream
1¾ cups marsala or other
   dessert wine
8 sugar cubes
½ cup rum

Cut a slice from the tops of the plums and set aside. Carefully remove the pits, being careful not to split the fruit. Whisk the cream in a bowl to stiff peaks, then fill each plum with it, reserving the remainder in the refrigerator. Top the plums with the reserved slices, choosing a red slice for a green plum, and a green slice for a red plum. Pour the wine into a large bowl and stand the plums in it. Chill in the refrigerator for 2 hours.

Just before serving, briefly soak the sugar cubes in the rum. Cover all the plums with the remaining cream and put the soaked sugar cubes on top. Standing well back, carefully hold a lighted match to the edge of a sugar cube, and ignite. Serve when the flames have died down.

Caramelized grapes

Uva caramellata

Preparation time: 1¼ hrs
Cooking time: 15 mins
Serves 4

almond oil, for brushing
1 bunch green Muscat or
   Italia grapes
¾ cup superfine sugar

Brush a serving dish with almond oil. Divide the bunch of grapes into several small clusters, each with just a few grapes. Put the sugar into a small pan, add 3–4 tablespoons water, and bring to a boil over very low heat, stirring constantly, until the sugar has dissolved.

Boil without stirring, occasionally shaking the pan, for a few minutes, until the caramel is golden. Remove the pan from the heat. If the caramel is too thick, stir in 1 tablespoon hot water. Dip the grapes into the caramel carefully, remove immediately, and put them on the prepared serving dish. Let set before serving.

Note: To make a chocolate version, break a bar of semisweet chocolate into pieces and melt in a heatproof bowl set over a pan of barely simmering water. Dip the grapes into the chocolate and let set in the refrigerator before serving.

Trieste-style potato gnocchi with plums

Gnocchi di patate con prugne alla triestina

Preparation time: 25 mins
Cooking time: 1 hr
Serves 4

12 plums
6 sugar cubes, halved
2¼ pounds potatoes
3 tablespoons butter
4 tablespoons fresh white
    bread crumbs
1 pinch ground cinnamon
1 pinch superfine sugar
1¾ cups all-purpose flour
1 egg
salt

Blanch the plums in boiling water for
5–7 minutes. Drain, halve, and pit them, then put
the halves back together again, stuffing each
plum with half a sugar cube. Cook the potatoes in
a large pan of salted boiling water for 25–30
minutes, until tender.

Meanwhile, melt the butter in a small skillet.
Add the bread crumbs and cook over low heat,
stirring frequently, for a few minutes, until
golden brown. Stir in the cinnamon and sugar and
remove the pan from the heat.

Drain the potatoes, mash while still warm, shape
into a mound on a counter, and make a well
in the center. Add the flour, egg, and a pinch
of salt to the well and knead to a smooth dough.
Shape the pieces of dough into egg shapes
and insert a plum inside each one, molding the
gnocchi dough around the plum.

Bring a large pan of water to a boil. Add the
gnocchi and cook them until they rise to the
surface. Remove them with a slotted spoon and
transfer to a warmed serving dish. Sprinkle with
the bread crumbs and serve.

Note: When plums are not in season, prunes can
be used instead.

/ Desserts /

Fritters
with rose petals

Frittelle alle rose

Preparation time: 30 mins

Cooking time: 5 mins

Serves 4

2½ cups superfine sugar
1 teaspoon anise-flavored
    liqueur
generous 1 cup all-purpose
    flour
1 teaspoon baking powder
1 cup milk
1½ tablespoons butter
2¼ cups whole-milk
    plain yogurt
scant ½ cup raisins
olive oil, for deep-frying
petals from 2–3 unsprayed
    pink roses

Put the sugar into a large pan, pour in 2¼ cups water, and bring to a boil, stirring until the sugar has dissolved. Reduce the heat and simmer, without stirring, for 5 minutes, until the syrup thickens. Stir in the anise-flavored liqueur, remove from the heat, and let cool.

Sift together the flour and baking powder into a bowl and stir in 2–3 tablespoons of the milk, then add the butter, yogurt, and remaining milk, and mix well. Shape the mixture into balls and push a few raisins into the middle of each piece.

Heat the oil in a deep-fryer or skillet to 350–375°F or until a cube of day-old bread browns in 30 seconds. Add the fritters, in batches if necessary, and fry for a few minutes, until golden. Remove with a slotted spoon and drain on paper towels, then dip in the syrup and sprinkle with rose petals. Serve hot.

Photograph p.371

Plums in wine (p.366)

itters with rose petals (p.369)

Ice Creams and Drinks

Gelati e bibite

The huge range of fruit that is in season during summer finds its perfect expression in countless Italian ice cream, sorbet, and granita recipes. Whether using cherries, apricots, melons, red currants, figs, blackberries, plums, strawberries, or raspberries, Italian ice cream recipes tend to be very simple, requiring only ripe fruit and a handful of other ingredients.

The fruit should be washed carefully but briefly before processing, because ripe fruit is easily damaged. Using an ice-cream maker, many ice creams can be prepared within half an hour, but the recipes are also achievable without a machine: they will simply require whisking for a few minutes every hour or so, until fully frozen.

There are also many tempting recipes for summer fruit-based drinks, both alcoholic cocktails and and nonalcoholic smoothies, which are perfect for refreshing the palate on long, hot summer days.

Pineapple ice cream

Gelato all'ananas

Preparation time: 5½ hrs
(including freezing)
Serves 4

1 fresh pineapple
1 pound canned pineapple
   in syrup
1 tablespoon confectioners'
   sugar, sifted
1 cup heavy cream

Cut a slice off the top of the pineapple and carefully remove the flesh with a sharp knife, without piercing the skin. Reserve the shell. Remove and discard the core of the fruit and coarsely chop the flesh. Put it into a food processor or blender, add the canned pineapple, together with its syrup, and process to a puree.

Pour the mixture into a bowl and stir in the confectioners' sugar. Put the bowl in the freezer and freeze for 1 hour, until thickened and partly frozen. Whisk the cream to stiff peaks, then fold it into the pineapple mixture.

Spoon the mixture into the pineapple shell and freeze for at least 4 hours.

Jasmine flower ice cream

Gelato ai fiori di gelsomino

Preparation time: 30 mins
(including freezing)
Cooking time: 10 mins
Serves 4

1 cup superfine sugar
50-60 fresh unsprayed
   jasmine flowers, plus
   extra to decorate
scant ½ cup heavy cream

Pour 2¼ cups water into a pan, add the sugar and jasmine flowers, and bring to a boil, stirring until the sugar has dissolved. Simmer over low heat, without stirring, for 10 minutes. Remove the pan from the heat and let the mixture cool.

Meanwhile, whisk the cream to stiff peaks in a bowl. Pour the jasmine mixture into an ice-cream maker, add the cream, and freeze for about 20 minutes, or according to the manufacturer's directions, then transfer to the freezer.

To serve, divide the ice cream among large champagne glasses or medium highball glasses, and decorate with a few fresh flowers.

Fruits of the forest ice cream

Gelato ai frutti di bosco

Preparation time: 30 mins
(including freezing)

Serves 6

14 ounces mixed berries,
    such as strawberries,
    blackberries,
    raspberries, and
    blueberries
juice of ½ lemon, strained
scant 1 cup superfine sugar
1 cup heavy cream

Put the berries, lemon juice, sugar, and cream into a blender and blend for 2 minutes. Pour the mixture into an ice-cream maker and freeze for 20 minutes, or according to the manufacturer's directions, then transfer to the freezer. Scoop balls into bowls to serve.

Photograph p.380

Mint ice cream

Gelato di menta

Preparation time:
3½–4½ hrs (including
cooling and freezing)

Cooking time: 5 mins

Serves 4

3½ cups very finely chopped
    mint leaves
scant ½ cup superfine sugar
2 ounces semisweet chocolate,
    broken into pieces
2 egg yolks
scant 1 cup heavy cream
whipped cream and mint
    leaves, to decorate

Combine the mint leaves and sugar in a bowl. Put the chocolate into a heatproof bowl set over a pan of barely simmering water and let melt.

Remove the bowl from the heat and let cool slightly. Add the egg yolks and stir until evenly mixed, then let the mixture cool completely. Whip the cream in a separate bowl until thick and stir it into the mint mixture, then fold into the chocolate mixture.

Rinse out a freezerproof mold with water. Spoon the mixture into the mold, cover with plastic wrap, and freeze for 3–4 hours. To serve, quickly dip the bottom of the mold in hot water, then turn out onto a serving dish, and decorate with piped cream and mint leaves.

Strawberry and yogurt ice cream

Gelato di fragole e yogurt

Preparation time:
1 hr 20 mins
(including freezing)
Cooking time: 35 mins
Serves 6-8

5¼ cups hulled strawberries
1 tablespoon orange-flower
  water
1 tablespoon lemon juice
generous ½ cup superfine sugar
1¼ cups heavy cream
4 egg yolks

For the strawberry sauce

5¼ cups hulled strawberries
2¼ cups plain Greek yogurt
scant ½ cup superfine sugar

For the raspberry puree

scant 2 cups raspberries
2 tablespoons superfine sugar
1 tablespoon orange-flower
  water

To make the ice cream, put the strawberries, orange-flower water, lemon juice, and ¼ cup of the sugar into a blender and blend to a puree. Pour the cream into a pan and gradually bring to a boil over low heat, then remove the pan from the heat. Beat the egg yolks with the remaining sugar in a bowl until pale and fluffy, then stir this into the warm cream.

Return the pan to the heat and cook over low heat, stirring constantly, until the mixture has thickened and coats the back of the spoon. Do not let the mixture boil. Transfer the custard to the blender with the pureed strawberries, and blend. Let cool, transfer to an ice-cream maker, and freeze for 20 minutes or according to the manufacturer's directions. Transfer to a freezerproof bowl. Freeze for 30 minutes.

To make the strawberry sauce, puree the strawberries in the blender. Scrape into a bowl and stir in the yogurt, sugar, and scant ½ cup water. Cover and chill in the refrigerator.

To make the raspberry puree, rub the raspberries through a strainer into a bowl. Stir in the sugar and orange-flower water. Remove the ice cream from the freezer and divide among sundae glasses. Pour the raspberry puree over it and then pour on the strawberry sauce. Serve immediately.

Iced raspberry
and strawberry soufflé

Souffle gelato di lamponi e fragole

Preparation time:

3 hrs 20 mins (including freezing)

Serves 4

generous 1 cup raspberries, plus extra to decorate
1¾ cups hulled strawberries
scant 1 cup superfine sugar
5 teaspoons strawberry liqueur, or other fruit liqueur
grated zest of ½ lemon
2¼ cups whipping cream
3 leaves gelatin

Cut a 1½-inch strip of wax paper to fit the circumference of a soufflé dish. Use adhesive tape to attach the paper around the rim of the dish.

Put the raspberries and strawberries into a blender, add the sugar, liqueur, and zest, and blend until smooth and frothy. Pour the mixture into a bowl and set aside. Put the cream into a bowl and whisk to stiff peaks.

Put the gelatin into a heatproof bowl and add water to cover. Set the bowl over a pan of barely simmering water and heat gently until the gelatin has dissolved. Add the whipped cream and gelatin to the berry mixture and fold in carefully, being careful not to knock air out of the mixture.

Pour the mixture into the dish and freeze for 3 hours. To serve, remove the paper from the dish and decorate the soufflé with raspberries.

Photograph p.381

Fruits of the forest ice cream (p.375)

Wild strawberry
and lemon ice cream

Gelato di fragoline e limone

Preparation time: 1¼ hrs
(including freezing)
Cooking time: 5 mins
Serves 6

For the wild strawberry
ice cream

3½ cups hulled wild
    strawberries
light white wine, for rinsing
1¼ cups milk
strip of thinly pared lemon
    zest
1 vanilla bean, split in half
2 eggs
1¼ cups superfine sugar
1½ cups heavy cream

For the lemon ice cream

juice of 6 lemons, strained
1¼ cups superfine sugar
1½ cups milk
1½ cups heavy cream

To make the strawberry ice cream, briefly rinse
the strawberries in the white wine. Pour the milk
into a pan, add the lemon zest and vanilla bean,
and bring just to a boil, then remove the pan
from the heat, and let cool.

Put the eggs and sugar into a blender and blend
until they turn pale and foamy, add the wild
strawberries, and continue to blend until pureed.
Add the cream, strain in the cooled milk,
and process again until combined. Transfer the
mixture to an ice-cream maker and freeze
according to the manufacturer's directions.

To make the lemon ice cream, put the lemon juice
and sugar into a blender and blend. Add the milk
and cream and blend again, very briefly. Transfer
the mixture into an ice-cream maker and freeze
according to the manufacturer's directions.
To serve, scoop balls of ice cream in different
sizes and arrange them in a pyramid in a glass
bowl or in individual dishes.

Note: Sherbets and ice creams made with fruit
contain proportionately more water than the
creamier types and have to be churned for longer
to prevent ice crystals form forming. Remember
that chilling mutes the flavors, so the fruit
must be very ripe and full of flavor.

Iced melon cream

Crema gelata di melone

Preparation time: 4½ hrs
(including freezing)
Serves 2

2 small melons
3–4 tablespoons millefiori or
    other honey
⅔ cup whole-milk plain yogurt

Halve one of the melons, remove and discard the seeds, and scoop out the flesh with a spoon. Put the melon flesh into a food processor or blender and process to a puree. Transfer the puree to a bowl, stir in 3 tablespoons of the honey, taste, and, if necessary, sweeten with another tablespoon. Stir in the yogurt. Transfer the mixture to a shallow, rectangular container. Place in the freezer and freeze for 4 hours. Meanwhile, halve the second melon and remove and discard the seeds. Using a melon baller, make small balls of the melon flesh, put them into a bowl, and chill in the refrigerator until required. Remove the iced melon cream from the freezer 10 minutes before serving and let stand. Turn out onto a serving dish, cut into slices, and decorate with the melon balls.

Peach ice cream

Gelato di pesche

Preparation time: 6¼ hrs
(including softening and
freezing)
Cooking time: 20 mins
Serves 4

1 pound 2 ounces peaches,
    peeled, pitted, and
    sliced
1½ cups confectioners' sugar
2 leaves gelatin
5 eggs, separated
½ cup rum

Put the peaches into a bowl, cover with the confectioners' sugar, let soften for 2 hours, then press them through a strainer into another bowl. Put the gelatin leaves into a small bowl of cold water and let soak for 5 minutes, then squeeze out. Put the egg yolks into a pan, add the peach puree, and cook over low heat, stirring constantly, for 15–20 minutes, until thickened. Put the gelatin into a heatproof bowl, add a little water to cover, set over a pan of barely simmering water, and dissolve. Stir it into the peach mixture and let cool. Whisk the egg whites to stiff peaks in a separate bowl and fold into the peach mixture. Brush a freezerproof container with the rum, pour in the peach mixture, and freeze for 4 hours. To serve, briefly dip the bottom of the container into hot water, turn out the ice cream onto a serving dish, and cut into slices.

Photograph p.386

Hazelnut ice cream

Gelato di nocciole

Preparation time: 1 hr
(including freezing)
Cooking time: 10–15 mins
Serves 6

scant 1 cup shelled hazelnuts
3 cups milk
2 tablespoons vanilla sugar
6 egg yolks
scant 1 cup superfine sugar

Preheat the oven to 400°F. Spread out the hazelnuts on a baking sheet and bake for 15–20 minutes, or until lightly toasted. Rub the hazelnuts in a clean dish towel to remove the thin skins of the nuts, then chop the nuts finely and transfer to a bowl. Bring the milk to a boil in a medium pan and stir in the vanilla sugar. Stir a few tablespoons of the milk into the chopped hazelnuts, then stir in the remaining milk. Beat the egg yolks with the superfine sugar in another bowl until frothy, then add them to the hazelnut mixture.

Transfer to a clean pan and cook over medium heat, stirring constantly, until the mixture just comes to a boil. Remove the pan from the heat and let cool. Transfer to an ice-cream maker and freeze for about 20 minutes or according to the manufacturer's directions. Transfer to a shallow, freezerproof container and place in the freezer.

Rose petal and cream ice cream

Gelato di panna ai petali di rosa

Preparation time: 3½ hrs
(including standing and freezing)
Cooking time: 10 mins
Serves 4

scant 1 cup champagne
scant 1 cup superfine sugar
2–2½ ounces fresh unsprayed
    rose petals
2–3 drops rose extract
scant ½ cup heavy cream
unsprayed rose leaves or rose
    petals, to decorate

Pour scant ½ cup water and the champagne into a pan, add the sugar, and heat gently, stirring until the sugar has dissolved. Remove from the heat. Stir 2–2¼ ounces of the rose petals into the syrup and let stand for 3 hours to let the flavors mingle. Strain the syrup into a bowl, add the remaining petals, and the rose extract. Pour the mixture into a blender and blend, then pour into an ice-cream maker. Whisk the cream to stiff peaks in a bowl, stir into the syrup mixture, and freeze for 20 minutes, or according to the manufacturer's directions. Divide the ice cream among dessert bowls, decorate with rose leaves or a few petals, and serve immediately.

Camomile semifreddo

Semifreddo di camomilla

Preparation time: 4–5 hrs
(including freezing)

Cooking time: 10 mins

Serves 4

7 ounces fresh unsprayed
    camomile flowers

½ cup superfine sugar

3 eggs, separated

¼ cup sweet marsala

juice of ½ lemon, strained

scant 1 cup heavy cream

chopped almonds, to decorate

Put the flowers and sugar into a large pan,
pour in scant 1 cup water, and bring to a boil,
stirring until the sugar has dissolved.

Boil, without stirring, until a thick syrup
forms. Pour the syrup through a fine strainer
into a bowl, lightly pressing the flowers to
extract the liquid, then let cool. Beat the egg
yolks into the camomile syrup until thickened,
then add the marsala and lemon juice.

In separate bowls, whisk the egg whites and cream
to stiff peaks. Fold the egg whites into the
camomile mixture, then fold in the cream. Line a
rectangular, freezerproof container with plastic
wrap, pour the mixture into the container, and
put in the freezer for a few hours. Sprinkle with
chopped almonds and serve.

Chilled wine with strawberries

Vino gelato alle fragole

Preparation time: 3¼ hrs
(including freezing)

Serves 4–6

juice of 2 lemons, strained

3–4 sprigs mint

4 strawberries, hulled and
    quartered

superfine sugar, for
    sprinkling

1 bottle dry white wine,
    chilled

Mix the lemon juice with 2¼ cups water in
a pitcher. Fill each segment of an ice cube tray
halfway with the mixture, put it into the
freezer, and freeze for 1 hour. Put a mint leaf
on the surface of each ice cube and fill the tray
with the remaining lemon mixture.

Return to the freezer and freeze for 2 hours.
Put the strawberries into a small bowl and
sprinkle with the sugar. To serve, put 2 lemon-
flavored ice cubes in each glass, pour in the
wine, and decorate with the strawberry pieces.

Photograph p.387

Peach ice cream (p.383)

Raspberry semifreddo

Semifreddo ai lamponi

Preparation time: 4½ hrs
(including freezing)
Cooking time: 15 mins
Serves 6-8

6 egg yolks
1¼ cups superfine sugar
1½ cups raspberries
3 cups heavy cream

Beat the egg yolks with the sugar in a heatproof bowl until they are light and foamy. Set the bowl over a pan of barely simmering water and cook, whisking constantly, until the mixture is thick enough to coat the back of a spoon.

Remove the bowl from the heat and continue to whisk until the mixture has cooled completely. Put the raspberries into a shallow dish and mash to a coarse puree with a fork. In a separate bowl, whisk the cream to stiff peaks, then fold in the egg mixture and the raspberry puree. Line a rectangular, freezerproof container with plastic wrap. Pour in the mixture and smooth the surface. Put the container into the freezer and freeze for at least 4 hours. To serve, briefly dip the bottom of the container in hot water and turn out the semifreddo onto a dish. Carefully remove the plastic wrap and cut the semifreddo into ½-inch slices.

Photograph p.390

Blackberry sherbet

Sorbetto di more

Preparation time: 3½ hrs
(including cooling and
freezing)
Cooking time: 12-15 mins
Serves 4

⅔ cup superfine sugar
2 tablespoons orange-flower
    water, plus extra for
    sprinkling
5¼ cups blackberries
whipped cream or blackberry
    jelly, to serve

Pour ⅔ cup water into a pan, add the sugar and orange-flower water, and bring to a boil, stirring until the sugar has dissolved.

Boil, without stirring, for 5 minutes, then remove the pan from the heat and let cool. Put the blackberries into a blender and blend to a puree. Stir the puree into the cooled syrup.

Pour the mixture into a freezerproof container and sprinkle with a little more orange-flower water. Cover with aluminum foil and freeze for about 3 hours. Serve the sherbet in scoops, with whipped cream or blackberry jelly.

/ Ice creams and drinks /

Red currant semifreddo

Semifreddo di ribes rossi

Preparation time: 10½ hrs
(including freezing)
Serves 4

2¼ cups heavy cream
¾ cup confectioners' sugar
5 ounces ladyfingers
1¾ cups red currants

Line a rectangular freezerproof container with plastic wrap. Whisk the cream with the confectioners' sugar to stiff peaks in a bowl. Divide the mixture between 2 bowls and chill in the refrigerator until required. Crumble the ladyfingers into one of the bowls of cream, then spread half the mixture over the bottom of the prepared container and freeze for 2 hours.

Set aside 2 tablespoons of the red currants. Put the remainder into a blender or food processor and process to a puree. Stir the puree into the second bowl of cream and pour into the container. Return the container to the freezer for 2 hours, then remove it from the freezer and fill with the remaining cream mixture. Smooth the surface and return to the freezer for another 6 hours. Briefly dip the bottom of the container into hot water, turn out onto a serving dish, decorate with the reserved red currants, and serve.

Plum sherbet

Sorbetto di prugne

Preparation time: 45 mins
(including freezing)
Cooking time: 10 mins
Serves 4

14 ounces purple plums,
    halved and pitted
grated zest of 1 orange
1¼ cups superfine sugar
½ cinnamon stick
1 egg white

Chop the plums, put them into a large bowl, and add the grated orange zest and 2 tablespoons of the sugar. Let stand for about 10 minutes. Meanwhile, pour 1 cup water into a medium pan, add the remaining sugar and the cinnamon, and bring to a boil, stirring until the sugar has dissolved. Boil, without stirring, for another 5 minutes, then remove the cinnamon stick and let the syrup cool. Transfer the plums to a food processor or blender, add the cooled syrup and egg white, and process to a puree. Pour the mixture into an ice-cream maker and freeze for 20 minutes or according to the manufacturer's directions. Pour into a shallow, freezerproof container and place in the freezer.

Photograph p.391

Raspberry semifreddo (p.388)

Zuccotto

Zuccotto

Preparation time: 4½ hrs
(including chilling)
Serves 8

11 ounces ladyfingers
⅔ cup Grand Marnier
3 cups heavy cream
1¼ cups unsweetened cocoa
    powder
2 tablespoons confectioners'
    sugar
3½ ounces semisweet
    chocolate, chopped
20 blanched almonds, chopped

Use some of the ladyfingers to line a hemispherical mold or bowl and drizzle with some of the Grand Marnier. Whip the cream to stiff peaks and divide it between 2 bowls. Sift the unsweetened cocoa powder and confectioners' sugar into one of the bowls and mix well. Add the chocolate and almonds to the other bowl and mix well. Pour the cocoa cream over the bottom of the lined mold, then tap the mold firmly against a counter to remove any pockets of air. Cover the cocoa cream with a layer of half the remaining ladyfingers and drizzle with half the remaining Grand Marnier. Pour the almond cream on top and cover with the remaining ladyfingers. Drizzle with the remaining Grand Marnier. Chill in the refrigerator for about 4 hours, then turn out onto a serving dish. If you prefer, freeze the zuccotto in the freezer.

Note: Zuccotto is a Florentine specialty. It is believed to be the first semifreddo in culinary history and its spherical shape is said to resemble the cupola of the Duomo in Florence.

Watermelon sherbet

Sorbetto d'anguria

Preparation time: 40 mins
(including freezing)
Serves 4-6

1 small watermelon
1 cup confectioners' sugar
juice of ½ lemon, strained
lemon slices, to decorate

Cut off a slice from the top of the watermelon and scoop out the flesh, reserving the "shell." Remove and discard the seeds. Cut up and put 2¼ cups of the flesh into a blender with the sugar, lemon juice, and 1¾ cups water. Process to a puree. Transfer the mixture to an ice-cream maker and freeze for 20 minutes, or according to the manufacturer's directions. Scoop out the sherbet into balls of various sizes and add to the watermelon shell. Decorate with lemon slices and serve.

Note: The same method can be used to make a melon sherbet, in which case add a glass of port to the water.

/ Ice creams and drinks /

Apricot sherbet

Sorbetto d'albicocche

Preparation time: 4½ hrs
(including freezing)
Cooking time: 15 mins
Serves 4

1 cup superfine sugar
14 ounces apricots, pitted
2 tablespoons white rum

Put the sugar into a pan, pour in scant ½ cup water, and bring to a boil, stirring until the sugar has dissolved. Boil, without stirring, for 10 minutes, then add the apricots and cook for another 5 minutes.

Rub the apricots through a nylon strainer into a bowl and stir in the rum. Pour the mixture into a freezerproof container and freeze for about 1 hour, until thickened. Scrape the sherbet into a bowl and beat well for 2–3 minutes, then return to the container and freeze for another 2–3 hours. Divide the sherbet among individual dessert bowls or sundae glasses and serve.

Basil sherbet

Sorbetto al basilico

Preparation time: 1¼ hrs
(including freezing)
Serves 4

16 basil leaves, plus extra
    to decorate
2¼ cups dry sparkling wine
½ cup confectioners' sugar
juice of 1 lemon, strained
4 egg whites

Put the basil leaves, wine, sugar, and lemon juice in a blender and blend at high speed for 1 minute, then transfer the mixture to a bowl. Whisk the egg whites to stiff peaks in a separate bowl and carefully fold them into the wine mixture.

Pour into a freezerproof container and freeze for about 45 minutes, or until the mixture is grainy. Remove from the freezer and divide among 4 sundae glasses. Decorate with a few whole basil leaves and serve.

Note: Adding stiffly whisked egg white makes sherbets creamier and less watery.

Cherry sherbet

Sorbetto di ciliegie

Preparation time:

2¼–3¼ hrs

(including freezing)

Serves 4
----

11 ounces ripe cherries,
    pitted
¾ cup superfine sugar
½ teaspoon almond extract

Put the cherries, sugar, and almond extract into a blender, pour in scant 1 cup water, and blend to a puree. Pour the mixture into a loaf pan and freeze, stirring 2–3 times at hourly intervals, for 2–3 hours. Remove from the freezer, divide the sherbet among 4 glass bowls, and serve.

Kiwi sherbet

Sorbetto al kiwi

Preparation time: 30 mins

(including freezing)

Cooking time: 15 mins

Serves 4
----

1 cup superfine sugar
4 kiwifruits
juice of 1 lemon, strained
strawberries, to decorate

Pour 2¼ cups water into a pan, add the sugar, and bring to a boil, stirring constantly until the sugar has dissolved. Boil, without stirring, for 15 minutes, then remove the pan from the heat. Peel and coarsely chop the kiwifruits, then process to a puree in a blender. Transfer to a bowl and stir in the sugar syrup and lemon juice. Pour the mixture into an ice-cream maker and freeze for 20 minutes, or according to the manufacturer's directions. Divide the sherbet among 4 glasses, decorate with the strawberries, and serve.

Blackberry ice pops

Ghiaccioli alle more

Preparation time: 3¼ hrs

(including freezing)

Cooking time: 10 mins

Serves 4
----

1 cup superfine sugar
2¾ cups blackberries
juice of 1 lemon, strained

Pour 2¼ cups water into a pan, add the sugar, and bring to a boil, stirring until the sugar has dissolved. Boil over very low heat, without stirring, for 5–10 minutes, until syrupy. Remove from the heat and let cool. Put the blackberries into a blender and blend to a puree, then strain them through a nylon strainer into a bowl. Stir in the lemon juice and cooled syrup. Divide the mixture among 4 or more ice-pop molds, insert an ice-pop stick into each, and freeze for 3 hours.

Apricot granita

Granita all'albicocca

Preparation time: 3¼ hrs
(including freezing)
Cooking time: 40 mins
Serves 4

1 cup superfine sugar
14 ounces apricots, pitted
  and chopped
1 teaspoon vanilla extract
juice of 1 lemon, strained
8 mint leaves

Put the sugar into a pan, pour in scant 1 cup water, and bring to a boil over low heat, stirring until the sugar has dissolved. Boil, without stirring, for 5–10 minutes, until syrupy.

Remove from the heat and let cool. Add the apricots to the syrup, return to the heat, and simmer very gently, stirring frequently, for 30 minutes. Remove from the heat and let cool. Rub the apricots, with their cooking syrup, through a nylon strainer into a bowl. Stir in the vanilla extract and lemon juice and pour the mixture into a freezerproof container.

Transfer to the freezer and freeze, stirring every 30 minutes, for 3 hours. Remove from the freezer, divide the granita among 4 small dessert bowls, decorate each with 2 mint leaves, and serve.

Strawberry granita

Granita alla fragola

Preparation time:
3 hrs 20 mins
(including freezing)
Cooking time: 10 mins
Serves 4

¾ cup superfine sugar
2¼ cups hulled strawberries
juice of 1 orange, strained
juice of 1 lemon, strained

Put the sugar into a pan, pour in 1 cup water, and bring to a boil, stirring until the sugar has dissolved. Boil over low heat, without stirring, for 5–10 minutes, until syrupy.

Remove from the heat and let cool. Set aside 4 strawberries for decoration and rub the remainder through a nylon strainer into a bowl. Stir in the orange juice and lemon juice, then add the sugar syrup. Pour the mixture into a freezerproof container and freeze, stirring every 30 minutes, for 3 hours.

Remove from the freezer and divide the granita among 4 tall glasses. Decorate with the reserved strawberries and serve.

Peach granita

Granita alla pesca

Preparation time: 3¼ hrs
(including freezing)
Cooking time: 40 mins
Serves 4

¾ cup superfine sugar
14 ounces peaches, peeled,
    pitted, and diced
juice of 1 lemon, strained
1 teaspoon vanilla extract
4 thick lemon slices, to
    decorate

Put the sugar into a pan, pour in scant 1 cup
water, and bring to a boil, stirring until
the sugar has dissolved. Boil over very low heat,
without stirring, for about 10 minutes,
until syrupy.

Remove the pan from the heat and let cool. Add
the peaches to the syrup, cover, and cook over
medium heat for 30 minutes. Remove from the heat
and let cool. Rub the mixture through a nylon
strainer into a bowl and stir in the lemon juice
and vanilla extract. Pour the mixture into
a freezerproof container and freeze, stirring
every 30 minutes, for at least 3 hours.

Remove from the freezer and divide the granita
among 4 glasses. Decorate each with a slice of
lemon and serve.

Raspberry and red currant granita

Granita di lamponi e ribes

Preparation time:
3 hrs 20 mins
(including freezing)
Cooking time: 10 mins
Serves 4

2¼ cups raspberries
1¼ cups red currants
½ cup superfine sugar
juice of ½ lemon, strained
lemon slices, to decorate

Push the raspberries and red currants through
a nylon strainer into a bowl. Put the sugar into
a pan, add scant 1 cup water, and bring to a boil,
stirring until the sugar has dissolved. Boil over
low heat, without stirring, for 5 minutes, until
the mixture is syrupy.

Remove from the heat and let cool. Stir the fruit
puree and lemon juice into the cooled syrup.
Pour the mixture into a freezerproof container
and freeze, stirring every 30 minutes, for
3 hours. Remove from the freezer and divide the
granita among individual glass bowls. Decorate
with lemon slices and serve.

Champagne barracuda

Barracuda di champagne

Preparation time:

2 hrs 10 mins

(including chilling)

Serves 4

4-5 strawberries, hulled

1½ tablespoons grenadine

1 bottle demi-sec (semisweet)
    champagne

wild strawberries, to
    decorate

Put the strawberries into a bowl and process
to a puree with a handheld mixer. Pour the puree
into a tall pitcher, and stir in the grenadine.
Chill in the refrigerator for 2 hours. Just
before serving, top off with the champagne and
stir gently. Pour into glasses, decorate with
wild strawberries, and serve.

Strawberries in marsala

Fragole al marsala

Preparation time: 1 month

(including standing)

Makes 4½ pounds

½ bottle marsala

2¼ pounds wild strawberries,
    hulled

1¼ cups superfine sugar

Pour the marsala into a bowl, add the
strawberries, and let stand for 30 minutes, then
drain, reserving the marsala. Make alternating
layers of fruit and sugar in a sterilized jar until
all the ingredients are used.

Finally, pour in the marsala to cover and seal
the jar. Store in a cool dark place for at least
1 month. Serve the strawberries in wide glasses
with their flavored wine.

Note: If the strawberries are kept too long, they
become soft, even squashy, and lose their color
and flavor.

Fruit in sparkling wine

Spumante alla frutta

Preparation time: 2½ hrs
(including chilling)
Serves 16

18 sugar cubes
Angostura bitters, for
    sprinkling
2¼ pounds mixed fresh fruit,
    cut into small pieces
2¼ cups brandy
1¼ cups Grand Marnier
4 bottles sparkling dry or
    sweet white wine, chilled

Put the sugar cubes into the bottom of a large
bowl and sprinkle with a few drops of Angostura
bitters. Arrange the fruit on top, drizzle with
the brandy and Grand Marnier, cover, and chill in
the refrigerator for at least 2 hours.

Just before serving, pour the sparkling wine over
the fruit salad and stir gently.

Photograph p.404

Raspberries in alcohol

Lamponi sotto spirito

Preparation time: 2¼ months
(including standing)
Cooking time: 15 mins
Makes about 2½ pounds

1 pound 2 ounces raspberries
1⅜ cups eau de vie or vodka
2 cups confectioners' sugar

Put the raspberries into a sterilized jar and
gently tap the bottom on a counter to settle the
fruit. Pour in the alcohol, cover, and let soak
for 8 days.

When the raspberries are thoroughly macerated,
make the syrup. Pour 1⅜ cups water into a shallow
pan, add the sugar, and bring to a boil, stirring
until the sugar has dissolved. Boil, without
stirring, for 15 minutes, until syrupy. Remove
from the heat and let cool. Pour the cooled syrup
into the jar, seal, and let stand in a cool dark
place for 2 months.

Fruits of
the forest cocktail

Cocktail ai frutti di bosco

Preparation time: 1¼ hrs
(including chilling)

Serves 4

1 pound 5 ounces mixed
    berries, such as
    strawberries,
    blackberries,
    raspberries, and
    blueberries
1½ cups superfine sugar
5 teaspoons brandy

To decorate

4 ice cubes
4 slices orange
4 sprigs black currants
8 mint leaves

Pour 2½ cups water into a large bowl,
add the berries, and stir in the sugar. Ladle
the mixture into a blender and process until
thoroughly combined. Add the brandy and
process briefly again. Pour the mixture through
a funnel into a carafe or pitcher and chill in
the refrigerator.

To serve, pour the cocktail into individual
glasses and add an ice cube. Decorate each with
a slice of orange, a sprig of black currants,
and 2 mint leaves.

Photograph p.405

Peach champagne

Champagne alla pesca

Preparation time: 5 mins

Serves 1

¼ very ripe pitted peach, cut
    into pieces and chilled
½ cup champagne, chilled
1 tablespoon Grand Marnier
    or vodka

Put the peach in a flute, pour in the champagne
and Grand Marnier or vodka, stir, and serve.

Fruit in sparkling wine (p.402)

fruits of the forest cocktail (p.403)

Melon fizz

Melon fizz

Preparation time: 2¼ hrs
(including chilling)

Serves 6

1 large melon
1¾ cups confectioners' sugar
1 cup gin
1 bottle dry sparkling wine

Halve the melon, remove and discard the seeds, and cut it into wedges. Peel the wedges and cut the flesh into cubes. Put them into a large bowl, sprinkle with the confectioners' sugar, drizzle with the gin, and pour over enough wine to cover. Chill in the refrigerator for at least 2 hours before serving.

Photograph p.408

Peaches with champagne

Pesche allo champagne

Preparation time: 1¼ hrs
(including standing)

Serves 6

1 pound 2 ounces peaches,
    peeled, pitted, and diced
½ bottle dry white wine,
    chilled
strip of thinly pared lemon
    zest
juice of ½ lemon, strained
½ bottle champagne, chilled

Put the peaches into a bowl and chill in the refrigerator until required. Pour the white wine into a large carafe, add the lemon zest, and let stand in a cool place for 1 hour. Just before serving, remove and discard the lemon zest from the wine and add the lemon juice, then add the champagne and the diced peaches.

Summer smoothie

Frullato d'estate

Preparation time: 10 mins

Serves 4

2½ cups low-fat plain yogurt
2½ cups crushed ice
¼ cup superfine sugar
juice of ½ small lemon,
    strained
4 daisies, to decorate

Pour the yogurt into a blender, add the crushed ice, sugar, and lemon juice, and process at medium speed until smooth and even. Divide the smoothie among 4 glasses, decorate each with a daisy, and serve.

Photograph p.409

/ Ice creams and drinks /

Blackberries or blueberries in grappa

More e mirtilli sotto grappa

For the blackberries:

Preparation time:
1–2 months
(including standing)
Makes about 2½ pounds

4½ cups blackberries
2½ cups grappa
¾ cup superfine sugar

For the blueberries:

Preparation time: 3 months
(including standing)
Makes about 3¼ pounds

2¾ cups blueberries
4 cups grappa
¾ cup superfine sugar

To prepare the blackberries, remove any leaves and stalks, rinse briefly, drain, and spread out on a clean dish towel. Let dry for several hours, then transfer to 1 or more sterilized jars.

Pour the grappa into a large pitcher, add the sugar, and stir until the sugar has dissolved. Pour the mixture over the blackberries and seal the jar. Let stand in a cool dark place, occasionally turning the jar over, for 1–2 months.

To prepare the blueberries, remove any stalks and leaves, rinse, drain, and spread out on a clean dish towel. Let dry. Spoon the blueberries into the base of a sterilized jar. Pour the grappa into a large pitcher, add the sugar, and stir until the sugar has dissolved. Pour the mixture over the blueberries and seal the jar. Let stand in a cool dark place, occasionally turning the jar over, for at least 3 months.

Watermelon smoothie

Frullato di cocomero

Preparation time: 10 mins
Serves 1

1 slice watermelon, peeled, seeded, and cut into pieces
juice of ½ orange, strained
juice of ½ lemon, strained
scant ½ cup dry sparkling white wine, chilled
1 tablespoon superfine sugar
1 small, unpeeled watermelon triangle, to decorate

Put the watermelon, orange juice, and lemon juice into a blender and blend until smooth. Transfer to a pitcher, pour in the wine, stir in the sugar until dissolved, and serve in a tall glass decorated with a small triangle of watermelon.

Melon fizz (p.406)

Strawberry smoothie

Frullato di fragole

Preparation time: 30 mins
(including soaking)
Serves 4

2 tablespoons white-wine
    vinegar
1¾ cups strawberries
superfine sugar, to taste
3 cups milk

Stir the vinegar into a medium-size bowl
of water. Add the strawberries, without hulling
them, and let soak for about 10 minutes. Drain
the strawberries well, hull them, and put them
into a blender.

Blend them to a puree, then taste and add a
little sugar if necessary. Add the milk and blend
briefly again to mix, then pour into 4 chilled
glasses and serve.

Rhubarb juice

Succo di rabarbaro

Preparation time: 20 mins
Cooking time: 15 mins
Serves 6-8

2¼ pounds rhubarb, cut into
    short lengths
1¼ cups sugar
1 cup apple juice

Put the rhubarb into a pan, pour in enough water
to cover, and add the sugar. Bring to a boil,
then reduce the heat and simmer for 15 minutes,
until the rhubarb has softened.

Remove from the heat and strain the cooking
liquid into a bowl, mashing the rhubarb with
a fork to extract all the juice. Discard
the pulp. Stir in the apple juice. Transfer the
mixture to a jar, close the lid, and store in
the refrigerator.

Recipe List

Antipasti, appetizers, and pizzas

Eggs and frittatas

First courses

Salads

Sauces, marinades, and flavored butters

Vegetables

Desserts

Index

mixed vegetable ring 225

mixed vegetable salad 97

panzanella with
vegetables 96

rustic vegetable pie 32

vinegar marinade 105

vino gelato alle fragole
385, *387*

vitello tonnato 309, *311*

W

walnuts

lettuce with skate and
walnuts 139

orange, walnut, and
fennel salad 66

warm figs with
mascarpone 212

watercress and eggplant
salad 76, *78*

watermelon

melon and watermelon
aspic 314–15

watermelon crowns 330

watermelon gelo 352, *354*

watermelon smoothie 407

watermelon sherbet 392

watermelon with shrimp
213

white wine marinade 105

wild duck with figs 286

wild greens

rustic vegetable pie 32

wild greens and
artichoke pie 35

wild strawberries

baked figs with wild
strawberry sauce 330

fruits of the forest
tart 337, *339*

mixed fruit in wild
strawberry coulis 340

wild strawberry and
lemon ice cream 382

Y

yogurt

cucumbers in yogurt 71

melon balls with mint-
flavored yogurt 348, *351*

summer smoothie 406, *489*

yogurt marinade 104

Z

*zabaglione di fiori
d'arancio* 334

*zucchine in insalata con
basilico* 93

zucchini

baby zucchini salad
93, *95*

baguette with
ratatouille 28, *31*

zucchini and beet
carpaccio 184

zucchini and mozzarella
tartare with tarragon
227

zucchini capricciose 181

zucchini flower soup 257

zucchini salad with
basil 93

zucchini, goat cheese,
and black olive frittata
38

zucchini with lemon 184

fried zucchini flowers
226

mixed zucchini salad 93

stuffed zucchini flowers
181, *183*

tomatoes with zucchini
176

zucchini al limone 184

zucchini capricciose 181

zuccotto 392

zuppa di ciliegie 325, *326*

Directory

The following stores stock high-quality Italian produce such as prosciutto, olive oil, balsamic vinegar, cheese, and other items used in the recipes.

USA

Zingerman's
422 Detroit Street

Ann Arbor, MI 48104

+1 734 663 3354

www.zingermansdeli.com

Di Pasquale's Italian Deli & Marketplace
3700 Gough Street

Baltimore, MD 21224

+1 410 276 6787

www.dipasquales.com

Buon Italia
Chelsea Market

75 9th Avenue

New York City, NY 10011

+1 212 633 9090

www.buonitalia.com

D Coluccio & Sons
1214–20 60th Street

New York City, NY 11219

+1 718 436 6700

www.dcoluccioandsons.com

Di Palo's Fine Foods
200 Grand Street

New York City, NY 10011

+1 212 226 1033

www.dipaloselects.com

Faicco's
260 Bleecker Street

New York City, NY 10014

+1 212 243 1974

Leo's Latticini
46–02 104th Street

New York City, NY 11368

+1 718 898 6069

Raffetto's
144 West Houston Street

New York City, NY 10012

+1 212 777 1261

Todaro Brothers
555 Second Avenue

New York City, NY 10016

+1 212 532 0633

www.todarobros.com

Corti Brothers
5180 Folsom Boulevard

Sacramento, CA 95819

+1 916 736 3802

www.cortibros.biz

Molinari Delicatessen
373 Columbus Avenue

San Francisco, CA 94133

+1 415 421 2337

DeLaurenti
1435 1st Avenue

Seattle, WA 98101

+1 206 622 0141

www.delaurenti.com

Vace Italian Delicatessen
3315 Connecticut Avenue

Washington, DC 2008

+1 202 363 1999

www.vaceitaliandeli.com

Convito Italiano
1515 Sheridan Road

Wilmette, IL 60091

+1 847 251 3654

www.convitocafeandmarket.com

Canada

Moccia's Italian Meat Market
2276 East Hastings Street

Vancouver, BC V5L 1V4

+1 604 255 2032

www.moccia.ca

Ottavio Italian Bakery & Delicatessen
2272 Oak Bay Avenue

Victoria, BC V8R 1G7

+1 250 592 4080

www.ottaviovictoria.com

Benito Meat and Deli
7900 Boulevard Provencher

Waterloo, 2017

Montréal, Quebec, H1R 2Y5

+1 514 723 2378

www.benitoinc.com

Photographs of Italy
by Joel Meyerowitz

Photographs of
recipes and ingredients
by Andy Sewell

Illustrations
by Jeffrey Fisher

Designed
by Sonya Dyakova

Phaidon Press Limited
180 Varick Street
New York, NY 10014

www.phaidon.com

© 2010 Phaidon Press Limited

ISBN 9 780 7148 5773 2
(US edition)

*Recipes from an Italian
Summer* originates from *Il
cucchiaio d'argento estate*,
first published in 2005,
and *Il cucchiaio d'argento*,
first published in 1950,
eighth edition (revised,
expanded and updated in
1997) © Editoriale Domus S.p.a

A CIP catalogue record for
this book is available from
the British Library.

Printed in Germany

The publisher would like
to thank Mary Consonni for
the translation, and Clelia
d'Onofrio, Carmen Figini,
Louisa Carter, Martin and
Vanessa Lam, Summer Nocon
and Philip Britten for their
contributions to the book.

Photographs page 14, 18-19,
22-3, 36-7, 52-3, 74-5, 98-9,
106-7, 110-1, 140-1, 144-5,
178-9, 188-9, 214, 215, 230-1,
240, 241, 250, 251, 268-9, 274-5,
280-1, 288-9, 300-1, 318,
319, 332-3, 372, 394-5, 400-1
© Joel Meyerowitz

Photographs page 26, 27, 30,
31, 40, 41, 46-7, 56, 57, 61, 64,
68, 69, 78, 79, 82, 83, 88, 89, 94,
95, 102, 114, 115, 118, 119,
122, 123, 126, 127, 130, 136, 137,
150-1, 154, 155, 157, 159, 166,
167, 174, 175, 182, 183, 193, 198,
202, 203, 208, 209, 218-9, 222,
223, 236, 237, 246, 247, 255,
258-9, 262, 263, 287, 292-3, 296,
297, 306, 307, 310, 311, 312, 322,
323, 326, 327, 338, 339, 344-5,
350, 351, 354, 355, 360, 361,
364-5, 370, 371, 376-7, 380, 381,
386, 387, 390, 391, 404, 405, 408,
409, 411 by Andy Sewell

Recipe Notes

Butter should always
be unsalted.

Pepper is always freshly
ground black pepper, unless
otherwise specified.

Eggs, vegetables and fruits
are assumed to be large size,
unless otherwise specified.

Milk is always whole, unless
otherwise specified.

Garlic cloves are assumed to
be large; use two if yours
are small.

Cooking and preparation
times are for guidance only,
as individual ovens vary.
If using a fan oven,
follow the manufacturer's
instructions concerning
oven temperatures.

To test whether your
deep-frying oil is hot
enough, add a cube of
stale bread. If it browns
in thirty seconds, the
temperature is 350–375ºF,
about right for most
frying. Exercise caution
when deep frying: add the
food carefully to avoid
splashing, wear long
sleeves, and never leave
the pan unattended.

Some recipes include raw or
very lightly cooked eggs.
These should be avoided by
the elderly, infants, pregnant
women, convalescents,
and anyone with an impaired
immune system.

All spoon and cup measurements
are level. 1 teaspoon=5 ml;
1 tablespoon=15 ml. Australian
standard tablespoons are
20 ml, so Australian readers
are advised to use 3 teaspoons
in place of 1 tablespoon when
measuring small quantities.

Pesci

Carni

Pasta

Oli

Vini

Erbe